3 IN 1

Practical Magick for the Solitary Witch

Starter Kit of Modern Witchcraft: Wicca, Hoodoo, Folk Magick, Prayers & Protection Magick; Manifestation Spells, Rituals & Breaking Curses

Author

Glinda Porter

© **Copyright 2021 Glinda Porter - All rights reserved.**

The content contained within this book may not be reproduced, duplicated or transmitted without direct written permission from the author or the publisher.

Under no circumstances will any blame or legal responsibility be held against the publisher, or author, for any damages, reparation, or monetary loss due to the information contained within this book; either directly or indirectly.

Legal Notice:

This book is copyright protected. This book is only for personal use. You cannot amend, distribute, sell, use, quote or paraphrase any part, or the content within this book, without the consent of the author or publisher.

Disclaimer Notice:

Please note the information contained within this document is for educational and entertainment purposes only. All effort has been executed to present accurate, up to date, and reliable, complete information. No warranties of any kind are declared or implied. Readers acknowledge that the author is not engaging in the rendering of legal, financial, medical or professional advice.

Table of Contents

Book 1: Modern Witchcraft Guide for Beginners   1

Introduction   2

Chapter 1: Understanding And Benefits   7
- Introduction to Witchcraft   7
- Brief History of Witchcraft   8
- Basic Principles, Beliefs, and Practices of Wicca   10
- The Role of The Sun   12
- The Role of The Moon   13
- Sabbats   13
- Being a Wiccan and Being a Witch   14
- Magick and how it Can Help You   15
- Different Types of Witchcraft and Magick   16
- The Do's and Don'ts of Witchcraft   17
- Psychic Abilities and Divination   19
- Divination   22

Chapter 2: Preparing   26
- Grounding and Drawing Energy   26
- Creating an Energy Circuit Through Grounding   27
- Centering Your Energy   28
- Getting Clear with Your Intentions   28
- Sacred Space for Practice   29
- Altars   31
- Basic Tools for Witchcraft - The Witch's Toolkit   31
- Step-By-Step Guides   43

Chapter 3: Casting Spells & Rituals   55
- Prosperity Spells   55
- Spells for Success   65
- Spells for Protection   69

Love Spells — 78
Spells for Health and Healing — 88
Third Eye Opening - Psychic Spells — 101
Personal Power Spells — 105
Spell To Perpetuate Energy And Power — 106
Cleansing Rituals — 108
Unhexing, Banishing, and Eradicating Curses — 112

Chapter 4: Maintenance & Disclaimer for Professional Assistance — 124
How to Know if Your Magick is Working — 124
Where Do You Go From Here? — 126
Spiritual Activities Requiring Professional Assistance — 127

Conclusion — 132

Resources — 135

Book 2: Beginners Witch Guide to Hoodoo & Folk Magick — 137

Introduction — 138

Part I: Understanding the Basics — 143
What is Hoodoo? — 144
Principles — 148
A Relationship with Your Ancestors — 150
Building Your Altar — 154
Working Altars — 158
Your Practice + the Elements of Hoodoo — 162
Working with Spirit — 163
Working with Nature — 163
Working with Waters — 164
Working with Place — 165
Working with the Mind — 165
Hoodoo Roots — 166
Seeds, Roots, Barks, Leaves, and Herbs — 170
Cleansing Oils — 179

Part II: Spells, Tricks, and Rituals — 181
Preparing to Work with Roots — 181

Equipment and Tools	185
Gathering and Drying Herbs	186
Mojo Bags	188
For Inner Peace	192
For Money	192
For Luck	193
For Love	193
For Self-Love and Inner Healing	194
For Health and Physical Healing	195
For Success in Career	195
For Protection	196
Magic Candles	197
Using a Lamp	198
Foot Track Magick	198
Spiritual Cleansing	200
Cleansing Rituals and Spirit Washes	202
On Knowing You Are Protected	209
Fires, Candles, and Incense Rites	211
For Spell Casting	213
Spells for Keeping the Peace	216
Peace Rituals: Using Waters	221
Peace Rituals: Using Dirt and Minerals	222
Spells for Money, Luck, Abundance, and Prosperity	228
Spells for Success	233
Spells for Justice	238
Spells for Protection	243
Part III: Eradication and Getting Professional Help	**248**
Unhexing, Banishing, and Eradication Work	248
What is a Hex?	250
3-Day Eradication Ritual	252
Spiritual Activities Requiring Professional Help	257
How to Avoid Getting Scammed	257
Why Hire a Professional	258
The End: Putting It All Together	**263**
Resources	**270**

Book 3: Prayers and Protection Magick to Destroy Witchcraft — 271

Introduction — 272

Chapter 1: Knowing & Signs — 278

- What is a "curse" and a "spell"? — 279
- Negative Soul Ties — 280
- Covenants — 281
- Agreements — 282
- Psychic Attack — 282
- The Dangers Of Witchcraft — 283
- Brief History of Witchcraft and Wicca — 284
- Types of Witchcraft — 285
- Angels for Prayer — 286
- Types of Curses — 288
- Reading the Signs: How to know if you are under a witchcraft attack — 290
- Destroying the Power of Witchcraft & Unholy Agreements — 291

Chapter 2: Prayers & Protection Spells — 293

- The Right to Reverse A Curse — 295
- Prayers To Destroy The Power of Witchcraft — 296
- Prayers to Destroy Curses and Spells — 298
- Prayers to Destroy Unholy Covenants and Agreements — 306
- Prayers for Deliverance from Destructive Habits — 309
- Prayers for Protection — 311

Chapter 3: Cleansing Rituals & Maintaining Victory — 320

- Cleansing Rituals — 321
- What cleansing is NOT? — 323
- Symbols, Stones, and Protective Objects — 324
- Understanding Blessings and Prosperity — 329
- Prayers for Manifesting Your Fruits — 330
- Stones and Crystals for General Abundance — 332
- Combinations for Specific Abundance — 333
- Maintaining Your Victory and Deliverance — 334
- Prayers to Maintain Victory — 336

Conclusion — 338

Resources — 341

Thank you! — 342

BOOK 1

Modern Witchcraft Guide for Beginners

Starter Kit of Wiccan History & Traditions; Practical Magick, Spells & Rituals with Crystals, Candles, & Herbs for the Solitary Practitioner

Introduction

Witch. What image does that word conjure up for you? The old Hollywood version of the hag with a mole on her nose, cackling as she flies across the backdrop of a full moon? Or perhaps the new Hollywood version of a pretentious English boarding school with mystical creatures hiding behind every door? I hate to be the bearer of bad news, but both images are equally incorrect.

The modern witch is your local baker, the CEO of a Fortune 500 company, that florist down the street, or the mail delivery person who waves at you every morning. The modern witch is physically indistinguishable from you and me (and very rarely has a lightning bolt scar on their forehead). The modern witch could be anyone who wants to unlock their highest potential, achieve their deepest desires, and delve into the powers held within themselves.

Getting started in witchcraft and/or the Wiccan religion can feel like a gargantuan task. Reliable information is scattered over many sources and can be difficult to differentiate from the misunderstood, incorrect, and just outright dangerous. But you can take a deep breath and relax. All the information, spells, rituals, etc. found in this book have been researched and come from a practicing Wiccan witch. Everyone working on the spiritual plane was once a beginner picking their way through a mountain of information, spells, and theory. But what was once a long, arduous process brought with trial and error, has been distilled and explained simply within this book.

This book will give you a great head start in gaining the knowledge and unlocking the abilities you need to begin your own personal journey into the world of witchcraft and Wicca. We will be discussing everything you need to know to get up and going, including:

- A history of Wicca and Witchcraft

- Beliefs, practices, and common rituals

- The difference between Wicca and Witchcraft

- An introduction to Wicca

- The seasons, holidays, and celebrations of the Wiccan calendar

- Step-by-step instructions to help you with basic rituals

- Simple spells to get started

- The relationship to nature, and the Gods/Goddesses

- Working within the spirit world

Although it is important to have a background and understanding of the theory behind spell work, practical and doable instructions for spells is what can lead to actual changes in your life. With that in mind, I have included over **45 simple spells** to attract money, draw good luck and love into your life, and protect yourself from evil - these are everything you need as a new witchcraft or Wiccan practitioner (or as an experienced witch looking for a refresher or some new spells).

We will learn to tap into our own magic as you are guided through each step of these Wiccan and witchcraft practices, including details on personalizing them to your specific situation. You will gain confidence in your own knowledge, inner force, and intuition. Learning to discover and harness your natural talents to perform work in the spirit realm will open up an entirely new world of possibilities.

We will dive deep into the world of moon, candle, herb, crystal, and incense magic, bask in appreciation for the natural elements of the universe, and walk beside the various Gods and Goddesses which inhabit the spiritual plane.

One very important lesson to learn in the pursuit of knowledge and magick is who you can trust. There are plenty of charlatans out there looking to separate you from your money at any cost; people who have never cast a spell in their life, writing books and "advice blogs" with absolutely zero real-life experience in the art of witchcraft. It can be devastating and dangerous to perform spell work that you do not understand or that has not been properly vetted. So, with that being said, let me tell you about my introduction to Wicca and witchcraft - the good, the bad, and the ugly.

I was introduced to Wicca, and eventually witchcraft, in 1994 through a friend. Once he realized it wasn't some kind of instant, get rich quick thing, he lost interest. But a belief system that properly appreciated and praised the beauty of nature was exactly what I was looking for. So, I began researching and practicing as a solitary practitioner. By 1995, I was a wide-eyed, fledgling Wiccan. Not all Wiccans are witches, and not all witches are Wiccan. However, my intent was to practice spell work within the Wicca belief system. Being new to the belief system and living in a rural setting, I did not have experienced Wiccans around me to provide guidance. Google did not even exist and the internet as a whole was still in its infancy. What I did have was access to a bookstore. So, I began to read everything I could to learn the ins and outs of the religion, as well as spell casting. I collected over a hundred spell books, not to mention the books on Wicca theology, symbology, and divination.

One of the biggest problems that I faced in those early days was understanding how to wade through so many spells which promised the same result but required the use of such different materials, tools, and incantations. Despite all of my reading, I had never found a source that explained to me how the spiritual realm actually worked or the reasoning behind the actions taken within a spell or ritual. They were all very good at telling me *what* to do but fell very short in explaining *why* I was doing it. Learning through trial and error was dangerous and I made some huge mistakes, including saddling myself with a demonic attachment instead of the intended positivity and prosperity! I remember thinking how ridiculous it seemed that I could be surrounded by books specifically written for a beginning solitary practitioner, and yet none of them contained a compilation of all the things I truly **needed** to know. From those first few baby steps onto the astral plane, and the ensuing years of study and practicing, comes the book I wish had existed for me - this book.

To practice any type of religion or belief system, there are certain items that are either necessary or, at the very least, recommended, and Wicca or witchcraft are no different. But fear not, because we will be discussing how you can begin building your witchcraft toolkit through different types of altars, crystal balls, divination accessories, wands, and knives.

Whether you have never approached this amazing world of realms, inner power, nature and magick, or have been practicing for years, you are about to embark on a journey of discovery unlike any other. So, secure your third eye in the overhead compartment, strap in and let's take your life to a whole new level.

And may I be the first to greet you officially - "Merry Meet"!

Quick Recommendation from the Magickal Witches team: We would like to make the magickal journey you are about to embark on as smooth as possible. As with any journey, preparations need to be made, and there are tools fit for each witch, new or experienced. In our case, we'd like to recommend the "Survival and Wellness Kit for Magickal Witches", which is completely free. Not using these tools is like making a trip to a rainforest and not taking any sort of tool to protect yourself from mosquitoes. You can do it, but the experience won't be quite as seamless as it could have been. It's discomfort that's not necessary and can even be risky. This analogy fits perfectly; if you don't have the right tools to go through with this process, it can be uncomfortable, and there is even a risk of not having a practice full of magick.

Please access the following link here or scan the code below: https://magickalwitches.gr8.com/

Introduction

It may not be completely clear why these components are essential quite yet, but in further chapters, you will notice that this information will be very helpful. When you actually begin the practical side of the magickal work, you will come to understand. These tools are meant to alleviate some stress and obstacles that may show up along the way. For the time being, let's dive into understanding some theories that are meant to enhance the magickal journey you're here for.

CHAPTER 1

Understanding And Benefits

Introduction to Witchcraft

There are an amazing amount of misconceptions about witchcraft; even as far as something seemingly as simple as providing a definition. The Merriam-Webster Dictionary definition of "witchcraft" is:

> *"The use of sorcery or magic; communication with the devil or with a familiar; rituals and practices that incorporate belief in magic and that are associated especially with neo-pagan traditions and religions (such as Wicca)."*

How can a single word have these three diametrically opposed definitions? Sorcery! Communication with the devil! A belief in magic associated with traditions and religions!

First and most importantly, modern witchcraft is NOT used to communicate with the devil! This is an example of how the folklore and superstitions of the past have bled into the present and continue to color the practice today.

In a general sense, witchcraft *should* be defined as behaviors that fall under the casting of spells that either have a positive or negative effect on the individual who is the focal point of the spell. Yes, witchcraft can be used to have negative effects on people; referred to as "black magick". However, we will be staying on the positive, affirming, "white magick" side of witchcraft. Witchcraft should be an act that promotes self-awareness, healing, and all-around the well-being of an individual.

The beautiful part of witchcraft is that it is completely driven by YOU! There is no liturgical or holy book, there are no services to attend every week, and there are no donation plates to pass around. Your witchcraft practice is dependent on your own intent on your time. The world is your sanctuary.

Brief History of Witchcraft

As much as I would love to be able to lay out an exacting history of witchcraft, with all of its twists and turns, I simply cannot. It would be very similar to writing down the exact history of plants… all of them. Since modern humans began to cluster together and care for each other, there have been "witches". They may have been referred to as healers, shaman, soothsayers, sorcerers, or any number of other terms throughout the ages, but their title within a given point in history does not make them any less a "witch" by the modern standard.

The first written record of the term "witch" comes from the Bible. In the book of 1 Samuel, written between 931 B.C. and 721 B.C., King Saul is said to have sought the Witch of Endor in order to summon the spirit of a dead prophet. Apparently, in the days of King Saul, consorting with a witch was acceptable. But by the time of Exodus, the opinion of the "witch" had soured - Exodus 22:18 says, "thou shalt not suffer a witch to live." So, yes, the Bible hasn't exactly been a great book for us throughout time.

The superstitious and the ignorant blamed witches for pretty much every disease, natural disaster, societal ill and stubbed toe since the medieval period. The term "witch" became synonymous with a woman who worshiped the devil, made unholy agreements, used the powers of black magick to cause harm, and lured pure souls into darkness. Being accused of being a "witch" would get you executed, but being a "sorcerer" would get you a royal appointment. A "sorcerer" was seen as an individual who used magick in furtherance of the wishes of the king. Not surprisingly for the time period, women were considered "witches" and men were considered "sorcerers". What? You didn't think sexism was a modern invention, did you?

How witches and witchcraft was viewed in society has been dependent upon the culture and their religious beliefs. For instance, healers and shamans are/were venerated and respected members of the community in the African and South American cultures. However, as a general rule, the more Christianized that a culture became, the more witchcraft was pushed to the outskirts of acceptability. Contact with the spirit realm was seen as demonic or in the service of the devil. The Christian God and his Son, Jesus Christ, exist for believers on the spiritual plane. However, for them, God, Jesus Christ, and the Holy Spirit are the only entities allowed to perform work on the spiritual plane. Any other work is considered "blasphemy".

Perhaps nowhere better exemplifies the zealous behavior of Christianity run wild than Salem, Massachusetts in 1692-1693. The Salem Witch Trials. The ironic part about the Salem Witch Trials is that there may not have been even one actual witch. The truth of the matter is that Puritan beliefs led to the punishment and deaths of 25 people. Of those twenty-five individuals, nineteen were executed by hanging, five died while in jail awaiting trial, and one died from being crushed under rocks. The entire period of "trials" was really more of a kangaroo court with no chance of survivability. The accused would be strapped to a dunk board (picture a large teeter-totter positioned either on a low bridge or on the bank of a body of water). The accused would be strapped to the board and lowered into the water. The Puritans believed that water was a pure element and would not accept the unclean. Therefore, if the accused sank and drowned in the river, then they were posthumously declared innocent. If the accused floated back up and lived through the trial, she was found guilty of witchcraft and was executed. With 25 people who died as a result of being found guilty, it is unclear how many individuals died as a result of the test itself.

Any history of witchcraft would be incomplete without a history of modern Wicca. Wicca is the nature-based religion surrounding the act of witchcraft.

The "father" of modern Wicca is Gerald Gardner, although he never actually called his belief system "Wicca" because he preferred the more ancient term "Witchcraft". In 1920, Gardner was initiated into the New Forest Coven in Britain. It was Gardner's belief and claim that the New Forest Coven was a surviving group of original witch-cult members.

In 1946, Gardner feared that witchcraft was a dying and disappearing practice. So he began his own coven, calling it the Bricket Wood Coven, with another former member of the New Forest Coven, Edith Woodford-Grimes. Gardner and Woodford-Grimes became the High Priest and High Priestess of the Bricket Wood Coven. Gardner implanted in his new tradition a lasting foundation of Wicca - the notion of an equal God and Goddess (this was terrifically unique and intriguing within the patriarchal, male-dominated society of 1940s Britain). In this same year, Gardner initiated Alex Sanders into the Bricket Wood Coven. Sanders would later leave Bricket Wood Coven to form a new system of belief known as Alexandrian Wicca.

Woodford-Grimes only stayed with the Bricket Wood Coven for 6 years, citing concerns over the publicity that Gardner was attempting to bring to the religion. Prior to Gardnerian Witchcraft, all aspects of witchcraft were practiced in extreme privacy for the safety of the practitioners. Gardner, however, aimed to change the pact of secrecy of the religion and to gain popular understanding and acceptance. This proved to be a brilliant and well-timed strategy, but it did tend to make some traditionalists rather uneasy.

In 1953, Gardner initiated Doreen Valiente into the Bricket Wood Coven and she became the new High Priestess of the coven. With the assistance of Valiant, Gardner wrote the Bricket Wood Coven Book of Shadows. Many of the rituals in the Book of Shadows came from late Victorian-era occultism, but much of the spiritual content is derived from older pagan religions and includes both Hindu and Buddhist influences. Valiant was able to rewrite many of the spells and incantations into poetic verse. The partnership with Valiant was also short-lived, as she left the coven due to Gardner's continued publicity hunt and the new rules and restrictions which he began placing on the Bricket Wood Coven and the other covens following Gardnerian Witchcraft.

Gardnerian Witchcraft was brought to the United States in the 1960s by a British Airways employee named Raymond Buckland and his wife. The Bucklands were initiated into Witchcraft in Britain by Monique Wilson, a Gardner adherent. Upon their move to the United States, the Bucklands began the Long Island Coven. The Bucklands continued to lead the Long Island Coven until 1973, at which time the Bucklands stopped strictly following

Gardnerian Witchcraft and formed a new tradition called Saex Wicca. Saex Wicca combined aspects of Gardnerian Witchcraft with Anglo-Saxon pagan iconography.

In 1971, American Zsuzsanna Budapest fused Wiccan practices with the burgeoning feminist ideals and politics to form Dianic Wicca. This tradition focused exclusively on the Goddess, Diana, and was completely made of female practitioners.

Although there are many different offshoots of Wicca and types of witchcraft, as we will soon see, Gardnerian Witchcraft was the first to step out of the shadows and show itself as a legitimate religious belief.

Basic Principles, Beliefs, and Practices of Wicca

Wicca is the "religion" of witchcraft. As we have seen, there is no central dogma, no governing body, and no unifying holy book for Wicca. So, if you ask ten Wiccans their spiritual beliefs, you are likely to get ten different answers. However, there are some core principles and beliefs which are common to the vast majority of modern Wiccan sects. Let's explore some of these overarching beliefs.

Wicca acknowledges the **duality** of the divine, meaning that both the male and female aspects of divinity - a God and a Goddess. Depending upon the tradition that the Wiccan ascribes to, the God and Goddess can be known by many different names: Isis and Osiris, Cerridwen and Herne, Apollo and Athena, etc. There are even traditions that honor a non-gender specific deity (still encompassing both the male and female aspects, but not identified as "male" and "female"). In many Gardnerian sects, the names of the honored deities are revealed only to initiated members and kept secret from all people outside of their sect.

The concept of duality is an overarching theme of Wicca. For light to exist, there must be darkness; for good to exist, there must be evil; for a sun, there must be a moon; for life, there must also be death. It is within this duality that respect and an awe for nature are found. Nature is the perfect example for all duality - out of life comes death, out of death comes life. As the plant is eaten by the rabbit, the rabbit must die and surrender its nutrients back to the soil for a new plant to grow. Wiccans hold nature in the highest regard for its perfect balance of duality, exemplifying the God and Goddess. We mourn the death and at the same time celebrate the life to come.

Within covens, we find the traditions of **initiation** and the **system of degrees**. Initiation is a formal acceptance into witchcraft and into a coven. It is a symbolic rebirth into the faith wherein you dedicate yourself to the God and/or Goddess of the chosen tradition. An initiation is akin to baptism in the Christian faith. Although initiation is usually observed by those joining a coven, it is certainly possible to undergo initiation as a solitary practitioner. Within Wicca, there is not a specific title of practitioner who is responsible for taking the prayers of believers before the God and Goddess. We are all sacred beings and interaction with the God and Goddess is not limited just to the priesthood or a select group of individuals. Anyone with the proper intent can approach the deities. As such, the solitary practitioner can perform their own initiation.

The degree system is used solely within covens. Degrees are obtained through the dedication of time to the religion and through study. A first degree is obtained at the time of initiation, a second degree can be obtained following 6 months of being in the faith and studying the craft, and the third degree can be obtained after 1 year and 1 day of being in the faith and studying the craft. In order to be named a High Priest or High Priestess of a coven, you need to have obtained a third degree.

The belief in and use of **magick** is nearly a universal principle among Wiccans. Magick is viewed within Wicca as the redirection of natural forces through manipulation on the spirit plane in order to realize or manifest the intent of the practitioner. This is where evil can become a problem within Wicca. There are spells (curses) that can be used to cause injury or negativity to occur to another individual. In order to perform that type of magick (black magic), the intent of the practitioner must be evil. The intent of the practitioner is extremely important to spell work. Magick can be used for good or magick can be used for evil and, oftentimes, the difference is found in the heart (the intent) of the practitioner.

The importance of keeping to the white side of magick cannot be understated. A guiding principle within witchcraft is the **Rule of Three** found within the **Wiccan Rede**. The definition of "Rede" is: "Advice passed on to another." The Wiccan Rede states as follows:

> *"Bide the Wiccan Law ye must,*
> *in perfect love and perfect trust.*
> *Eight words the Wiccan Rede fulfill;*
> *If ye harm none, do what ye will.*
>
> *What ye send forth comes back to thee,*
> *so ever mind the Rule of Three.*
> *Follow this with mind and heart,*
> *Merry ye meet and merry ye part."*

The Rule of Three states that any dark magick one performs will be returned to the witch threefold. Fear and respect for the Rule of Three, along with morality, is what keeps the white witch from performing painful, destructive, and disturbing black magick spells or rituals.

Wiccans, regardless of their tradition, hold the principle of **personal responsibility** near and dear. Everyone is responsible for their own actions. Whether a member of a coven or a solitary practitioner, we must all be willing to accept the consequences, both good and bad, of our behavior here on the physical plane and in the spiritual plane.

And the final overarching principle of Wicca is **respect for the beliefs of others**. You will not see Wiccans out on a street corner professing why you also should become a Wiccan. Each person has the right and, indeed, the responsibility to choose their own spiritual path. Quite frankly, Wicca is not for everyone. If the beliefs and principles of Wicca do not fall in line with your personal beliefs, find a different path. It is important for the conviction of the

Wiccan that they search out Wicca, not have Wicca thrust upon them, nor should they expect everyone around them to convert to Wicca. Although we do not necessarily receive the same from other organized religions, Wiccans are to fully respect the spiritual beliefs of others.

The Role of The Sun

Although witchcraft and Wicca generally bring to mind thoughts of spells and rituals cast by moonlight, the sun plays an equally important role. The sun is the realm of the God and is seen as the masculine aspect of the daily cycle. The God is often referred to and depicted as the Horned God, his horns thought to be a symbol of virility. The Horned God is also usually seen as having the upper half of a man and the bottom half of a goat, much like the vision of Pan in earlier Pagan religions.

Another form common to the God in modern Wicca is that of the Green Man. Within this iteration, the God's natural forest aspect is brought to the forefront. The God is connected with the sun, hunting, death, forests, and animals.

Any spells or rituals having to do with the more "masculine" powers of hunting, death, forestry, plant life, or animals would, as such, be performed with honorifics to the God in whatever form to which you ascribe. These spells and rituals would most effectively be performed during the day and while the sun is at its peak in the sky.

Sunlight can also be used to charge magickal items, or to imbue non-magickal items with magickal properties, to be used in the realm of the God. For instance, perhaps you are a bowhunter. On the day prior to your hunt, leave your bow and arrows in the sunlight. Allow these daily items to become more than mere tools of your own ability, but feel that they have been soaked in the God's power.

Or follow the tradition of the Vikings who would place their axes outside their dwellings on sun-filled days, but never allow moonlight to touch them as they believed moonlight would dull the blade by stealing its virility. As an aside, it is this tradition that led, through the twists of many generations, to the practice of a fighter or soldier not engaging in sexual encounters in the days leading up to a fight, lest he "lose his edge".

Also, due to the elliptical orbit of Earth, the sun is not always the same distance from us. The Earth is at its closest to the sun in the first week of January, known as "perihelion", and at its farthest from the sun in the first week of July, known as "aphelion". So from January to July, the bond between the Earth and the sun (the bond between us and the God) is weakened each day; and from July to January, that bond grows stronger each day. Wiccans and witches use our position relative to other celestial bodies to time spells, rituals, and holidays for the greatest effect.

The Role of The Moon

No other object holds as much symbolism to Wicca as the moon. The moon is the realm of the Goddess, the feminine aspect of the daily cycle. In line with the duality of Wicca, the Goddess is the antithesis of the God in all things. So, in relief of the hunter, killer, animalistic God, comes the rejuvenating, life-giving, magickal, human-loving Goddess.

As we have discussed earlier, the Goddess can be known by a wide pantheon of names. The most common in modern Wicca, however, is "Diana" of the Greek tradition. I have always found it telling that the masculine, hunting, "tough guy" aspect of the duality would be known as the Green Man (which seems mysterious and kept at arm's length), while the feminine, nurturing, motherly aspect would be known as Diana (a more relatable, human, and welcoming name).

Traditionally in Wicca, the Goddess is seen as a "Triple Goddess", meaning that she embodies the aspects of maiden, mother, and crone. She is at once the eternal virgin as well as the bringer of life. The Triple Goddess symbol has, in more recent times, been adopted as a universal symbol for Wicca and witchcraft. The symbol is the three moon phases connected at tangents - the waxing crescent moon, the full moon, and the waning crescent moon.

Moonlight is the raining down of the Goddess' love and life forces onto her adherents. Because of this deep connection, moonlight is used in a large number of spells, rituals, and celebrations. Moonlight is also used to charge any crystal or magickal item with positive energy.

The moon's phases also play a large part in the effectiveness of spell work, not in that it is necessary to only cast spells or perform rituals on full moons. In fact, the waxing (building up) and waning (breaking down) phases can also be key depending on what type of spell or ritual is being performed. Also, the new moon phase (rejuvenating of power) is suggested for many spells because of its universal openness and promise of things to come.

Most spells found in books or online will have suggested moon phases in which they should be performed. However, if they do not, match the spell's intention with the proper moon phase - A new moon is best for spells to manifest new joys, emotions, or powers into your life; a waxing moon is best for spells that increase existing joys, emotions, or powers; a full moon is best for maintenance spells, devotional spells, or spells of protection from evil; and a waning moon is best for spells which decrease bad habits or negative emotions in our lives.

Sabbats

The 8 major "holidays" of Wicca are referred to as "Sabbats". The exact timing of each Sabbat is based upon the solstices and equinoxes, as well as the moon phase. The yearly Sabbats equally divide the calendar and are often represented by a circle divided into 8 sections (picture an empty Trivial Pursuit game piece). This circle is called the Wheel of The Year.

- Yule - Midwinter Solstice. Usually occurring in December. Common practices are giving of gifts, feasting, decorating using sprigs of holly, mistletoe, ivy, yew, and pine (known as the "Yule Log"), bringing in and decorating of an evergreen tree.

- Imbolc - Candlemas. Imbolc falls on February 1st. It marks the earliest rumblings of the forthcoming spring (in the northern hemisphere). It is commonly used as a time for pledges, rededication, initiations, purification, and cleaning.

- Ostara - Ostara marks the vernal equinox. It is a time when the day and the night are equal and balanced. Ostara is celebrated as a time of new beginnings and of life emerging from the deadly grip of winter.

- Beltane - Known as "May Day" in the modern world. As in ancient Irish pagan religions, the day is celebrated by dancing around the maypole. The festival of Beltane is meant to recognize life at its fullest, the greening of the world, and youth.

- Litha - Summer Solstice. Litha falls at the end of June/early July. It marks the day when the sun shines the longest during the year. Litha is a highly anticipated celebration each year and festivities have been known to last 24-36 hours.

- Lammas - Also known as Lughnasadh. This is the only festival dedicated to specifically honoring and celebrating the God. It is traditionally celebrated by baking and eating bread in the figure of the God. Lammas is meant to symbolize the sanctity and importance of the upcoming harvest. This is the first of three harvest festivals.

- Mabon - Autumnal Equinox. Mabon typically falls in September. Mabon is a celebration of thanksgiving for the fruits of the earth and a recognition of the need to share the bounty to secure blessings during the harsh upcoming winter months. It is the second of the three harvest festivals.

- Samhain - Halloween. The third harvest festival. Samhain (pronounced sow-wen) is a night-long celebration of the lives of the dead; paying respects to passed relatives, elders of faith, and loved ones. In some rituals, the dead are invited to attend the festivities along with the living. It is considered a night festival during which the veil between the world of the living and the world of the dead is at its thinnest allowing for movement between worlds and easier communication across the plains.

Being a Wiccan and Being a Witch

Being Wiccan does not necessarily mean you are a witch, and being a witch does not necessarily mean you are Wiccan. However, practicing modern Wicca *nearly always* involves practicing witchcraft. It is for this reason that I believe we can comfortably call all Wiccan followers "witches", but we cannot assume that all witchcraft practitioners are "Wiccan".

Wicca is a religious belief. Witchcraft is an action. Think of it this way, Christianity is a religious belief, while prayer is an action. All Christians pray, but not everyone who prays is a Christian.

What separates a Wiccan who practices witchcraft from a practitioner of witchcraft is the belief in the Wiccan Rede/Rule of Three. A Wiccan believes that any negativity or any evil released onto the spiritual plane, intentionally doing harm to another, will be returned to the caster threefold. A witchcraft practitioner believes that there is no consequence to them personally regardless of the energy released during the casting of a spell.

Magick and how it Can Help You

Have you thought the use of the "k" at the end of magick was a typo? It is not. Magick with a "k" is the spelling of the word which differentiates what witches practice versus magic with a "c" which is the sleight of hand which magicians and illusionists perform. Magic with a "c" pulls a rabbit out of a hat, while magick with a "k" casts a spell to free a rabbit from being held captive in a hat.

Now, how can magick help you? Magick is an action meant to materialize a blessing, something that the spell caster has set their intentions upon. Magick is a result of intent. The intent of the castor of a spell functions differently on the spiritual plane than it does here on the physical plane. Magick (through manifestation) can provide changes in our lives through manipulation of energies and vibrational frequencies.

I am often asked, "If you are a witch, why not just do a spell to win the lottery or materialize a new car." Trust me, those questions will come your way sooner than you think. My response is usually along the lines of "It just doesn't work that way." You will find spell books that include spells for material possessions (money, a new house, a new car, etc.). However, that does not mean that, if you perform this spell you will awaken tomorrow morning and trip over stacks of $100 bills. You must remember that we work on a spiritual plane, an ethereal dimension, where energy is the only material and time is irrelevant. A spell to manifest money may present itself in your life as a more lucrative job opportunity, or a gift from someone, or an inheritance, etc. Magick can and will help you manifest your desires in your life, but most times we do not have the ability to dictate just *how* those desires arrive. This is the very factor that makes magick so useful in other areas.

Magick seems ready-made for self-improvement pursuits, such as introspection, control of negative emotion, enhancement of positive emotion, finding love, spiritual growth and enlightenment, protection from negative and evil forces, healing both physically and emotionally, discovering and developing psychic abilities, etc. These are the types of areas wherein magick reveals its true capabilities and its nature. Yes, materialism is certainly a part of the world and a part of each Wiccan as well, however, it should not be the main focus or the impetus which draws the practitioner. One must always remember that in Wiccan belief, there is a balance in all things. Therefore, there is a negative to every positive and the adherent must be willing to accept that negative as readily as the positive.

Different Types of Witchcraft and Magick

There is a seemingly endless number of types of witchcraft and magick which one can practice. It seems that there are as many categories, sub-categories, and specializations as there are practitioners! But let's focus on 7 categories.

Folk Magick - A "traditional" or "Folk Witch" practices the magick of his or her ancestors, or of their general geographic region. The Folk Witch tends to take their magick as historical because it would have been practiced well prior to the formation of Wicca as a religion. The Folk Witch would most likely be a wealth of local information, having access to local availability of talismans, crystals, herbs, charms, and spells. Many Folk Witches have begun to blend the use of their "traditional" magick with more updated beliefs and modern tools.

Green Magick - The Green Witch focuses on their interaction with nature and the magic to be garnered daily from nature itself. A Green Witch is typically a rural witch and highly influenced by folk magic, with the center of their magical world being the home. The use of herbal remedies tends to be the specialty of most Green Witches and they often grow and harvest the herbs themselves, as opposed to purchasing herbs from vendors. Also, Green Witches are usually quite versed in aromatherapy using local herb blends.

Gardnerian Wiccans - Gardnerian Wiccans are one of only two forms of modern witchcraft that can trace its lineage back in an unbroken line to the very beginning of Wicca, i.e., Gerald Gardner. Gardnerian Wicca is a British form of Wicca which is bound by oath to practice reasonable witchcraft. Gardnerian Wicca tends to be extremely practical with very little ceremony.

Alexandrian Wiccans - Alexandrian Wiccans are the second form of modern witchcraft able to trace its lineage back to those early days, i.e., Alex Sanders. Alex Sanders was one of Gerald Gardner's very first human beings initiated into Wicca. Alexandrian Wicca is typically a blend of ceremonial and Gardnerian Wicca.

Eclectic Witchcraft - Eclectic witchcraft is a catch-all term for witchcraft that doesn't specifically fit into any other category. The Eclectic Witch may be a blend of many different traditions, faiths and folk practices. The Eclectic Witch can be thought of as the consummate do-it-yourselfer. They may take some traditional beliefs, some things read online, some things learned from a workshop they attended, and their own personal experiences; roll them all together, and come up with a practical method of witchcraft that works for them.

Ceremonial Magick - Ceremonial witchcraft, also called High witchcraft, uses very specific tools and incantations to call upon the deities and entities of the spirit world. Ceremonial witchcraft is a blend of ancient occult/pagan teachings. This type of witchcraft is held highly secret and many practitioners do not even identify with the word "witch" at all out of an abundance of caution.

Hereditary Witchcraft - Hereditary witchcraft is a belief and practice system in which the knowledge is handed down from one generation to the next (mother to daughter; father to son). It is very unusual for any family outsider to be included in Hereditary witchcraft and it is just as unusual for the existence of such knowledge to even be discussed in the presence of an outsider, including sons-in-law or daughters-in-law. The relationship need not necessarily be a genetic one, as adopted children are seen as worthy candidates for Hereditary witchcraft. It is more a family tradition basis than a strictly biological tradition.

The Do's and Don'ts of Witchcraft

Starting to practice witchcraft or learning about the Wiccan belief system is hard, there is simply a TON of information and it feels like you need to instantly retain it all. Right? Relax. You are not going to go from "interested" in witchcraft to some full-blown, mega-wizard, master of all realities by reading a book one time. This is a huge opportunity to affect both your inner being and your physical life, but it is a process. For those times when you become overwhelmed at the length and breadth of the information available to you, and you will, I have compiled here a list of Witchcraft Do's and Don'ts so you can easily reference them later. Think of this as a cheat sheet of highlights for your magickal journey.

DO your homework. Research everything… twice! I say this for two reasons. First, if you are just starting out, you still need to determine if Wicca and/or witchcraft is really what you are looking for in your life. Take the time to research as many world religions as you can, compare and contrast your personal beliefs and feelings with the teachings and precepts of these religions, and then decide. Please understand, of course I want as many strong Wiccan brothers and sisters as possible and I want you all to experience the freedom that comes from practicing witchcraft to experience a more fulfilling life. But more than that, I hope that everyone finds their own personal path to happiness and peace. If that is through Wicca and/or witchcraft, welcome! If it is not, then go in peace and I wish you only joy on your journey.

DON'T rush out and spend a bunch of money on your ritual tools right away. The practice of witchcraft was being performed in times where purchasing items was not even a consideration. Everything necessary was made by hand. Now, thankfully for us craft-challenged individuals, we are able to buy some of the ritual items. That is nice but can get extremely expensive very quickly. So, until you are certain that you want to practice witchcraft or enter the Wiccan religion, and have researched what you will need to purchase versus what you can make for yourself, there is no need to run up that credit card bill.

DO choose your ritual items carefully and mindfully. Once you have made the commitment and decision to move forward into the Wiccan religion or practice of witchcraft, you will need a few items (a starter tool kit, if you will). Some things you may be able to make yourself. Others you may need to purchase. Take your time in finding these items. Hold them, touch them, feel their energy, and note the way your energy responds. This is not the time for bargain online shopping I'm afraid. Allow your intuition to guide you to the proper items through physical contact.

DON'T choose witchcraft out of a thirst for revenge. I am talking about hexes and curses here. Don't do it. That is the path of black magick. Yes, it exists. And no, it is in no way good for you. The type of negative energy that it takes to hex or curse a person marks you, that kind of evil stains you. Witchcraft and Wicca were not intended to be used to harm others. The side of light will lead to peace and balance - while darkness will always lead to destruction and decay.

DO commit to following the Rule of Three and the Wiccan Rede. It is human to be upset and out of a fit of anger wish some type of harm on another. But as a practitioner of witchcraft or Wicca, we need to end those negative thoughts quickly, before they turn to intent or action. By committing ourselves to the Wiccan Rede, the basic principle of which is "Do No Harm", we are committing ourselves to a world of light. Let that anger pass through you and move on. It is not worth the threefold return just to gain some fleeting moral victory. Let it go.

DON'T expect everything to turn out perfectly instantaneously. Witchcraft is more an art than it is a science. Some spells just do not work for me. It happens. We may try the exact same spell using the exact same ingredients yet receive completely different results. It is no different than if you gave two artists the exact same type of brush, paint, and canvas, along with instruction to produce a painting of the same mythological animal. There is very little chance that their paintings would be identical. Do not let spell work that does not produce your desired result overly frustrate you. Keep a good, up-to-date grimoire so that you are able to see what works for you and what does not.

DO what feels best and works for you. Witchcraft is not a list of boxes to check off on the way to a promised prize. Witchcraft is the ultimate customizable life-changer. There is no *wrong* way to practice! As long as your intention is clear to you and you are staying on the white witch side of things, you do you. The spell calls for a copper bowl, but all you have at the ready is a Tupperware container? As long as you believe it will suffice, it will suffice. Halfway through a ritual and forget the exact language you are to recite? As long as what you say holds the same meaning and power to you, wing it. The spell calls for the use of thyme, but you are allergic to thyme? Rosemary it is. Remember that witchcraft is about your intent being manifested on this plane through the manipulation of forces and energies on the spiritual plane. Your intent is the key.

DON'T reject meditation. Meditation provides clarity through a knowledge of self. Knowledge of yourself strengthens your ability to remain grounded. Remaining grounded allows your focus to be on your intent. And your intent is what is released onto the spiritual plane, or into the universe, during a spell or ritual. You don't need to become some kind of monk, just give yourself 10 minutes per day, three or four times per week, to meditate. You will be surprised at the results it will have on your practice and the effectiveness of your spell work.

DO trust yourself while walking along this path. You have made the decision to participate in something which exists solely to create joy, peace, comfort, and happiness in your life and in the lives of those you care about. There are so many self-destructive ways you could be spending your time, ways that would only serve to hurt you and those you love in the long run. But instead, you have consciously chosen to embark on a journey to better your life. By learning and practicing spell work, rituals, and enhancing your natural psychic abilities, you are doing just that - walking toward a better and more fulfilling life.

Psychic Abilities and Divination

Psychic Abilities

Psychic abilities are not necessarily a precursor or a result of witchcraft or Wicca. However, the development of these abilities does seem to be extremely common in both the religion of Wicca and in the practice of witchcraft, and for good reason. Wicca and witchcraft require one to be very self-aware; a state achieved through deep introspection. The more comfortable that we are able to become with the true nature of ourselves through introspection, the more obvious and pronounced your natural psychic abilities become. That is why, if you spend 10 minutes at any Wicca or witchcraft event, you will get 15 offers to have a tarot reading performed for you.

Everyone has at least a small amount of natural psychic ability lying dormant within them. The question becomes whether or not they will discover, nurture, and grow this talent. There are different types of psychic abilities and a number of ways to explore and develop these abilities.

First, let's discuss the types of abilities:

- **Precognition** is the ability to know future events. A Precog may receive clear, definite messages or visions of the future, or they may receive more vague messages or even flashes of images and emotions.

- **Intuition**, or **intuitiveness**, is the ability to just "know" things. An Intuitive usually makes an excellent Tarot Card reader because they are able to interpret the meaning of the cards correctly for the client without knowing any specifics of the client's life.

- **Clairvoyance** is the ability to visualize situations or objects not within the physical space. A Clairvoyant is excellent at remote viewing and is the type of "psychic" used by police in locating missing people.

- **Empathy** is the ability to sense the feelings, emotions, and energies of other people. Empaths often find themselves to be very effective spiritual healers as they are able to sense disturbances in the energy fields of their clients, which lead them to a specific part of the body that may be causing a health issue. Empaths are also the most likely to be affected by negative energies given off by evil or negative spirits and, as such, often find themselves feeling drained or exhausted just by being in the presence of specific people.

- **Mediums** are individuals who are able to communicate with the spirit world through the use of spirit guides. Mediums may see and/or hear the spirits themselves and be able to hold a dialogue, or they may only receive messages via dreams or visions without the ability to control the messages, like a telephone call where you can hear the other person but they cannot hear you.

- **Telepathy** is the ability to communicate with another living individual by mental means alone. Telepaths have been referred to as "mind readers", but that is not completely accurate. In truth, a Telepath is able to receive messages from another individual AND send messages to another individual. The other individual need not be a developed Telepath themselves but does need to be focused on sending or receiving a message.

- **Telekinesis** is the ability to move a physical object using only the power of their mind (intent). A Telekinetic is the Jedi of the psychic world. Telekinesis is a rare ability and is a favorite of charlatans to fake.

As I stated earlier, everyone has at least a little psychic ability and talent tucked away within them. This ability can be drawn out through introspection and meditation. But what then? There are a number of ways that you can begin to develop your natural psychic ability further. Let's take a look at some of them.

- **Listen Intently to What Is Said AND What Is Not Said**

  - When people have a conversation, there is as much to be gleaned and learned by what is omitted as there is in what is actually discussed. For example, let's say that you are having a passing conversation with a female friend. You say, "How are you doing?" And she answers, "I'm fine. The kids are doing good and growing like weeds." Although that seems like a positive answer, you will notice that she glanced over herself quickly and never even mentioned her husband. Perhaps they are not doing so well as a couple as she would have you believe. Learn to stretch your intuitive legs.

- **Deliberate Clarity**

  - Achieving deliberate clarity simply means becoming aware of everything around you. It is being purposefully observant - another word for this is "mindfulness". Pay attention to changes in the sunlight and shadows, notice a shift in the wind, note who enters a room and who exits. Take mental notes of everything. Becoming deliberately clear will help you by being able to separate real psychic messages from imagination and wishful thinking.

- **Meditation**

- One of the best ways to develop intuition is to implement a regular schedule of meditation. When we meditate, we explore and open the depths of our subconscious mind. Intuitiveness is a function of the subconscious. Learn your way around so you are able to connect to your subconscious and retrieve those intuitive thoughts.

- **Trust Your Gut**

  - Your "gut feeling" is your intuition trying to express itself. Those feelings are your subconscious thoughts struggling to come to the surface. Pay attention. Explore those thoughts. Learn to trust your intuition and see where it takes you.

- **Journal**

  - Have you ever had a dream about a specific person or an event? Have you ever felt like something important was about to happen but didn't know exactly what? Write it down! Keep a journal so you can track your sensory messages and be able to review them for significance. It will help you gain confidence in your abilities and learn to trust them more. Of course, there will inevitably be messages you are never able to confirm. And that is okay. It doesn't mean that they were not accurate, it only means that you were not able to verify the message.

- **Practice Makes Perfect**

  - Well, practice may not make you "perfect", but it will make you better. Try learning about different forms of divination and, when you find one that interests you, keep practicing it until you can verify that the messages you are receiving are valid. When you have practiced enough, keep practicing! There is no finish line here, you can always improve or learn new skills. Challenge yourself to stretch and grow by developing new skills and strengthening those you have begun to develop.

- **Test Yourself**

  - If you believe you are receiving messages from someone or someplace else, try to confirm it. When your phone rings, try to feel who is calling before checking the caller ID. When you are meeting a friend for coffee, focus and try to feel what kind of music they are listening to on the drive. Then ask them when they arrive. Simple exercises like this will help you develop your natural abilities. Never shy away from a chance to test yourself.

And realize that, as you start out, you may well be wrong more often than you are right. But, hopefully, with practice, your correct percentage will rise to heights that will surprise you.

Divination

Divination is the practice of seeking knowledge of the future or the unknown through supernatural or magickal means. As with psychic abilities, there are many ways to practice divination and some may match better with your innate abilities than others. Let's discuss some of the practices and see if anything particularly resonates with you. If not, try them all until you find one that works best with your personal abilities.

- **Tarot Cards**

  - If you are not familiar with divination, it may seem as though someone who reads Tarot Cards is "predicting the future" through the cards. That is not exactly accurate. The cards provide an outline or a course of energy. It is the job of the reader to interpret the meanings and possible outcomes of the flow of energies.

- **Celtic Ogham**

  - The Ogham are mostly used as a divination tool by Wiccans who follow a Celtic tradition. In this practice, the Ogham alphabet is inscribed on wooden dowels. The dowels are then dropped, and the message is interpreted by the reader.

- **Norse Rune Stones**

  - According to Norse pagan tradition, Odin created a set of sacred symbols, known as Runes, as a gift to humans. Over the ensuing centuries, the Runes evolved into a collection of 16 letters. Each of these Runic letters holds both a metaphorical and divinatory meaning. The reader casts the lot of 16 stones and interprets the message based on how each Rune is positioned and oriented.

- **Tea Leaves**

- The reading of tea leaves became popular in the western world in the 17th century, although the Chinese have been using the method for divination for much, much longer. In this practice, a cup of unstrained tea is made and consumed by the reader. When the tea is gone and the leaves remain, the cup is swirled three times to distribute the leaves into a pattern. The reader is then able to interpret the message based upon the pattern formed by the tea leaves. Today, there are even specially designed tea cups with patterns and symbols inscribed onto the rim and sides of the cup to make the process of interpretation easier.

- **Pendulum**

  - Pendulum divination is one of the simplest forms to understand and interpret. This form is based on the asking of yes or no questions. Based upon the resulting pattern of a swing of the pendulum (usually a crystal at the end of a length of rope or chain), the yes or no answer is determined. The trick to this type of divination is not so much in interpreting the result as it is in learning to ask the right questions.

- **Osteomancy**

  - If you knew that "Osteomancy" meant "divination through reading bones", you were a step ahead of me! However, reading bones has been performed by cultures all around the world for thousands of years. Although there are many techniques, the purpose is the same - foretelling the path of future energies through interpreting a cast of bones.

- **Scrying**

  - This practice of scrying can be done using a number of different types of medium - water, mirror, crystal ball, etc. Pretty much any reflective surface can be used for scrying, although you may have noticed a pattern in the three media I listed (water, mirror, and crystals are all energy enhancers). Scrying is practiced by entering a state, not unlike meditation wherein you access your subconscious mind while keeping the client's question at the forefront of the conscious mind. By directing your energy and brain waves into the chosen media, an image or message can become clear to the reader (usually visually), either physically visible within the media or as a subconscious vision. It is then the job of the reader to interpret the message for the client. The practice of scrying does come with a caveat. When opening ourselves up to the spirit world in this manner and essentially becoming a blank slate for another realm to draw on, there is no guarantee that the entity answering your call is a being of light. In other words, much like with the use of Ouija Boards, once the doorway is opened, there is no way of knowing exactly what is going to step through. This puts the reader in spiritual, mental, and possibly physical danger during and after each reading. Explore, but be safe.

- **Numerology**

  - Many pagan spiritual traditions, as well as Wiccans and witchcraft practitioners, incorporate the practice of numerology. Numbers have great significance within the spiritual and magickal realms. Some numbers hold more power than others, and specific combinations of numbers can even be developed for magickal use in spell work. There are also links to be drawn between numbers and planets and/or other celestial bodies.

- **Automatic Writing**

  - One of the most popular modern methods of divination is automatic writing. In this practice, the practitioner holds a writing instrument, enters into a meditation-like state, and allows words and messages to flow through them onto the paper without any conscious thought or effort. The idea of automatic writing is to channel the message from the spirit realm directly onto the paper without running the information through the practitioner's conscious mind first. I have personally even seen automatic writing practiced with the eyes closed, writing phrases, keywords, and drawing shapes or pictures. Following the writing, the practitioner usually offers to go through the writing with the client to attempt to "divine" meaning from what may seem like an incoherent jumble of words.

In the section on scrying, you will notice that I mentioned Ouija Boards. I would be remiss if I did not at least mention that Ouija Boards (otherwise known as "Talking Boards" or "Spirit Boards") are used as a tool of divination. I did not include Spirit Boards in the list because I feel that they are extremely unsafe. Yes, I have heard it before, "you are warning me about a board game made by Milton-Bradley". And I completely understand the ridicule of my hesitancy. However, allow me to explain why Spirit Boards are so dangerous.

The cardboard and plastic used to make a Spirit Board and planchet are not the issue. The problem is that the board itself only serves as a focal point. The true power of a Spirit Board comes from the player(s). Most of the time, a player goes into a Spirit Board session completely unprotected and having no idea the danger that they are placing themselves in. Imagine going from playing flag football to playing against an NFL team - oh and you do not have any pads or a helmet. That is essentially what is going on when the common person, or even an inexperienced witch, communicates using a Spirit Board.

When a Spirit Board session begins, the player(s) opens him/herself to the spiritual plane and hopes to come into contact with a positive entity. That is like throwing open the door of a shark cage and hoping that Nemo is who swims in with you. Sure, it may be a positive entity, but are you truly prepared to deal with the consequences if it is not? Are you actually willing to roll the dice that it is Nemo as opposed to a great white shark? Quite honestly, the risk is simply too high and unnecessary.

There is absolutely no way to determine what type of entity or energy is speaking to you through a Spirit Board. And once that door is opened and something has been invited onto our plane, it is not a simple task to return it. Evil exists. Evil is real. Evil will do what evil does - cause nothing but pain, chaos, and turmoil. So, while you may think you are speaking with your dearly departed Aunt Edna, truthfully you may have just become the next target of a fresh new demon.

For these reasons, I could not in good conscience include Spirit Boards on the above list. I recommend that this type of divination be avoided for the safety of everyone involved.

Chapter 2

Preparing

Grounding and Drawing Energy

Do you realize what is happening at this very moment as you read or listen to these words? Your brain is experiencing a literal lightning storm. Billions of times per second, the neurons in your brain are firing electrical pulses of ions across tiny gaps (much like a spark plug), within the trail of each lightning bolt are charged particles of chemicals that relay a biological message to the accepting neuron, directing what it does next. And this process is repeated constantly throughout the brain, simultaneously. Our bodies, our brains, our thoughts, feelings, and emotions are all electrical impulses - they are energy. My body, your body, a slug, a cow, a fox, and a meerkat, every living organism in the physical world is made of energy. And where do we receive our charge? What is the power plant that can keep all of these electro-chemical machines running at full capacity? Mother Earth! Our planet generates a constant, radiating stream of electromagnetic energy. Within this natural link between us and our planet can be found all the energy that we will ever need throughout our lives, both physically and metaphysically speaking. It is like all living creatures are plugged into the same electrical outlet.

This relates to our discussion of magick in two ways. First, magick requires a large output of energy from the Wiccan or witch. It is, after all, a blast of our intentions sent out into the universe and across the spiritual plane. And secondly, we humans have a tendency to step on our own power cord and we end up getting "unplugged", unfulfilled, and unsure how to fix our problems.

There are two important steps that we must take to ensure our magick and our spell work are being done with the proper energy - creating an energy circuit by grounding ourselves and centering our energy.

Creating an Energy Circuit Through Grounding

For centuries, humans never had to worry about whether their energies were or were not properly grounded because they were very rarely out of direct contact with the earth. But today we wear rubber-soled shoes, live and work many stories above the planet, spend our time on asphalt, and drive in rubber-tired vehicles. When was the last time you were in direct contact with the surface of the earth? For many, it might have been years! After all, rubber, asphalt, wood, and plastic are all non-conductive, which means we all pretty much exist in a bubble separating ourselves from the natural energy flowing from the Earth. Now, please do not misunderstand. I am not trying to convince you to go full hermit, move to the forest, and walk around barefoot in the middle of nowhere. I am quite happy to have my modern conveniences. But that makes it all the more important to make a designated effort to ground our energy from time to time in order to recharge ourselves and to rid ourselves of negativity. We cannot make a working energy circuit with only a "positive" wire or with only a "negative wire". Just like the electricity flow in our homes, we need to have a full, uninterrupted circuit with a positive, negative, and ground wire.

If you happen to live in a rural setting with warm average temperatures year-round, then you have hit the grounding jackpot. Take off your shoes and take a walk through the forest. Be mindful of the connection you are making with the earth, take time to appreciate the feeling of being in your rightful place in the natural scheme and in your biome. Stand with the grass between your toes and visualize the positive energy of the earth flowing up through your left leg, all the way up to the top of your head, and down your right side back into the ground. As this positive energy enters you, it shoves any and all negativity that you have taken on out of the way ahead of it and out through the bottom of your right foot. Once you have only the positive, white light flowing in and out of you and all of the negative, dark energy has been removed and cleansed from you, picture the light growing and branching into every part of you, every cell of your body, until you simply appear to yourself to be made of the light energy. That is how you want to feel when approaching spell work or rituals or any other spirit plane tasks - like you are so full of energy that you ARE the energy.

If you do not live in a countryside utopia, or like me, you only have "no shoe" weather for about 3 months per year, it doesn't mean that you cannot ground yourself. First of all, find a park and when it is warm enough, take off your shoes. But any other time that you need to ground, you can accomplish it through intense visualization.

First, find a chair with a straight enough back that you can sit comfortably with both of your feet flat on the floor. Close your eyes. Take 3 deep breaths, slowly in and slowly out. With each exhale, visualize roots extending from the bottom of your feet and going straight down towards the ground. By the third exhale, these roots reach all the way from wherever you are sitting, through the structure you are in, and into the ground beneath. Next, visualize the positive energy of the earth flowing up through your left leg, all the way up to the top of your head, and down your right side back into the ground. As this positive energy enters you, it shoves any and all negativity that you have taken on out of the way ahead of it and out through the bottom of your right foot. Once you have only the positive, white light flowing in and out of you and all of the negative, dark energy has been removed and cleansed from you, picture the light growing and branching into every part of you, every cell of your body, until you simply appear to yourself to be made of the light energy. That is how you want to feel when approaching spell work or rituals or any other spirit plane tasks - like you are so full of energy that you ARE the energy.

Centering Your Energy

Learning to center your energy is one of those big breakthrough moments in life. Being centered is a necessity in spell work, but it is also useful in daily, mundane life as well. It is all about controlling our emotional responses to stress and channeling them into a positive outcome.

Let's think about it this way. Have you ever had to give a speech or presentation in front of a group of people? You know that feeling of "butterflies" you had beforehand, the sweaty palms, the dry mouth, the increased heart rate, how it seemed like time was actually speeding up? That was your body responding to the stress you were under by dumping adrenaline into your bloodstream. Then came all of those negative thoughts about not being properly prepared, not being as eloquent as you should be, tripping over your words, and coming off as awkward instead of relaxed. Well, what if I told you that at that moment, just before you were ready to stand up and start speaking, you could visualize your way to using all of that adrenaline to your advantage? It is very similar when we are working on the spiritual plane, casting a spell, or performing a ritual. We get nervous that we are not prepared or are going to forget something. So, let's see how to center our energy and use all of that adrenaline to our advantage.

First, concentrate on your breathing. Take slow, deep breaths in through the nose and out through the mouth. This will flood your cells with oxygen as well as work to slow your heart rate to a reasonable level.

Secondly, know or figure out where your center is. This is your physical center of gravity. Usually, it is located about two fingers below your navel. This is the spot on your body with the greatest ability to balance. Focus on your center.

Next, visualize all of the energy in your body as being spread out into the points farthest from your center. For most, this will be your hands, feet and top of your head. Visualize yourself pulling all of this scattered energy into your center. This energy becomes a super dense, bright light at your center.

Then visualize everything that is left in the places where your energy had been as a dark "Silly Putty" substance. Picture pulling all of this negativity, all of the negative thoughts, the worries, the stress of the situation out into the palms of your hands and shaping it into a ball. Then throw all of those lies and self-deprecation as far from you as you possibly can.

Now as you relax, you will feel a renewed sense of calm and confidence. You are once again clean and full of light. You are able to see your intentions clearly and are able to channel your adrenaline into positive thoughts.

You are centered.

Getting Clear with Your Intentions

It can be so disheartening to spend time and energy learning, preparing, and casting a spell just to have it not produce any results. You could have found the perfect spell and performed everything flawlessly, but nothing happens. I learned long ago that in times like these, it is usually a problem with intention.

Any intention is the "what you want to result from the spell" part of practicing magick. And, sure it sounds like it would be obvious. "If I perform a money spell, then I must want money." But do you? Is that what you mean? There are three good reasons to set intentions.

First, you want to set an intention so your desires are clearly communicated. Remember, you are powering your spell with this intention, so you need to send out this intention into the universe. No intention behind a spell is the same as just performing a scene from a play.

Secondly, setting a clear and concise intention will guarantee that you do not manifest something that you do not actually want, or that you manifest something in a detrimental way. For example, let's say you want to be able to quit your current job and go into business for yourself, but to make that transition you will need money. So, you set the desire, "I desire money. I WILL have enough for all of my desires." At first glance, that makes sense. You need money, so you ask for money. A short time later, you get called into your boss' office and they give you a substantial raise (with additional responsibilities). Although you will now have enough money to start your own business, you will need to continue to work for your employer to receive it, plus you now feel beholden to your employer for giving you such a raise. It turns out that you are actually *further* from reaching your desire of becoming an entrepreneur. That is because your intention was not clear and concise. You thought you just needed money, but that was not correct. Perhaps changing your intention to, "I desire to work for myself doing what I love while it brings me financial abundance month after month" would be the more specific and true intention. That is what you actually want, so ask for it.

The final reason to set an intention is for power. As we have discussed, the fuel behind sending your intention into the universe is the intention. So how strong do you want your spell to be? You won't overpower the universe, so give it everything you have! Once you have that clear and concise intention in your mind, harness and use that power by making sure all your thoughts and feelings support your intention.

Sacred Space for Practice

For many practitioners, there is inherent magick to be found in having a sacred space to practice. In setting this space, you are not only setting up a physical space, but also a space where the physical plane meets the spiritual plane. The space that you choose for yourself can either be a permanent sacred space specifically set aside for your practice, or it can be a temporary space that you set up each time you practice or during months that you are able to be outside. It can be inside your home or it can be outside among nature. It really is up to you when it comes to where you practice and what you make your sacred space. There are a few tips on choosing and creating your sacred space.

- Take your time and choose wisely.

  - Just because you happen to have a spare corner in your basement, does not necessarily mean that is where you want to practice your Wicca or witchcraft. You will want to choose somewhere that makes you feel welcome, comfortable, and peaceful. Right there beside the furnace may not be a great choice! Outdoor sacred space can be perfect and powerful but keep inclement weather in mind. You may either need a backup plan for those rainy days or, like me, you may only be able to use an outside space a few months per year and be inside the remainder of the year. Personally, I keep a "permanent" sacred space inside my home but create a "temporary" sacred space in a nearby forest whenever the weather cooperates. Also, consider lighting conditions, foot traffic, noise, etc.

- Make it your own.

  - Customize the space to yourself or your intention. This space is for *you* and it should reflect *you*. Perhaps you have decided to use your college student's now spare bedroom. Then down come the puppy posters and the mirror with band stickers all over it. Give it a cleaning. Hang some of your things on the walls, put some of your books and knick knacks on the shelves, hang that painting of the Green Man that caught your eye. Bring in your straight-backed chair for meditation. Add a small table you can use as an altar or workspace. Don't forget your candles and some colored scarves. Whatever you need to do to make the space feel like it is yours and yours alone.

- Cleanse the space.

  - Once you have chosen your space and redecorated it to amplify your personality, you will want to perform a ritual cleansing of your new sacred space. This will eliminate negativity or evil that may be remaining in the area. This is a very important step in preparing your sacred space. There is nothing that will cause more unwanted or dangerous repercussions to your magick than having evil within your work area. Negativity will attach itself to your intentions anytime it possibly can and, at the very least, nullify any positivity you are attempting to manifest. At most, it can literally change a spell with pure intention into a manifestation of evil. When you are using a permanent installation of sacred space, you should cleanse through smudging at least once per month. Also, for this type of sacred space, consider performing a simple incantation in order to clarify your intent to dedicate this space to the practice of white magick and banishing all negativity and evil from the space. If you are setting up a temporary sacred space, smudge every time you set up your space.

After you have chosen a sacred space, made it yours, and cleansed it of negativity, you will need an altar. Don't panic, it is not as difficult to prepare as it sounds. Let's explore altars and see just what you will need.

Altars

Just as with a sacred space, some Wicca and witchcraft practitioners have the ability to maintain a permanent altar, while others choose the temporary option. Truthfully, it depends on your circumstances, your available space, and your location.

Altars are available through Wicca supply stores, but they are not truly an item that is necessary to purchase as opposed to making your own. Pretty much any flat surface can be used as an altar (a table, a desk, a coffee table…). The only caveat to altars I would offer is that it be made of a natural material like wood, stone, concrete, or glass. Synthetic materials, although easier to find, are just not as conductive to energy transfer as natural materials. Personally, my inside altar is a table made of repurposed pallet wood and my outside, natural altar is a tree stump found in the forest behind my home.

Altars can be decorated in whichever way you prefer. Perhaps try some colorful scarves to match the intent of the spell or ritual you will be performing, or the time of year you are performing your ritual. Maybe you would like to scatter some flower petals on the altar to signify spring or some colorful leaves when autumn is in full bloom. Feel free to place some of your favorite crystals on the altar, just be sure that the crystals have been cleansed.

The most important items on your altar will be your tools. We will be covering the necessary tools in the next section. Just know that on your altar, you will need to leave a comfortable amount of room for the appropriate tools.

The only person who needs to like your altar is you. So never feel as if you would be performing better magick with a fancier altar. The altar is meant to celebrate what you have been given through nature, thank the God and Goddess for your blessings, and help to reflect your intentions into the universe. Nowhere in that list is the altar to show how much spending power you wield. Nature has no use for money so you will never gain favor from a tree spirit simply by having LED lights around your chalice. Make your altar reflect your intention and your commitment to the God and Goddess and you cannot possibly go wrong.

Basic Tools for Witchcraft - The Witch's Toolkit

The Cauldron

The witch's cauldron is a very recognizable iconic symbol that even people outside of Wicca or witchcraft are familiar with and will recognize. In Wiccan traditions, the cauldron is a symbol of creation and transformation, as well as fire. It is a sacred tool to the Goddess due to its shape and symbology of creativity and transformation. It can be used in a number of different ways during your practice. Because cauldrons are metal, they are excellent for use in fire spells, as incense holders, as a place to burn candles until completely consumed, or as a place to make and burn charcoal.

Don't worry, you won't be making soup, even though the word "cauldron" automatically draws forth the vision of mysterious ingredients in a witch's broth. Actually, the roots of that pop culture fallacy are traceable back to none other than William Shakespeare!

> *"Double, double toil and trouble;*
> *Fire burn and cauldron bubble.*
> *Fillet of a fenny snake,*
> *In the cauldron boil and bake;*
> *Eye of newt and toe of frog,*
> *Wool of bat and tongue of dog,*
> *Adder's fork and blind-worm's sting,*
> *Lizard's leg and howlet's wing,*
> *For a charm of powerful trouble,*
> *Like a hell-broth boil and bubble."*
> - William Shakespeare (from Macbeth)

Cauldrons are, unfortunately, quite expensive and can vary greatly in size. However, the thought of the huge cauldron hanging over the open fire is really unnecessary. Those were literally cooking vessels and are not exactly in fashion in the modern world. So, if you are able to afford a small cauldron for your altar, wonderful! If you have a difficult time convincing yourself that a cauldron is a necessary expense, like me, feel free to use a sturdy and thick metal bowl. It will fill the role just fine.

The Elements

Traditionally, and in the vast majority of practices, there are four elements that are focused on in Wicca. The four elements are earth, air, fire, and water. Each of the elements are associated with cardinal directions, traits, as well as being guardian beings invoked for protection when casting a sacred circle.

The following cardinal directions are for the northern hemisphere. If you are in the southern hemisphere, use the opposite cardinal direction.

Earth - The element of earth is fertile and stable. The earth is considered the ultimate feminine element and is associated with the Goddess. The earth is circular and, as the Wheel of the Year turns, we are able to watch the seasons change and we watch the cycle of life play out because of it: birth, life, death, and rebirth. The earth is nurturing and stable, solid and firm, full of endurance and strength. Earth's cardinal direction is north.

Air - The element of air is connected to the soul, breath of life, and communication. Air carries away our strife and troubles and, as such, is associated with positive thoughts and peace. It is a good element to focus on if your spell deals with wisdom or powers of the mind. Air's cardinal direction is east.

Fire - The element of fire is connected to both creation and destruction. Fire is purifying with a masculine energy connected to strong will and is associated with the God. Fire's cardinal direction is south.

Water - Water is used for healing, cleansing, and purification. It is associated with passion and emotion. Water is used and sacred in many world religions, and Wicca is no different. "Holy Water" is saltwater that has been blessed by a long-time practitioner of the faith. Some Wiccan covens use their own holy water to consecrate the circle and tools used in spell work and rituals. Water's cardinal direction is west.

There are some modern traditions that include a fifth element - that of spirit. Spirit is also sometimes referred to as Akasha or Aether. The spirit element acts as a bridge between the physical plane and the spiritual plane.

Just like everything in the Wiccan belief, how much you incorporate the elements is completely your choice. However, it is important to keep in mind that the elements are used as a foundation in the vast majority of Wiccan and witchcraft spell work that you will come across in your reading and research.

The Chalice

The chalice is also sometimes referred to as a "goblet". Traditionally, the chalice is silver, and its use depends upon the spell or ritual being performed. It can contain wine, ale, water, or remain empty (to be symbolically filled during the ritual). The chalice is considered a tool of femininity and represents the Goddess, the element of water, and is a not-so-subtle symbol of fertility.

Although the chalice is not a Wiccan "necessity", it is a tool that I highly recommend for its powerful symbolism and its versatility.

Incense and Smoke

Incense has been used by every religion dating back to antiquity. The smoke of incense is associated with the spiritual world. It also is the only tool that represents two of the four elements - those are the elements of air and fire. Incense is a core component of every Wiccan ritual and in the practice of magick.

Incense is available in a seemingly unending number of scents, however, the scent is secondary in its use of magic. The more important portion of incense for our uses is the smoke itself which has the symbolic ability to carry our desires into the universe under the power of our intent. It is even possible to learn how to create your own incense with customized scents.

Traditionally, incense was used in witchcraft rituals by placing a blend of dried herbs in a censer or cauldron. However, in modern practice, most use either incense sticks or cones because they are inexpensive, and gathering your own herbs and charcoal is time-consuming.

The Candles

Since humans have learned to create lasting light, we have been using candles. Candles are now used as a major part of every Wiccan and witchcraft ritual. Simply put, no Wiccan gathering is complete without candles.

In each sacred circle, the cardinal directions are marked with specifically colored candles - Green or brown for the north, yellow or white for the east, red or orange for the south, and blue for the west. Also, on the altar would be 2 pillar candles to represent the God and the Goddess.

Within different spells, any number of candles may be lit and extinguished during the spell work.

The mere act of lighting a candle can be a powerful expression or energetic doorway-opener of intention. It can make a strong and deep connection between you and the magick which you are attempting to manifest. They are great for focus and meditation as well.

The Crystals and Stones

Each crystal and stone have unique properties which make it useful in different types of magick. Some are good for protection and grounding, while others excel at enhancing the connection between the practitioner and the spirit realm.

We will only be exploring a few of the thousands of stones and crystals which hold magickal significance because there are thousands of reference books out there dedicated solely to the subject. However, we should have a working knowledge of the following stones and crystals.

- **Black Tourmaline**
    - Black Tourmaline is a power healer and protector crystal. Specifically, it is useful in blocking psychic attacks and negative thought patterns. It is even used as protection against harmful electromagnetic radiation caused by modern electronics.

- **Black Obsidian**

    - Black Obsidian is formed when molten lava is cooled very quickly, like when it comes into contact with water. It works wonderfully as a protective shield against negativity and evil. It soaks up bad energy like a sponge and holds it. Because of its retention ability, you will want to cleanse your obsidian regularly by simply holding it under running water and visualizing all of the negativity washing from the stone, down the drain, and out of your life.

- **Selenite**

    - Selenite has been a favorite among crystal lovers dating back to Ancient Greece. Some Greeks actually made windows from thin slabs of Selenite. It is found deep in the caves of Mexico, Morocco, and Madagascar, and the raw crystal formations in the caves can reach up to 35 feet long. The caves are absolutely beautiful, assuming you would find Superman's Fortress of Solitude to be beautiful! Selenite is very useful in cleansing and clearing a home or office because it dispels negative energy and creates calm in any space. Selenite lamps are also a great alternative to Himalayan salt lamps because it not only looks great when lit but is also self-cleansing and can cleanse other crystals in its environment.

- **Amethyst**

    - Amethyst has been used since the middle ages as a healing crystal. It is widely used for its ability to protect its bearer emotionally and spiritually by helping to break anxious or addictive thought patterns and ties to stressful energies. Also, a piece of amethyst on your nightstand or under your pillow can help protect you from nightmares.

- **Carnelian**

    - Carnelian is an absolutely beautiful, polished stone with swirls of red, orange, and brown. It is a great way to stay energized but calm at the same time. It will keep you grounded even when the atmosphere around you is buzzing. Carnelian can make you feel comfortable without the effects of laziness or complacency.

- **Clear Quartz**

- Clear quartz is an extremely dynamic and versatile crystal. It is useful in both deflecting negativity and attracting positivity. Also, clear quartz is easily able to pick up and funnel intention. Just as it does in its use in laser functionality, in television projection tubes and in early computer motherboards, clear quartz is a ready-made energy storage and amplification device.

- **Smoky Quartz**

  - This opaque gray crystal is a personal favorite. Smoky Quartz helps you in manifesting your desires out of the ethereal plane and into the material world. But the beautiful part is that, once you have made your ideas into reality, smoky quartz will also protect those intentions from any evil or negative energies that may attempt to get in the way.

- **Black Jade**

  - Black jade can help you stay clear of negative people and situations by helping you tune into the root source of the negativity. Sometimes it is just easier to avoid contact with negativity than it is to try to rid yourself of it. Black Jade is also known to assist you in tapping into your intuition.

- **Smithsonite**

  - Smithsonite is a soothing stone that can help calm your emotions and connect you to your center. Having a calm mind and a grounded center is absolutely vital to the success of many of the spells, rituals, and prayers we have discussed. Plus, who couldn't use some help relaxing after a stressful day or event!

- **Limestone**

  - Any witch who already practices, or spiritualist familiar with crystals, is undoubtedly confused by this addition. Limestone is not usually included in a list of stones or crystals used in any kind of spell work. However, limestone is very special. Limestone is found as bedrock in non-sandy environments and is often used to build the foundation of many of the homes in these non-sandy environments. And a special quality of this common stone is that it contains natural clear quartz and silica. Within the metaphysics community, limestone is seen as a storage vessel for energy. There is also the paranormal theory that limestone allows for storage and release of high-energy situations (the stone tape theory). For these reasons, I always include a piece of limestone with me during a cleansing session, and keep one nearby during meditation.

The Crystal Ball

The crystal ball is an iconic image of witchcraft, and of the psychic abilities associated with witchcraft. The crystal ball is used in the divination practice of scrying. We talked about scrying in Chapter 1.

I keep my crystal ball on my altar during rituals and spell work in order to keep it charged with magickal energy. Also, it seems to facilitate communication with the spiritual plane. In my opinion, the crystal ball acts as a two-way door, allowing the physical plane to access the spiritual plane and also giving the ethereal access to our world.

The Herbs

The use of herbs in magick is among the oldest practices in witchcraft. The earliest forms of "magick" was little more than an understanding of the health and aromatherapy benefits of natural herbs. Anything that the general public does not understand has always been considered "magick" or "supernatural". Modern Wicca and the practice of witchcraft has grown from those early times of healing. Now we have gained significantly more knowledge, experience, and a deeper understanding of the benefits of herbs and herbal remedies.

In the practice of magick, herbs can be used in three different forms - fresh, dried, or oil. Fresh and dried herbs are self-explanatory. An herb oil can be made by infusing either coconut oil or olive oil with an herb. Add the herb to the oil, allow it to sit for up to 48 hours, remove and discard the herb, and cover the oil for future use.

There is a world of herbs. A discussion of each and every herb would take volumes of encyclopedia-sized books. So instead of getting into all herbs, we are going to focus on a handful of herbs that are the most commonly used in magick.

- **Basil**

    - Basil has been used for hundreds of years as a spice in the Mediterranean, and most people would have basil in their kitchen. The magickal properties of basil include love, wealth, purification, and the banishing of negative or evil spirits. Basil corresponds to the masculine energy and is associated with the element of fire.

Medically, basil is known to produce a mild sedative effect when consumed as a tea. The essential oil produced from basil displays natural anti-fungal and antibiotic properties.

- **Bay Leaf**

  - Commonly used as a spice in culinary recipes, bay leaf grows as a shrub with shiny leaves. Medicinally, bay leaf is used for relieving symptoms of the common cold, and treatment of headaches. The essential oil produced from bay leaf is used as a treatment for arthritis and sore muscles.

- **Burdock**

  - Burdock is associated with the element of water. Burdock has feminine energy and is used during rituals to protect the practitioner against negative energy, for healing, and for protection in general.

- **Chamomile**

  - Chamomile is probably best known as a calming tea, but when growing it produces beautiful daisy-like flowers. The magickal properties of chamomile include purification, protection, meditation, and luck with love and money. Chamomile corresponds to the masculine energy and is associated with the element of water.

- **Cinnamon**

  - Cinnamon is a spice with a rich history. Its origins can be found as an Asian evergreen tree with the spice produced from the bark. The cinnamon tree also produces flowers and berries that are still used in Eastern medicine today. Cinnamon can be used for protection, luck, love and passion, healing, and economic prosperity.

- **Coltsfoot**

  - Coltsfoot is the first flowering plant that appears at the beginning of the growing season, often as early as February. It is a useful herb for springtime rituals, such as Imbolc, Ostara, and Beltane. Coltsfoot is connected to love, tranquility, and money. It is associated with the element of water.

- **Comfrey**

  - Although Comfrey is lesser-known in modern times, it has been used for treating skin conditions for over 2,000 years. The magical properties of comfrey include healing, protection of travelers, protection against theft, good luck, and cleansing. Comfrey corresponds to the feminine energy and is associated with the element of water.

- **Dandelion**

  - Even though this flower is often considered a weed, it is not widely known that it is an edible flower and has been traditionally used in spring salads, teas, and in wine. The magickal properties of dandelion include purification, relaxation, and a return to child-like innocence.

- **Lavender**

  - The fragrant purple flower of this herb is well known and is used in perfumes, soaps, and oils. The magickal properties of lavender include cleansing, luck, evoking spirits and entities, happiness, and rejuvenating sleep. Lavender corresponds to the masculine energy and is associated with the element of air.

- **Mint**

  - Mint is not just for mojitos anymore! If you are growing your own herbal garden, mint should be grown in a container because it will spread and can easily take over your entire garden. There are also many different varieties of mint, so you should research which variety would work best depending on the form you plan to use (fresh, dried, or oil). The magickal properties of mint include wealth, luck, healing, and protection. Mint corresponds to the feminine energy and is associated with the element of earth.

- **Oregano**

    - Oregano is an ancient spice which we are all familiar with through its uses in food preparation. However, the magickal properties include happiness, tranquility, harmony, and spiritual growth. Oregano corresponds to the feminine energy and is associated with the element of air.

- **Red Hibiscus**

    - Hibiscus is a beautiful and sweet-smelling flowering decorative plant. Magickly, red hibiscus is associated with love and lust.

- **Rosemary**

    - This herb is the most commonly used in ritual and spell work. The magickal properties include protection, cleansing, courage, and knowledge. Rosemary corresponds to the masculine energy and is associated with the element of fire.

- **Rue**

    - Rue is a very strong and useful herb that will help to banish negativity from your life. Rue can be sprinkled around the outside of your home to ward it against negative influences and entities, or added to a magickal bath to cleanse yourself of negative thoughts and to help in breaking bad habits. Spell bags made with rue will help in breaking malicious spells and magick and help to protect you from further interference.

- **Sage**

    - The indigenous people of North America have been harvesting sage for thousands of years. The magickal properties of sage include wealth, purification, good health, wisdom, and protection. Sage corresponds to the masculine energy and is associated with the element of air.

- **St. John's Wort**

    - St. John's Wort is an extremely versatile and powerful herb. I would go so far as to call it a "must-have" for any Wiccan or practitioner of witchcraft. When used in a spell bag or sachet, St. John's Wort will help you in overcoming challenges, find that hidden pocket of personal courage, keep you moving forward through difficult times, increase your divination success, help you develop your psychic abilities, as well as protect you from negative magic and malevolent entities. Placing a sachet of St. John's Wort under your pillow at night can trigger prophetic dreams. Further, storing your St. John's Wort near your divination tools will help to cleanse them of negativity and increase your connection with the tools.

- **Thyme**

    - One of the first recorded uses of thyme is in the Egyptian mummification process, even before it was recorded being used as a food spice. The magickal properties of thyme include healing, courage, attraction, and the enhancement of psychic abilities. Thyme corresponds to the feminine energy and is associated with the element of water.

- **Valerian**

    - Valerian root has been used medicinally for at least the past 500 years. It has been described as having a sedative effect similar to the modern class of drugs known as benzodiazepines. The magickal properties of valerian include love, protection, mending of relationships, and restoration. Valerian corresponds to the feminine energy and is associated with the element of water.

The Pentacle

The pentacle is undoubtedly the most commonly misunderstood symbol and tool of Wicca. The pentacle is an *upright* five-pointed star inside a circle, along with eight holy symbols (meant to symbolize the drawing together of the four elements and the divine). Many mistake the pentacle for the satanic pentagram. A pentagram is an *upside-down* five-pointed star inside a circle (meant to draw together the elements and the power of Satan from below). Remember - up to raise yourself, down to lower yourself.

The pentacle is usually placed in the center of the altar and items to be consecrated are placed upon it, in order to offer assurance and power in your magickal works.

The Wand

As cliche as it may sound, the wand is actually a very important tool for the male witch. The wand replaces the besom, or broom, of a female witch.

A wand can be made of any natural material, however wood is the most common. It is used for the stabilization of energy within a coven. It is an obviously phallic representation and is associated with masculinity, vitality, strength, and virility. The wand is associated with the elements of air and fire, depending upon the type of spell work or ritual being performed.

In its docile form, the wand is used to represent power, will, and intent. The wand is especially useful in sanctifying a hallowed space or in the conjuring of spirits.

The Tarot

As with the crystal ball, the tarot card deck is a tool of divination. In the hands of someone who does not understand the meaning behind the cards, a tarot deck is little more than a collection of pictures. However, if the reader has taken the time to learn to develop their ability, the tarot deck can be a powerful tool of guidance and self-discovery.

The Besom

The besom is a straw broom, either full-sized or more the size of a feather duster. It is used to "sweep" a ceremonial or ritualistic space, clearing out and expelling any negative energy which may be present.

The besom is associated with femininity. The besom signifies a purifier and is associated with the element of water. Within the toolkit of a male Wiccan or witch, the besom may be replaced with the wand.

The Athame

An athame is a dagger-style, double-edged knife. The handle of the athame is traditionally made of dark wood, however I have seen some beautiful examples with handles made of shaped crystal. Some covens require both an athame and a separate sword, but more modern magickal practices have foregone the sword. The athame is used in the casting of the sacred circle. Because the athame is used to direct energy into the casting, it is quite important that the athame remains cleansed and that it is consistently charged with moonlight. An athame is usually held as one of a Wiccan's or witch's most personal and important tools. We are pouring such a large amount of our trust and power into the athame while casting a sacred circle, that the athame becomes a prized possession.

An athame is not used as a physical blade. It is not to be used to cut anything on the physical plane. This is magickal work taking place on the spiritual plane and it should be reserved for that use only.

Step-By-Step Guides

Step-By-Step Guide to Creating an Altar

Your altar is your space to demonstrate devotion. It is your most personal space because it is the artistic expression of you, your magic, and your practices. An altar is a physical manifestation of your personal spiritual journey, a display of your internal magickal self.

There are no hard and fast rules for creating your altar, and it can easily be changed and updated as your practices grow by adding or taking items away.

1. The first step in creating an altar is finding an appropriate placement. An altar can be inside your home or outside amongst nature. For obvious reasons, it is preferable to make your altar in a natural setting. But, for the majority of us, that is just not an option due to climate or access to forest land. As such, the majority of modern altars are made inside of our homes.

You will want to choose a location inside your home with minimal traffic. This is a sacred personal space meant to reflect you and you alone. It should be a place where you can feel completely safe and open to meditation, concentration, and communication with the spirit plane.

2. Next, you will choose the physical object which will be the altar. This object can be any flat surface made of a natural material - a table, a bookshelf, a coffee table, a large cardboard box, etc.

3. Use some colored fabric (I use different colored scarves, some with patterns, some with symbols) to cover the top of the altar. The colors can represent the type of spell work you will be performing, or the ritual you will be performing, or the season, or the deity associated with the work you will be performing. This fabric is the base of the energy or intent you are attempting to transmit into the universe.

4. Next, place your pentacle onto the altar. The pentacle is normally positioned in the horizontal center, and just above the vertical center, of the altar. From the time when the pentacle is placed on the altar, all tools or items which should be consecrated should be touched to the pentacle prior to being placed on the altar.

5. The next step is to place your tools on the altar, first touching the tool to the pentacle for purification and symbolic devotion of the item to the magick to be practiced. The location of each tool is completely up to your personal wishes.

6. Lastly comes the placement of two pillar candles on the altar to represent the God and Goddess. White is always a good choice for these candles as it symbolizes purity, but I have also seen a green candle for the God and a blue candle for the Goddess, or an orange candle for the God and a black candle for the Goddess (day and night).

Step-By-Step Guide to Spell or Ritual Preparation

Properly preparing for spell work or a ritual is vital. Once the doorway is opened, you do not want to be shrouded in doubts, negativity, or uncertainty.

1. Get clear with your intentions. As we have discussed, knowing what it is that you actually desire is crucial in getting the results you want.

2. Words are important. Misspeaking, mispronouncing, or forgetting a section of language can be very detrimental to your spell or ritual, and could actually be quite dangerous spiritually in the case of names (the names of angels and demons can be very similar, on purpose some would say). If you are not reading directly from a spellbook, it is a good idea to write the wording down. Better yet, write the entire spell or ritual into your grimoire (magickal journal) so that you can then note any effects which were seen.

3. Be clean when stepping onto the astral plane. Prior to beginning your spell or ritual, take the time to cleanse your physical being with protection and to draw energy. If you can bathe, add some salt or a small sachet of herbs and salt to your bathwater. If showering, use a bit of salt as a scrub. It can help you feel more relaxed to know you have removed any negativity from yourself that may taint your magick.

4. Gather all of the ingredients you will need for your spell work or ritual. It may sound silly but trust me it happens. You are halfway through a spell and realize you left the rosemary on the kitchen table! Been there, done that. So, check and double-check that you have everything you will need at the ready.

Step-By-Step Guide to Casting A Circle

Casting a circle is the beginning of any session of spell work or ritual. The circle serves two purposes - as a doorway to the spiritual plane, and as a protective barrier keeping the practitioner safe from evil while performing the spell work or ritual. Think of it as a tunnel connecting your spiritual self (your energy which is tethered to your body) with the spiritual plane. Opening the circle is crucial to your magickal being and closing the circle upon completion of your spell work or ritual is crucial to your physical being.

You need to cast a circle **every time** you are going to perform a spell or a ritual, no matter how little or gigantic the energy output or the time involved in the work. Practicing while not in a circle can lead to demonic attachments, negative soul ties, or possibly unleashing something even older and more evil than a demon. When we practice without a circle, we make *ourselves* the doorway into the spiritual plain and there is no telling what may walk through that doorway. We need not approach magick or the spiritual plain with fear, but with respect. In the words of Friedrich Nietzsche,

> *"He who fights with monsters might take care lest he thereby become a monster.*
> *And if you gaze for long into the abyss, the abyss gazes also into you."*
> -Nietzsche

1. Establish the amount of space you will need for your ritual or spell. For a single person, a good rule of thumb is to stretch your arms straight out from your sides, mark those points. Then from those points, take one large step away from the center. This will be the outer marks to cast your circle.

The point is to have a circle that is small enough as to be easy to cast and control, but not so small that you end up stepping outside the circle at any time during your spell or ritual. Once the circle is cast, do not step or reach over the boundary line. "Breaking" the circle can, and does, result in the same negativity and attachments as performing magick without a circle. Should something occur and you must exit the circle prior to closing it: visualize a door through the edge of the circle, open the door, walkthrough, close the door behind you. It is only as strong as your ability to visualize, so it is certainly not ideal.

2. Next, you will need to cleanse your circle of any negative energy or entities which may be present. This can be done by ritually sweeping them outside of the circle using the besom, ordering them out using the wand, burning incense, or sprinkling salt water within the circle. Whichever method you choose, visualize the negative energy dispersing from the sacred space as you perform the ritual.

3. If you are practicing outside among nature, the physical circle can be drawn using your athame by either carving in the soil or by symbolically tracing the circle. If you are casting the circle in your home, you can either use salt poured over the athame or by symbolically tracing the circle. However, if merely tracing the circle, be cautious that you remember the outline so as not to prematurely break the circle prior to closing. Either way, you would walk clockwise (known as "sunwise" in Wiccan and witchcraft traditions) starting at the eastern point of the circle. As you make your transits, visualize that you are pouring out energy, power, and protection into the barrier. Personally, I visualize each transit adding blue flaming rings which reach up and disappear into the sky above me.

4. You will want to make a number of complete transits. I suggest either 3, 6, or 9 transits as they are strong protective numbers in numerology. As you reach each cardinal direction point, call it out and, if you are using crystals or other markers to signify the directions, place your marker down on the first transit. To call out the cardinal directions, use the following words:

"I call upon the energy of the (north, east, south, or west). Welcome to this circle of light. Join in my magick. So mote it be."

When your transits are complete and you feel that you have created a space that feels healthy and balanced, the circle casting ritual is complete.

Step-By-Step Guide to Rituals

Wouldn't it be wonderful if I could just write down exactly how to perform every ritual! Alas, that is not how the practice of Wicca and witchcraft works. There is an endless number of rituals one can perform or participate in, and an endless number of ways to perform or participate in each one. Most likely, the first ritual a beginner Wiccan or practitioner of witchcraft will perform should be a dedication ritual, dedicating oneself to Wicca and to the God and Goddess. A dedication ritual would be performed as follows:

1. Cast a protective circle.

2. Light a candle representing the God, a candle representing the Goddess (or candles representing your chosen deities), and a dedication candle representing your intention. The deity candles can be extinguished following the ritual, but the dedication candle should be left to burn out on its own.

3. Light an incense to carry your intention to the spiritual realm.

4. The language recited should be similar to the following:

"I call upon the power of the God and of the Goddess (or Universe, Angels, Spirit, Ascended Masters, Protectors, etc.). It is my intention to dedicate myself to you and your praise. I will follow the Wiccan Rede and ask that you, in return, bless my magick and my life with your light and power; keep me safe physically, mentally, emotionally, and spiritually throughout my journey. All the many splendors of nature bow to you, as do I. Thank you for the blessings you have and will pour out onto me. My devotion is yours. So mote it be!"

Step-By-Step Guide to Closing A Circle

When your magickal session or ritual is finished, you will need to close the circle. Closing the circle will close the doorway you have opened to the spiritual plane and signify that you have finished your work, allowing your intentions to be dispersed.

1. Begin by addressing each element of earth, air, fire, and water. As an example, I use the language:

"Thank you to the earth element which grounds me. Thank you to the air element which blows me forward on my journey. Thank you for the fire element which lights my way. Thank you to the water element which cleanses and purifies me and my works."

2. A thank you should be expressed to the God and Goddess for lending their power to your magick or ritual.

3. Beginning again in the east and walking counter-clockwise (or "moonwise"), make the same number of transits around the circle as you did at the casting. This time, visualize the power and energy returning to you.

4. When you have reached the eastern point after the correct number of transits, end the session with, *"So mote it be!"*

Step-By-Step Guide to Crystal Magick

As we discussed earlier, there are simply too many different crystals to provide an exhaustive list within this book. However, crystal magick is extremely powerful and useful to all Wiccan and witchcraft practitioners. Because of the power and popularity of crystal magick in modern Wicca, It would be remiss if we did not at least cover some basics of the practice.

Having the proper crystals present at the time of a spell or ritual is like running your magick through a spiritual amplifier. The crystal will focus the magical energy, add additional correspondences to strengthen the work, and store magickal energy for future use.

Crystals are also used in holistic healing practices. The theory behind the use of crystals is one of vibrational frequency. Everything in nature has a vibrational frequency, including you and me. The higher the vibrational frequency, the closer the object is to the spiritual plane. Crystals have been shown to have extremely high vibrational frequency. This property is what allows for enhanced communication between the two planes when using crystal magick. Crystals placed on the body, in the area of disease or pain, can raise the vibrational frequency of that area and the surrounding aura, leading to faster and more comprehensive healing. In my opinion, it is also this property that makes modern cancer treatments even slightly effective. When delivering radiation therapy, doctors pass radioactive isotopes between two neodymium magnets and then through a quartz crystal which focuses the isotopes into a laser-like beam. I believe that they could actually focus non-radioactive, magnetized materials through a quartz crystal and get the same result. It is not the poisonous radiation that is causing the healing, but the higher frequency of the ions after passing through the quartz crystal.

Preparing

The first thing that you must do when you buy or receive a new crystal is to cleanse it and power it with your personal magick and light.

Your crystal may have been dug from the ground or grown under controlled conditions. Following that, it most likely went through some sort of tumbling and polishing process. Then it was sold to a wholesale crystal company, who then likely sold it to a pagan, new age, or Wiccan supply shop (or even Amazon!). It sat in this shop for an undetermined amount of time until being selected by you and taken into your home. Throughout this entire process, your new crystal has been absorbing energies of people who came into contact with it or were even in its immediate vicinity. How sure are you that each of these people was positive, enlightened, upbeat people with no negative or evil attachments? Exactly. And that is why we need to immediately cleanse every new crystal.

To cleanse your crystal, I would recommend one of two methods. You can cleanse your crystal by holding it under running water for several minutes. In this method, you will want to visualize all of the negativity absorbed by the crystal being purged from inside the crystal and being washed down the drain or down the stream. The other method is to place your new crystal in salt for a few days. Much like you put your wet cell phone in rice to leach out water, placing your crystal into salt will leach out any negativity which it may have absorbed. Place the salt and crystal in an airtight container and keep it in a dark, cool location. After three-four days, you can retrieve your crystal and dispose of the salt. Do NOT consume this salt or use it as protection in any way. It is tainted with negativity and evil. Dispose of it immediately either in your trash can or by burial. Also, it is a good practice to cleanse your crystals and reset their intent at least once per month. Crystals pick up negativity like sponges (keeping it from you) and they can become evil-logged over time. Yes "evil-logged". I just created that word, but you knew exactly what I meant!

Once cleansed, it is time to imbue your crystal with your personal magick and light. This is accomplished simply by holding your crystal in your hands and focusing a meditative 5 or so minutes on directing your power, your intent, and your light into the crystal. A crystal should be an extension, a link between its owner and the spiritual plain. The more you are reflected by your crystal, the stronger the link. You can customize your crystals while empowering them as well by saying out loud what your intention for each is (i.e., "You will be used for healing", or "You will be used for protection").

Next, it is time to charge your crystal. Just like a battery, your crystal needs to have power stored inside in order to function properly. To charge your crystal (or some refer to this process as "mounting your crystal"), place them either in direct sunlight for a _minimum_ of five straight hours, or place them under the light of a new or full moon overnight.

Now your crystal is ready to use! Depending on the crystal and your intent, wear it as jewelry, put it in your pocket as a talisman, hold it while meditating as a palm stone, keep them in a safe place for use in healing, place it near your bed or under your pillow to facilitate more peaceful sleep and positive dreams, put it on your altar for spell work… The uses are as boundless as your desires and imagination.

Step-By-Step Guide to Candle Magick

Candles have only been widely used for magickal purposes since the early 1800's. Prior to that period, colored candles were simply too expensive to be afforded by anyone but the upper class. However, with advances in candle-making techniques and the discovery of new coloring elements, colored candles have become extremely popular and among the cheapest types of magick to practice. Today, candles can be found in any color imaginable, in a wide variety of sizes, made from many different materials, with or without fragrance, and in the shape of pretty much anything your heart desires.

Because many spells call for the candle to be left to burn itself out of the duration of the efficacy of the spell, I tend to stick with short to medium-sized candles made of natural materials such as beeswax for the majority of spells, even opting for votive candles for short-duration spells. I do suggest large candles as the representation of the God and Goddess, as they are the focal point of any Wiccan spell or ritual and should last the longest.

The colors of candles are meant to focus and reflect your intent, as every color has a different meaning and can influence a person's emotions. Scientifically speaking, color is perceived due to the frequency of the light wave reflected from an object to our eyes. So just as crystals emit higher frequencies of energy, colors are reflected at different frequencies. The concept of vibrational frequency can be found at every level of nature and colors are no exception.

To aid you on your first journey into candle magick, I have included this listing of basic colors and meanings. This is by no means exhaustive, as there are different shades to consider, whether herbs are included inside the candle, fragrances, etc.

Black - Black is not dangerous or evil. Black is the color perceived when the object absorbs all of the colors of the spectrum and reflects none. Therefore, black is excellent at absorbing negative energy, pulling it from the air around you. You can use this inherent property to protect yourself. or to repel, reverse, or banish negative and evil energy from your surroundings

Blue - Blue is a color of relaxation and tranquility. It is often used to heal and strengthen the mind during spell casting. It is also useful to encourage sleep, allowing your intention to sleep to flow into the candle before burning it for a few short minutes and then extinguishing it.

Brown - Brown is largely considered a color of nature, from the soil beneath our feet to the color of many animals. Brown is often used in conjunction with other colors in order to tie a spell to the natural world - influencing the physical world around you rather than another person or yourself.

Green - Green is a very versatile color. Foremost, it represents the Earth element. Green also represents growth, fortune, prosperity, and success. It can also be used effectively in healing.

Gold - Gold is primarily associated with the God, the sun, and masculinity. Gold is fantastic at attracting knowledge or developing a power of influence.

Orange - Orange is energetic and attentive. Orange is a great attractor of energy, influence, intentions, or lost objects. It is positive, spiritual, and physical energy and is associated with being encouraging and allowing for clear thoughts.

Pink - Pink is about connection, be it love or friendship. It is nurturing, encouraging the art of communication. Pink is often found at marriage ceremonies as it fosters affection and romance through communication.

Silver - Silver is primarily associated with the Goddess, the moon, and celestial bodies, and femininity. Silver encourages goodness to overcome evil, encourages the use of intuition, and encourages self-reflection through meditation.

Red - Red conveys passion and health and is associated with energy and vitality. Red bolsters the soul against corruption by negativity. It is closely associated with the element of fire and, as such, lends itself to representing burning desire, lust, and sexual passion.

White - White is pure and unifying. Its purity allows it to be used in virtually any context, though it is most commonly associated with truth and illumination. Primarily a defensive color, it can also be used as a replacement for any color you do not have on hand or if you are unsure which color to use. It will help to connect you with the spiritual plane and to prevent evil from taking you over.

Yellow - Yellow is associated with knowledge, discovery, and innovation. It is the perfect color to use when studying any subject because it will help you to absorb the material and make the necessary logical connections. Yellow is also representative of the fulfillment of your dreams.

Violet - Violet is power. It encourages prowess in the magickal world, the spiritual plane. You can think of violet as magick steroids. Any spell you are casting or ritual you are performing will be magnified on the spiritual plane by incorporating violet. Casting a love spell? Burn a violet candle along with your pink candle to really bolster the effects of pink's affinity for love.

Choosing the proper candle for your needs does, of course, involve more than color. Candles can also vary greatly by size. Similar to other important aspects of life, it is not always a matter of "bigger is better", it depends on how it is used.

Many spells require that you allow a candle to burn itself out prior to either ending the spell or to move on to the next step of the spell or ritual. When you come across a long-duration spell, you may want a much larger candle. However, for short-duration spells and rituals, many use votives, short tapers, or menorah candles. Menorah candles are perfect for much candle magic because they are readily available at any local grocery store, they are white and unscented, and they are short enough to be confident that they will burn themselves out in a reasonable amount of time.

Something to remember is that we cannot reuse leftover candles or candles that have been extinguished during other spell work. Once a candle is charged, impregnated with your intent and lit, its use is set. While burning, a candle may attract and hold negativity or evil. We would not remove bubble gum from our mouth, use it to clean dirt from the bottom of our shoe, and then pop it back into our mouth! Once we have begun to chew the gum, its use is set. It is the same concept. So always use fresh, or "virgin", materials in each spell work. This rule does not apply to the God or Goddess candle, as those candles are cleansed by their very intent.

Candles are also available in a variety of shapes or forms. They can be shaped as humans, animals, deities, etc. Here is just a short list of possible candle shapes and their uses.

Female Figure - This is used to attract or repel someone specific but can also be used to represent someone close to you who identifies as female.

Male Figure - This is used to attract or repel someone specific but can also be used to represent someone close to you who identifies as male.

Couple - Candles shaped like a couple are used to bring a married couple closer together.

Genitalia - This one is pretty obvious. It is used for arousal, passion, sexual desire, and fertility.

Buddha - This shape is often used to bring good fortune, abundance, and luck.

Devil - A devil-shaped candle is used for temptations, whether to encourage or banish them.

Cat - This shape is used specifically for money spells, luck spells, and for protection.

Skull - A candle shaped as a skull is used to repel unwanted feelings or thoughts. It is also used for healing and cleansing spells.

Knob - The seven knobs which make up the body of this candle shape represent seven wishes. Use them for what you desire.

Now that you have chosen your candle (the shape, the size, the color), how do you prepare the candle for use in spell work? Let's get into how we prepare candles for our magick.

1.　　Dress Your Candle - Imbuing your candle with your intent for the spell work is completed through the process of "dressing". Dressing your candle requires using a natural oil, such as grape seed oil. Apply the oil to the candle by rubbing it onto the candle from the top to the center point, then from the bottom to the center point.

2.　　Consecrate Your Candle - I actually combine the consecration of the candle with the dressing of the candle, instead of repeating a very similar process twice. To consecrate your candle, anoint the candle with a natural oil. While applying the oil, verbally dedicate the candle to your magick and to the purpose (intent) of the spell it will be used to facilitate.

At this point, your candle is ready to be used in your spell or ritual. The simplest spell in candle magick is one that simply carries your intent to the spiritual plane. It can be used for pretty much any manifestation-style desire.

Simple Candle Spell

You will need:

1. A prepared candle
2. A piece of paper and pen
3. A cauldron or metallic bowl

Steps:

1. Cast a sacred circle.

2. Light your prepared candle.

3. Write your intended desire on a piece of paper.

4. While reciting your intended desire aloud, light one corner of the paper on fire by holding it in the flame of the candle.

5. Place the burning paper into the cauldron or metallic bowl and allow it to burn out naturally.

There are also ways to "read" the candle flame in order to ascertain the strength of the spell and spiritual energy being invested into the manifestation of your desire. It is a form of divination related to spell efficacy. It can certainly be helpful to have some idea whether you might need to repeat the spell or whether you appear to have nailed it on the first try. We will take a quick glance into this spell-focused divination.

High and Strong Flame - Manifestation is proceeding quickly.

Low and Weak Flame - There is a low amount of spiritual energy invested in your intentions. You may want to begin preparations to repeat the spell or ritual.

Thick Black Smoke - Active opposition exists to your work. This could mean that there are Wiccan or witchcraft practitioners actively casting negativity against you, or that your own subconscious mind is working against your intentions.

Dancing Flame - Indicates a highly energetic, but chaotic, manifestation.

Flickering Flame - Spirits are present within your circle and your prayers and intentions are being acknowledged.

Popping or Sputtering Flame - This signifies interference in the communication of your spell or ritual intent due to outside forces. It could be that something or someone is working against you, or that you may need to add more concentration and spiritual energy to your spell or ritual.

Flame Goes Out - A flame that suddenly extinguishes during your spell or ritual indicates that a stronger (more energetic) opposing force has ended your spell or ritual. You will need to deal with this negative force before you can be successful in the spell work or ritual.

Cannot Extinguish Flame - A flame that seems to refuse to be extinguished signifies that your work is not done. You should spend more time and invest more energy into the spell or ritual.

Step-By-Step Guide to Herb/Plant Magick

Herbal and plant magick is where the devotion to the Earth Mother or Goddess meets the art of nature. Wicca embraces the world of nature as a religion, and as we learn to cast spells and perform rituals, we invoke the energies and deities of nature to assist us on our path. It only makes sense that, as we worship all that nature brings, we also offer our devotion to the magick and healing abilities contained in the plants and herbs which support our practices. Because of this basic deeply rooted connection between herbs and Wicca, we would be hard-pressed to find a Wiccan or witch who does not use plants or herbs in their practices.

Plants and herbs offer our magick both a literal and an ethereal link to Mother Earth - growing from the minerals found in the soil, using the elements of earth, air, fire, and water. Even if the plants are grown using hydroponics, natural minerals must be included in the water in order for the plants to grow. Plants depend upon the wind to scatter their seeds in order to reproduce, not to mention their production of oxygen from carbon dioxide. They use the fire produced by the sun to provide their basic living function of photosynthesis. And plants use and store water in ways quite similar to those of animals. They are truly perfect examples of living in balance with the elements.

I am often asked about whether Wiccan and witchcraft practitioners must grow their own herbs for them to be effective in spell work or rituals. Simply put, the answer is "No". Is it better to grow herbs and plants yourself?

Absolutely. But store-bought herbs can be just as effective. Whether it is due to a lack of space, climate, or if, like me, your thumb is more black than green, sometimes it is just necessary that you buy the herbs you will be using. That is fine. Remember, it is the intent of the spell caster which gives power to a spell.

There are four forms in which we can use herbs in our magickal sessions – Raw, Sachets, Tinctures, or Elixirs. Each has its own pros and cons and some of the herbs limit their useful forms all on their own. The purpose and duration of the spell, along with the herb(s) being used, are all factors in the form best suited for use in the spell work or ritual.

Any herb or plant can be used in its **raw** form. In their raw state, herbs maintain their highest grounding energy. Further, some herbs are poisonous and cannot be ingested. Obviously, the raw form or sachet form are the only forms in which these herbs should be included in your spell work.

Sachets can be a convenient form of carrying bits of your magick with you throughout the day, much like an amulet or talisman. A sachet is a small cloth pouch containing the ingredients of a spell. They can be kept in a pocket, worn around your neck, tucked away in a purse, dangled from a rear-view mirror, floated in a cleansing bath, etc. Whether the herbs themselves are fresh or dried, a sachet can serve as the perfect vessel for maintaining the power of a spell near you for the duration of the magick.

A **tincture** is a naturally infused mixture of herbs, water, and alcohol. It is most often applied like a balm or salve and used in healing either the body, the mind, or the spirit. A tincture is created by placing the fresh or dried herbs in a glass jar, then adding equal parts water and alcohol (usually vodka or a high alcohol content rum). The jar is then sealed airtight and the mixture is left to steep for up to a month before use. When ready to use in the spell, the tincture is opened and the liquid and any solids which still remain are rubbed onto the skin as directed by the spell.

And finally, an **elixir**. Elixirs are made from herbs that can be safely ingested. They can be made and consumed as a tea, or steeped in a fashion similar to a tincture by steeping without heat. Most elixirs have the added ingredient of a natural sweetener to make them more palatable, such as honey or agave nectar.

Chapter 3

Casting Spells & Rituals

Prosperity Spells

Money. The root of all… well… everything in modern society. At least on the physical plane. I get it. We all need money to pay rent, buy food, pay the electric bill, buy books on Wicca and witchcraft, etc. There are times when it may very well be necessary to use your magick to attract money. It can absolutely be done. I want to just throw out this caveat, do with it what you will.

Everything in magick has a give and take, everything has a yang to its yin. Do you see a large Wicca and witchcraft community in the world driving Porsches and wallpapering their homes with cash? There is a reason for that. Money has absolutely no spiritual value. Money is paper or, in our digital world, no more than a set of ones and zeros in a database. We do not want to waste our energies on things that do not bring us true joy or glorify the God or Goddess or beauty of the universe. Working on the spiritual plane to attract items that do not have any effect whatsoever on the spiritual plane can lead to mixed and, sometimes, undesired results. Perhaps it would make more sense to perform spell works that include specific wants or needs rather than the general "money" that many spell casters end up requesting. Try substituting money with "payment of my rent" or whatever it is that you truly desire.

MONEY CHARM BAG

This spell should be performed during a waxing crescent or full moon to lead to earthly success, abundance, and prosperity.

You will need:

- Incense: Use any scent associated with money (orange, cinnamon, etc.)

- A small bowl of salt

- A small bowl of water

- A red candle

- Basil (fresh or dried)

- Crystal: Any crystal associated with money (Citrine)

- Nail and hair clippings

- A silver coin from the year of your birth

- A token representing your work

- A small green pouch

- String

Instructions:

1. Cast a sacred circle.

2. Ground and center yourself.

3. Light the red candle and the incense.

4. Meditation and visualization play a vital role in this ritual. Meditate and visualize your life and where the money you want is already with you.

5. Focus on every detail that you are visualizing, how you feel after getting the money that you need, how you are spending it and how it is affecting your life.

6. Take the basil into your hand and visualize yourself happy and prosperous. Place the basil into the pouch.

7. Take the crystal into your hand and visualize that you are holding the earth's agreement to fulfill your desire. Place the crystal into the pouch.

8. Take the nail and hair clippings into your hand and visualize yourself happy and prosperous. Place the clippings into the pouch.

9. Take the coin into your hand and visualize yourself happy and prosperous. Place the coin into the pouch.

10. Take the token of work into your hand and visualize yourself happy and prosperous. Place the object into the pouch.

11. Close the pouch and tie it shut with the string.

12. Pass the pouch through the smoke of the incense. Pass the pouch over the fire of the candle. Sprinkle a pinch of the salt onto the pouch. And splash a bit of the water onto the pouch.

13. Close the sacred circle. The red candle should be allowed to burn itself out.

13. Keep this pouch on a windowsill, covered porch, Greenhouse, somewhere that the pouch will get both direct sunlight and direct moonlight.

14. After the ritual's results have manifested, or after 30 nights - whichever comes first, open the bag and remove the crystal. The bag should then be re-tied and buried.

15. Do not forget to cleanse the crystal before using it for any other magickal or spiritual purpose.

MONEY OIL

This potion can be used in any money or prosperity spell, to dress candles for instance. It can also be used to anoint objects (like a resume) or as a part of a ritual bath (just a few drops is enough). Its potency lasts for up to a year, so it is a good idea to just have some on hand when you need it.

The oil should be made during a waxing moon.

You will need:

- A jar with an airtight seal

- 3 whole cinnamon sticks (or the equivalent in dried spice form)

- Enough almond oil to fill the jar

Instructions:

1. Take a deep breath and intentionally remind yourself that your intent in making this oil is magickal.

2. Place the cinnamon sticks into the jar (breaking the sticks is fine if need be). If using dried spice, just pour the proper amount into the jar.

3. Fill the jar with the almond oil and seal it shut.

4. Shake the jar thoroughly.

5. Keep the jar where it can receive direct sunlight.

6. Shake the jar every two days.

7. The oil will be ready when the moon returns to the same position it was when you began the preparation, approximately 4 weeks.

DOORSTEP BLESSING

This ritual will create a money-attracting herbal wash for your front door threshold. Because it will keep for years, it also makes a thoughtful and appreciated Yule gift for your Wiccan or witchcraft friends.

The mixture should be prepared on the first Thursday following a full moon and used on the first Thursday following a full moon.

You will need:

- A metal mixing bowl

- Fresh basil leaves

- Fresh dill

- A couple bills of large denomination (don't worry, these are not going anywhere)

- A handful of coins

- A saucepan

- White vinegar

- A jar with an airtight seal

- A small amount of Money Oil

Instructions:

1. Put the bills, coins, basil leaves, and dill into the mixing bowl.

2. Mix the ingredients together by hand. While mixing, recite the following: "The herbs herein are coated in money. Money is their nature. Success and money are drawn to these herbs as the moth is drawn to the flame."

3. Remove the bills. Place the remaining ingredients into the jar.

4. Bring the vinegar to a simmer in the saucepan. Then **carefully** pour it into the jar.

5. Allow the jar to cool enough to touch.

6. Seal the jar.

7. Place your hand on the lid of the jar and recite the following:

> *"By the power of the Lady and Lord,*
> *By the power of my will and word,*
> *Money follow where you go,*
> *Money follow where you are,*
> *Money blessings at the door.*
> *So mote it be."*

8. Use the Money Oil to mark a pentacle on the lid of the jar.

9. Store the jar in a cool, dark place for one week.

10. After one week, the potion is ready to use.

11. To use the potion, wipe it onto the threshold of the most often used doors in your home. As you do so, concentrate your energy on the abundance this potion will bring to you and your household.

12. You can renew the spell by rewashing the threshold every season. The shelf life of the potion is up to 5 years if kept sealed (other than for use) and stored in a cool and dark area.

SPELL FOR A GROWING PAY STUB

A pay stub is a physical representation of how much money our time is worth to our employer. We all believe that our time should be worth more than it is. So let's see how we can magickly grow our worth and watch the number on that pay stub increase!

This spell can be performed either outside in a garden or inside with a potted version. The location is not nearly as important as the time of year - late spring during a waxing moon.

You will need:

- A pay stub (or printout)

- A small amount of Money Oil

- A basil seedling

Instructions:

1. Anoint the pay stub with Money Oil. While doing so, recite the following:

"This seedling shall grow,
And my bank overflow.
May the universe allow
That I reap what I sow."

2. Dig deep into the soil and place the pay stub in the hole.

3. Put some soil over the pay stub.

4. Plant the basil seedling on top of the pay stub.

5. Nurture and grow this plant throughout the growing season.

PROSPERI-TEA

If you have any doubts about the power of intention and clear communication with the spiritual plane, look no further than this tea. This is a daily beverage of thousands of individuals, but without the directed intent and the practice to communicate clearly with the spiritual plane, it is not magickal in any fashion. The tea includes fresh tea leaves and bergamot. Fresh tea leaves and bergamot are also the ingredients of Earl Grey tea! Tea leaves and bergamot also both happen to be associated with wealth. Further, this tea is sweetened with honey - a natural substance associated with prosperity, long life, and good fortune.

Begin this spell on the first Thursday following a full moon and continue to make and drink one cup per day until the next full moon.

I do recommend that you buy the Earl Grey tea from a specialty shop or high-end market to ensure you are receiving the freshest and least processed tea. I also recommend that you source your honey so that it is as local and fresh as possible.

You will need:

- Earl Grey tea

- Honey

Instructions:

1. Make a cup of tea. Sweeten it to taste with honey.

2. Prior to your first sip, recite:

> *"I take abundance into me.*
> *Abundance comes to me.*
> *Through air, fire, water, earth.*
> *Abundance comes to me.*
> *So mote it be."*

3. Drink your cup of tea as you visualize yourself receiving the rewards you seek.

SPELL TO ATTRACT MONEY

You will need:

- Five candles (1 yellow, 1 white, 1 green, 1 red, and 1 blue)

- Hyacinth petals or oil

- Salt

Instructions:

1. Dress the candles by rubbing them with the hyacinth petals or oil.

2. Cast a sacred circle.

3. Inside the circle, draw a pentacle using the salt.

4. At each point of the pentacle, place one of the unlit candles.

5.   Light each candle beginning with the upper point and proceeding clockwise (moonwise). As you light each candle, summon the power of the element represented by that candle's color. You can choose the order of the incantations by choosing the order of candles, but the incantations would be as follows:

"Through this yellow candle, I summon the power of the Air!
Through this green candle, I summon the power of the Earth!
Through this red candle, I summon the power of Fire!
Through this blue candle, I summon the power of Water!
Through this white candle, I summon the power of Spirit!"

6.   Stand in the center of the pentacle. Visualize energy from each of the colors flowing from the candles and joining your aura; your being.

7.   Recite the following incantation six times:

"With the powers of earth, air, fire, and water. With the power of spirit, you must hear my plea.
It is money I need; money is my desire. I call upon God to grant this to me."

8.   At the end of the sixth recitation, add *"So mote it be."*

9.   Allow the candles to burn themselves out.

10.   Close the sacred circle.

11.   Bury the candle remains.

SIMPLE CASH FLOW SPELL

This cash flow spell requires very few ingredients and a very short incantation. The true power of this spell comes from the visualization and our desire for money to mimic nature (an unending flow). The pink candle is used in this spell for its amplification power. This spell should be performed when the flow of moonlight is at its highest (a full moon).

You will need:

- A green candle

- A pink candle

- Small amount of patchouli oil

Instructions:

1. Dress the candles with patchouli oil.

2. Cast a sacred circle.

3. Stand at the center of the circle.

4. Ground and center your energy.

5. Visualize yourself standing in a free-flowing stream filled with shining coins and floating paper notes (bills). Focus until you can actually *feel* the excitement of being surrounded by this unending flow of cash.

6. As you hold onto that feeling, light the green candle and then the pink candle.

7. Recite the following:

    "With this fire, I summon the forces
    of nature and the elements. Money now flows to me from all
    sources. So mote it be."

8. Allow the green and pink candles to burn themselves out.

9. Close the sacred circle.

SIMPLE MONEY SPELL

This simple money spell relies on your intention being carried to the spiritual plane. It is best performed on a new moon. With each successive night, as the moonlight grows more plentiful, so should your money.

You will need:

- 3 green candles in candle holders

- 3 one-dollar bills

- Either one or a blend of the following dried herbs: basil, cinnamon, clove, ginger, nutmeg, mint, dill, and patchouli

Instructions:

1. Cast a sacred circle.

2. Place the three-dollar bills on the ground, separated.

3. Sprinkle the dried herb(s) onto each bill.

4. Place one of the candles (in its holder) onto each bill.

5. As you light each candle, recite the following:

    "Money, fall down on me. Pour down on me in plenty. May I be wealthy and cause harm to no one."

6. Following the 3rd recitation, conclude it with

    "So mote it be."

7. Close the sacred circle.

8. Allow the three candles to burn themselves out.

Spells for Success

Aside from the simple acquisition of wealth and money, there is another way to achieve financial gain - being successful in your profession. The ability to encourage success, respect, and esteem in the workplace means not only being able to earn more money, but also leveraging your reputation in the marketplace to earn your true worth. For those who want to grow and improve their career, these spells and rituals offer a wonderful opportunity.

SPELL FOR SUCCESS

This spell can be useful in a number of professional circumstances, whether you are searching for a job, looking to improve or increase your current salary, thinking of starting a new business, or improving the fortunes of your current business. This spell should be performed during the time of a waxing moon.

You will need:

- A picture of the individual whose career you are attempting to improve

- One white candle

- Four green candles

- A small amount of basil oil

- Cinnamon incense

- A small amount of dried bay leaf

- Two green fluorite stones

- A few coins of various denominations

- A metal bowl

- A small white satchel

Instructions:

1. At the center of what will be your sacred circle, arrange the four green candles in line with the cardinal

directions. Place the white candle between you and the green candles. Place the incense to your left. Place the metal bowl to your right. Place the picture between you and the white candle.

2. Cast the sacred circle.

3. Put the bay leaf, the stones, the drops of basil oil, and the coins into the metal bowl. This will now be referred to as the "offering bowl".

4. Center your energy.

5. Light the green candle to the north, then the east, then the south, then the west.

6. Lastly, light the white candle.

7. Use the flame of the white candle to light the cinnamon incense.

8. Wait a few seconds until the white candle produces some melted wax. Drip some of the wax onto the photo.

9. Remaining focused on the photo, lift the offering bowl with your right hand and hold it at head height in front of you.

10. While holding the bowl and focusing on the picture, recite the following:

> *"Success is coming soon to me.*
> *Prosperity is flowing unto me.*
> *So mote it be."*

11. Place the bowl back down in its original location.

12. Visualize how professional success might manifest in your life and what it would look like. Imagine and visualize the route, the process it might take to reach you and make you more successful. The longer and more detailed you are able to hold this image in your mind, the more powerful your intent will be on the spiritual plane.

13. Extinguish the green candle to the south, then the east, then the north, then the west.

14. Lastly, extinguish the white candle.

15. Close the sacred circle.

16. Place the items from the offering bowl and the picture into the white satchel. Bury the satchel in the ground on the property where you live.

SPELL TO GET A DESIRED JOB

This spell is designed to bring you success in landing that perfect job… whatever that job is in your mind. This is your route to a financially and personally rewarding job or career.

This spell should be performed during a waxing moon. The symbol marked on the resumé should be something you specifically associate with the job you desire (like a badge shape for a police officer job, for example).

You will need:

- A small amount of Money Oil

- A small amount of saltwater

- A green candle

- A printed copy of your resumé

- An envelope

- A pen

Instructions:

1. Cast a sacred circle.

2. Light the green candle.

3. Visualize your ideal job. Concentrate on the details (what are you wearing, what type of work environment is it, are there co-workers, how does your boss treat you, how much money do you make).

4. Holding that image, wave your resumé through the smoke of the green candle. DO NOT ALLOW IT TO CATCH ON FIRE! This is called "censing".

5. As you cense your resumé, recite the following: *"By air and fire, the job is mine."*

6. Wet the corners of your resumé with the saltwater.

7. While wetting your resumé, recite the following:

"By water and earth, the job is mine."

8. Dip your finger in the Money Oil and draw the symbol of your desired job on your resumé.

9. As you anoint your resumé with the Money Oil, recite the following:

"The Sun does shine.
The job is mine.
The Moon does glow.
To work I go."

10. Fold the resumé and seal it in the envelope.

11. Address the envelope to: "Perfect Employer, Perfect Location"

12. Close the sacred circle.

13. Keep the sealed envelope in your sacred space for the next 30 days.

Spells for Protection

It is an unfortunate reality that, from time to time, we need to protect ourselves physically, emotionally, or spiritually. Just as there is light, beauty, and wonder in the world, there is also negativity, evil, and destruction. We can find ourselves purposefully targeted by other Wiccan or witchcraft practitioners who wish to do us harm or ensure that our magick does not produce results. These are types of black magick known as hexes and binding, respectively.

We can also find ourselves under attack from evil forces and entities which are not under the control of a human and have never walked through our plane in human form. I refer to these entities as "demons". Understanding that my choice of the word "demon" carries with it a certain amount of religious connotation, you are absolutely free to pick whatever word you wish for these bringers of darkness.

No matter the linguistic line you choose, we do need to know how to protect ourselves against them and their effects on our lives.

As modern Wiccans or practitioners of witchcraft, we enjoy a unique relationship with the spiritual plane. We purposefully open doorways between planes, alternate realities, and universal communication networks. No matter the intent we may have, it is important that we understand and accept the dangers we face as a result of our actions on the physical and spiritual planes. Despite our best attempts to remain spiritually safe, there is simply no way to ensure that the pathways we open will only be used by beings of light. So, what can we do to protect ourselves, our family, and our property from attachment by dark energy, negativity, and evil entities? Well, just like most needs, Wicca has some spells for that!

SPELL FOR PROTECTION FROM EVIL ENEMIES

You will need:

- A piece of paper

- A black pen

- A piece of black string

- Small amount of saltwater

- A freezer (if not performed in sub-freezing outside temps)

This spell is a type of binding to be performed when another Wiccan or witchcraft practitioner is using their magick to cause negativity in your life. The ritual is best performed during a new moon.

Instructions:

1. Cast a sacred circle.

2. On the piece of paper, write the name of the person(s) affecting you.

3. Tie a single knot in the middle of the string. While tying the knot, focus on the negative effects this individual has been causing in your life.

4.   Fold the paper up with the piece of string tucked into the middle. Moisten the paper with the saltwater (you do not want to soak it and obliterate the name or names).

5.   Place the paper in the freezer (or in a protected spot outside if performing the spell in sub-freezing temperatures) and leave it there until the situation has passed and the individual is no longer affecting your life negatively.

THE WITCH'S BOTTLE

The Witch's Bottle is used to protect your home from negative energy and evil entities. Witch's bottles have been used for at least 400 years to protect the home by creating a magickal double of yourself. The supplies needed are a bit odd, but this is ancient magick after all.

The idea behind a Witch's Bottle is that the evil spirits are drawn to the bottle instead of you, and then get trapped by the nails, pins, and knotted string and confused by the broken glass/mirror (like a funhouse mirror maze).

You will need:

- A bottle with a tight cork or cap

- Nails and pins (preferably bent)

- Broken glass pieces and/or broken mirror pieces

- Pieces of string, knotted multiple times

- Your own nail, hair clippings, and bodily fluids (i.e., urine)

- A black candle (just to seal the bottle cap)

Instructions:

1.   Put the nails, pins, glass pieces, mirror pieces, string, nail clippings, and hair clippings into the bottle. While adding the ingredients, recite the following:

"Harm be bound away from me".

2. Add the liquid ingredient.

3. Close the bottle and seal it with the wax.

4. Bury the bottle upside down outside the front door of the home, or under the floorboards, or hidden in a remote corner of the lowest point of your home.

SPELL FOR PROTECTION OF FRIENDS AND FAMILY

You will need:

- Salt

- Rosemary

- Angelica

- White Dandelion Fluff

- Small Crystal of Either Blue Lace Agate, Carnelian, or Garnet

- Slip of Paper with The Name of The Person to Protect

- White Sachet

Instructions:

1. Cast a sacred circle.

2. Place the salt, rosemary, angelica, dandelion fluff, crystal, and the slip of paper into the sachet.

3. Focus on a visualization of the protected person. As you hold the visualization of this individual in your mind, recite the following:

"I send you protection from all that may harm you. I send you the wish of safety. I send you the energies to keep you out of harm's way."

4. Tie your sachet shut and gently kiss it focusing on your desires to send your friend or family member protection.

5. Close the sacred circle.

6. Place the sachet in a slightly open window to help send the energies to the friend or family member.

7. Leave the sachet untouched for a minimum of one hour.

8. Following removal from the window, the sachet can be emptied and cleaned for future use.

SPELL FOR SPIRITUAL AND MENTAL PROTECTION

This ritual will allow you to create an amulet for the purpose of protecting yourself spiritually and mentally from negativity and evil forces. Wear or carry the amulet whenever you feel the need for spiritual and mental protection. The amulet can be recharged from time to time by using a new golden candle.

You will need:

- A gold candle

- A pair of earplugs

- A flat stone, or piece of wood, or piece of metal (as amulet)

- Gold paint and a brush

Instructions:

1. Cast a protective circle.

2. Light the gold candle and recite the following:

"This is the power of silence."

3. Put in the earplugs.

4. Concentrate on the power of spiritual and mental stillness as is found in the candle flame. When you feel calm and still, paint the bindrune on the amulet.

5. Feel the power of the silent stillness flowing from the candle, through you, and into the amulet.

6. Close the protective circle.

INCANTATION FOR PROTECTION OF BODY AND SPIRIT

This quick incantation and visualization allow you to protect yourself when an unexpected threat appears. Repeat the incantation a total of seven times. During each incantation, visualize an electric blue ring of flame encircling you until you have a seven-ring spiral from head to toe.

Instructions:

1. Recite the following incantation (even if under your breath):

> *Power of the Goddess (or Goddess, Universe, Angels, Spirit,*
> *Ascended Masters, Protectors, etc.).*
> *Power of the God (or Goddess, Universe, Angels, Spirit,*
> *Ascended Masters, Protectors, etc.).*
> *Cool as a breeze.*
> *Warm as a stove.*
> *Flowing like a stream.*
> *Solid as a stone.*
> *So mote it be!*

CREATING A TALISMAN TO PROTECT LOVED ONES

There are times when what the world may see as a string of bad luck, we are able to recognize as signs of a negative or evil attachment to a loved one. Nothing makes you feel more helpless than when you *know* what is wrong with a spouse, close friend, or family member and yet they will not believe you or allow you to fix it. There is, however, a way that we can protect those whom we care about from being saddled with these attachments in the first place - a protective talisman. This is an object that they would carry with them most, if not all of the time which would act as a shield or hedge of protection around them and keep them safe from dark magick, negativity, and evil entities. Kind of like a good luck charm that works not by bringing good luck, but by keeping bad luck away.

You will need:

- 5 candles (1 yellow, 1 white, 1 green, 1 red, and 1 blue)

- A coin or object for each person you wish to protect

- Salt

- The juice from 1 lemon

- A small amount of ground clove

- A small black sachet

- An empty cup

Instructions:

1. Dress the five candles by rubbing them with lemon juice and ground clove.

2. Place the coins or objects in the black sachet.

3. Cast a sacred circle, using salt as the border.

4. Draw a pentacle within the sacred circle using the salt, with each point touching the border.

5. Place the yellow candle at the upper left point of the pentacle, the green candle at the lower-left point of the pentacle, the red candle at the lower-right point of the pentacle, the blue candle at the upper-right point of the pentacle, and the white candle at the top point of the pentacle.

6. Place the black sachet and the empty cup in the middle of the pentacle.

7. Because this spell draws heavily on elementals for protection, as you light each of the candles, say the name of the element represented. (Yellow for air, blue for water, green for earth, red for fire, and white for spirit).

8. At the center of the pentacle, take one of the coins or objects from the sachet and recite the following:

> *"Oh Goddess and God of all that is.*
> *Hear me and listen to my cry.*
> *Give protection to the person carrying this {coin or object}!*
> *Protect them with all your might.*
> *Let no evil befall them.*
> *Let no darkness cast its shadow upon them.*
> *So mote it be."*

9. Place the talisman into the empty cup.

10. Repeat this process for as many talismans as you are creating, one at a time.

11. Allow the five candles to burn themselves out.

12. Place the talismans back into the satchel.

13. Close the sacred circle.

14. Take the remainder of the burned-out candles and bury them.

15. The talismans are now ready for you to give to those who they will protect.

SPELL TO BREAK A CURSE AND REVERSE THE EVIL

Although we try to protect ourselves from negativity, curses, and evil entities, there may be times when another follower of Wicca or witchcraft practitioner uses dark magic against us. Having a curse placed on you is a very dangerous situation to live through. As such, we need to be mindful that these instances do occur and that what may at first seem like a run-of-back luck may actually be something much more targeted and sinister.

The Wiccan Rede, and specifically the Rule of Three, can help us to break a curse that has been placed upon us and return the effects of the curse to the caster threefold.

You Will Need:

- A mirror

- A piece of paper

- A black pen

- A white candle

- A piece of white fabric

Instructions:

1. Cast a protective circle.

2. Light the white candle.

3. Lay the mirror on the altar, reflection side up.

4. Next, on the piece of paper, write all of the symptoms you are experiencing from the curse.

5. Then, lay the paper upside down on the mirror and cover it all with the fabric.

6. Recite the following:

> *"Your magick delivered*
>
> *A curse unto me.*
>
> *I remove and return*

Your curse back to thee."

7. Press on the mirror through the fabric until it breaks (or smash it with a tool).

8. Gather all of the pieces for disposal. Be careful not to either cut yourself on the shards, or see your reflection in any of the shards.

9. Close the protective circle.

10. You can either bury the mirror shards or dispose of them in your trash.

Love Spells

By far the most commonly performed type of spell is the love spell. Some spells can help you to open your heart to romance, while others can attract love to you.

There is a very clear distinction made within Wicca and witchcraft between "love" and "lust". There are spells for each, but it is quite important to be cognizant of which you truly desire. Love involves the possibility of a lifelong commitment, to sharing the ups and downs of life, and establishing an emotional bond. Lust involves the quenching of carnal desires, the possibility of a very short-term relationship, and keeping the establishment of a physical bond. It is certainly possible for one to lead to the other, however when magick is used, it is more likely that you get what you ask for - no more, no less.

There is also one caveat that I would keep in mind when performing love spells. Take, for instance, a scenario wherein you perform a successful love spell aimed at a specific individual. That person does, in fact, develop strong feelings for you although they may not realize exactly why. What happens if it turns out that you are not able to reciprocate their feelings? What if you made an error in judgment and they are not the wonderful person you thought they were? What if they are unable to control their feelings for you when you lose interest in them, because the feelings are a result of magick? This scenario is not purely hypothetical. It has been played out before, to the detriment of the casting practitioner. You may have just magickally created your own stalker, or worse. I simply urge caution when performing love spells. It is fine and fulfilling to cast spells that open *your* heart or mind to love, or to attract souls with love to offer to you. But more often than not, danger lurks when one attempts to manipulate another unsuspecting individual into feelings or thoughts through the use of magick.

BASIC LOVE SPELL

This is a rather basic love spell designed to attract to you an individual who exemplifies the traits you desire in a love interest. After this spell is performed, keep your eyes open for new people joining your life or the development of new feelings for someone already present in your life.

This spell is best performed during a new moon when the stars are visible in the night sky.

You will need:

- 1 red candle with candle holder

- Rose petals

- Rose or lavender incense

- A rose quartz crystal

- 1 piece of paper

- A pen

Instructions:

1. Cast a sacred circle.

2. Light the red candle and place it on the altar.

3. Light the incense using the wick of the red candle

4. On the paper, write down all of the qualities that you are hoping for in a partner. Be as specific as possible. Try to envision the person, experience the feeling of being near them.

5. Read the list of qualities aloud. Then fold the paper and place it under the candle holder.

6. Take the rose petals and crystal into your hands. Look to the sky and find a star that appeals to you.

7. Hold your hands out, palms up, to expose the rose petals and the crystal to that star's light.

8. Recite the following:

"The love star, always burning bright,

Help and enable me in this spell tonight.

Unify my true love with me,

As I ask, so mote it be."

9. Sprinkle the rose petals around the base of the candle holder.

10. Place the crystal in front of the candle holder.

11. Recite the following: "Hear me as I call to you. Come to me, my love so true."

12. Allow the red candle to burn itself out.

13. Close the sacred circle.

LOVE KNOT

A love knot binds two people together so that they may come to realize they love each other and begin a romantic relationship. It is a very powerful spell and should be monitored, lest it leads to compulsion as described in the caveat above.

You will need:

- A length of silk string

- Pink chalk or salt

- 5 pink candles

- A small amount of ground cinnamon

- A small amount of Adam-And-Eve Plant root

Instructions:

1. Dress the 5 pink candles by rubbing them with the ground cinnamon and Adam-And-Eve Plant root.

2. Cast a sacred circle using either the pink chalk or salt to show the outer border.

3. Inside the sacred circle, draw a pentacle using either the pink chalk or salt. The five points of the pentacle should touch the outer border of the sacred circle.

4. Place one of the pink candles at each point of the pentacle.

5. Light the pink candles beginning with the uppermost point and proceeding moonwise.

6. Standing in the middle of the pentacle, take the piece of silk string and tie it into a knot.

7. While tying the knot, recite the following:

"As I tie this knot, bring the love of {the name of the spell's target} to me!"

8. Repeat the tying of the knot and incantation a total of 6 times.

9. When all 6 knots have been tied and the incantation has been said 6 times, burn the silk string in the flame of the uppermost pink candle of the pentacle.

10. All the pink candles need to burn themselves out.

11. Close the sacred circle.

12. Take the remnants of the pink candles and bury them in 5 separate holes.

LUST SPELL FOR INCREASED LIBIDO

There are times when love may not be what is missing. Married couples who have been together for a long time know exactly what I am talking about. Sometimes it can feel like your physical ship has sailed and you may struggle to find that red hot flame of passion that once burned so bright inside. If you would like to reignite your libido, this spell should put you directly on the path to a smile-filled, reinvigorating, evening with your partner.

This is a spell that is to be performed during a sunny day, as it draws upon the power of the God (sun). Best results will be seen by performing this spell on a Friday.

You will need:

- A red candle with a candle holder

- A food or drink thought of as an aphrodisiac (for example, hot peppers, whiskey, ginger candies, cherries, or olives)

- A small amount of patchouli oil

Instructions:

1. Dress your red candle by rubbing it with the patchouli oil.

2. Take your dressed candle and your aphrodisiac of choice outside into the sunlight. Pick a spot where you can sit, meditate, and not be disturbed.

3. Light the red candle.

4. Gaze into the flame of the candle and allow yourself to be consumed by the moment. Imagine the fire coming into you and filling you with its heat. Feel it explicitly enflaming your groin and arousing your natural carnal instincts.

5. As you concentrate on this sensation, recite the following: "I am fire. I am heat."

6. Eat or drink your aphrodisiac. Feel the heat of it as goes into your body. Let your skin tingle. Let the experience radiate into your entire body.

7. As you concentrate on this sensation, recite the following:

"I am fire. I am heat."

8. Extinguish the red candle. Take it home with you and place the candle near your bed.

9. At the earliest possible convenience, have sex with your partner in the bed. Throughout, refer to the

visualization of the fire being a part of your body, of keeping the flame alive within you. Allow the heat to be a part of you at your very core.

CREATING A FIRST DATE CHARM

Is there anything more exciting AND terrifying as a first date? The jitters, the hope of a blossoming relationship, the fears of will you like them and will they like you! There is a way to stay calm and enjoy those feelings without becoming overwhelmed by them. A first date charm. It may not guarantee that this person will be your one true love, but at least it will keep you relaxed long enough to find out for sure.

The blue paper in this charm ritual is meant to represent calm and to help keep your head clear. The red ink is here to encourage an open heart to receive romance.

You will need:

- A piece of blue paper

- A pen with red ink

- A pair of scissors

Instructions:

1. Visualize your intention clearly - a relaxed, happy date going well. Picture laughter and ease. Nothing forced or disingenuous. Just feel a glow of peace and hope for the future.

2. While holding this visualization, write the first name of your date on the paper.

3. Draw a circle around the name. Carefully cut the paper along the circle.

4. Fold the paper into thirds. While folding, recite the following:

> *"With this I have*
>
> *the eyes to see.*
>
> *True love or not,*

So mote it be."

5.Place the folded paper in your shoe during the date.

As a testament to this charm's efficacy, I used this exact ritual prior to going on the first date with the person who became my partner, my one true love. This year, we celebrated our 20th wedding anniversary.

BRINGING LOVERS TOGETHER

Here is an example of a decidedly modern spell meant to solve a modern problem. In the age of internet dating, it is more possible than ever before to fall in love with someone far away from your location - from a different city to halfway around the world. But that does not have to mean that you are destined for a solitary life with short bursts of happiness achieved through Zoom or FaceTime.

This is a spell designed to bring long-distance lovers together. The point of this spell is to already be in a loving and committed relationship, but living far apart, with the intent of either cohabitation or at least living in much closer proximity. Spread out over 10 consecutive nights, this spell should be performed during a waning moon.

You will need:

- A small amount of saltwater

- Lavender incense

- A map, showing where each of you live (a printout or something you create yourself would be fine)

- Scissors and tape

- A pen

Instructions:

1.After lighting the incense, consecrate the map by anointing each corner with saltwater. Then pass the map through the smoke of the incense.

2. On the map, mark each of your locations with a hand-drawn star.

3. Cut the map in two, closer to the star representing where you live.

4. Cut away a strip of the distance between you.

5. Tape the map back together. As you do, recite as follows: "We are coming closer together. So mote it be."

6. Repeat steps 4 and 5 each night for 10 consecutive nights.

7. On the 10th night, cut away all the remaining distance. When you tape it together, the stars should touch each other? On that night, recite the following:

"We are together. So mote it be."

8. Fold the map so that the stars are on the inside.

9. Take the map outside and burn it. The ashes that scatter to the breeze flies to your joint destiny. If you are unable to burn the map outside, burn it safely indoors and scatter the ashes to the breeze later.

RITUAL BLESSING OF ROMANCE

If you are already in the romantic relationship you have always wanted, but wish to have it blessed, there is a beautiful ritual you can perform. This ritual is meant to stabilize a romance desired by both parties. It is not intended to be, nor should it ever be used, as a one-sided spell.

For best results, carry out this ritual on a Saturday night during a waxing moon.

You will need:

- 2 glass beads (one the color of your birthstone and one the color of your partner's birthstone).

- At least 1 foot of brown thread.

- A small amount of saltwater

- Incense (preferably something earthy, like patchouli or lemongrass)

Instructions:

1. Cast a sacred circle.

2. Light the incense.

3. Pass the bead representing you through the incense smoke and then dip it into the saltwater.

4. Recite the following:

    "By air and fire. By water and earth.
    This is me in relation to {the name of your partner}."

5. Pass the bead representing your partner through the incense smoke and then dip it into the saltwater.

6. Recite the following: *"By air and fire. By water and earth. This is {the name of your partner} in relation to me."*

7. Pass the thread through the incense smoke and recite the following:

    "Air binds our minds to earth. Fire binds our passion to earth."

8. Dip the thread in the saltwater and recite the following: *"Water binds our hearts to earth. Earth binds us together."*

9. Thread the two beads together on the string and tie the string together using 7 knots.

10. With the tying of each knot, recite the following:

    "With the power of seven, we are blessed. Blessed be."

11. Take the amulet outside and bury it.

SPELL FOR NEW LOVE

This spell is designed to bring love into your life by focusing on attracting a loving energy.

For best results, perform this spell on a Friday night during a waxing moon.

You will need:

- 7 pink candles

- 7 red candles

- Incense (Rose or Valerian)

- A list of 9 attributes that your dream partner would possess (Available for love, live in my state, athletic… for example)

Instructions:

1.	Set up the 14 candles in a heart shape surrounding you. They should be arranged alternating pink, then red, then pink, then red…

2.	As you light each pink candle, recite the following:

"I light for love".

3.	As you light each red candle, recite the following:

"I light for passion".

4.	Once all 14 of the candles have been lit, read your list aloud, preceding each trait with a plea to the Goddess in the form of *"Goddess send me…"*. Just as an example, perhaps you would say, "Goddess send me a woman who wants to have children".

5. This list is your prayer, treat it as such. Channel all of your mental and spiritual energy into this prayer. Continue to send your energy into the universe until the candles burn themselves out. As they begin to extinguish themselves, close the prayer with *"So mote it be."*

Spells for Health and Healing

The majority of work that a white witch does is in the arena of health and healing. The person being helped can be yourself, a loved one, or a client and the type of healing can be physical, mental, emotional, or spiritual. As you can imagine, with these many options, the permutations of spells and rituals which can be performed are quite vast. Finding the correct spell for the correct individual to heal the correct problem at the correct time is not simple. It is, however, extremely rewarding; and an excellent way to use the powers you are developing magickly as well as psychically.

Let me take a moment to make one thing very clear. The use of spell work to physically heal the body is NOT meant to be a substitute for modern medical treatment. Your work on the spiritual plane can, and will, have tremendous effects on physical illness; however, it should be seen as a companion to treatment from a medical professional. The two should work hand in hand with each other to heal a physical ailment. What modern medicine views as "miraculous" only appears that way to those unaware that much magickal work may have gone into securing that result.

Let's start by taking a look at some ways to address and heal emotional trauma, both in ourselves and in others.

RITUAL FOR A POSITIVE ATTITUDE

It can be downright amazing just how mean we can be to ourselves. Beyond just the old adage of "I'm my own worst critic", some of us face negative thoughts about ourselves which actually make us "Our own worst enemy". Many of us find it easier to forgive others for their own shortcomings than to forgive ourselves for the same.

I was in this pattern of negativity myself at one point in my life, living in an unending loop of "I am a loser and so I do not deserve love, yet if I had love I would be less of a loser." However, what I came to realize was that this line of thinking ignored all of the positive aspects that made me a unique and wonderful soul. That negative line of thinking was a self-fulfilling prophecy whispered into my ear from a very young age by darkness and deceit, by an unseen enemy in order to convince me of my worthlessness. Darkness, evil, the devil - whatever you wish to call it - whispers to us all at one point or another in our lives. It is up to us individually to decide whether we will listen or not.

One way of breaking free of negative thoughts and a negative attitude towards ourselves is by performing this ritual.

It is a very simple undertaking and, as such, you will get out of it what you put into it. Take your time in creating the lists and try to search your subconscious mind to gain these insights. We are all beautiful balls of positive energy contained in a meat-suit on this plain. Try not to get distracted by the meat-suit and focus on the light within.

There is no specific day of the week on which to perform this ritual. For the best results, I suggest performing the ritual during a waxing moon.

You will need:

- A sheet of paper

- A pen

- A pair of scissors

- A white candle

- A metal bowl or cauldron

Instructions:

1. Prior to beginning any magickal or cleansing rituals (including a ritual bath), draw a line down the center of the sheet of paper. In the column on the left, write all of the negative things you have thought or heard about yourself. Be specific, honest, and don't hold back. This is your opportunity to purge yourself of all of the negativity which has been holding you back.

2. After writing the negative side of the list, follow-through and complete any pre-ritual cleansing that is planned.

3. Cast a sacred circle.

4. On the right side of the divided paper, write a list of all of your positive attributes; all of the positive things you have thought or heard about yourself. Again, be honest and specific. The only rule is that you must have at least as many positives as you do negatives written down.

5. Light the white candle.

6. Cut the paper down the centerline, separating the positive list from the negative list.

7. Using the flame of the white candle, light the negative list on fire and place it in the metal bowl or cauldron to burn.

8. As the negative list burns, read aloud the positive list. Take your time and focus on each attribute. Read each as follows: "I am _____. Blessed Be. I am _____. Blessed Be…"

9. After reading the final attribute, end the ritual with "So mote it be."

10. Allow the white candle to burn itself out.

11. Close the sacred circle.

12. Keep the positive list with you and read a few of the positive attributes any time that negativity attempts to re-enter your mind and steal your light.

ANTI-NIGHTMARE MOJO BAG

A "mojo bag" is a common technique employed in magick. It is a small sachet bag, which is filled with many different items depending upon the spell. The mojo bag might then either be kept with the practitioner or buried to act as a barrier.

If you have been plagued by nightmares, you know the negative effects that the disruption to your sleep schedule, and the terrifying images that accompany the nightmares, can have on your daily life and your health. Nightmares can be a sign of an evil attachment, a signal that you are being attacked psychically through black magick, or the purging of violence and fear by your own subconscious. No matter the cause, being awoken several times per night by nightmares can lead to devastating impacts on your physical and mental well-being. For the self-care aspect of avoiding consistent nightmares, this mojo bag is being included in the "Health and Healing" section.

One of the steps in this preparation is to anoint your "third eye" with water. The "third eye" is the pineal gland located inside the brain. However, we can approximate the third eye with a spot located about one inch above where our eyebrows would meet. This is the spot to anoint in this spell.

You will need:

- A small white or blue sachet

- A piece of silver ribbon

- A silver marker or paint pen

- Cedar shavings or cedar chips

- A piece of charcoal (for censing the cedar shavings)

- A small amount of saltwater

- Anise seeds, rosemary, and thyme

Instructions:

1. Cast a sacred circle.

2. Draw a crescent moon on the outside of the sachet with the silver marker or paint pen.

3. Light the charcoal and place the cedar shavings or chips on top.

4. When the cedar begins to smoke, cense yourself with the cedar. As you cense yourself, recite the following:

    "I bless my dreams by the power of air and the power of fire."

5. Cense the sachet through the cedar smoke.

6. Anoint your third eye with the saltwater. As you anoint, recite the following:

    "I bless my dreams by the power of water."

7. Splash a small amount of saltwater onto the sachet.

8. Point your athame at the mixture of anise seeds, rosemary, and thyme. Direct your energy through the athame and into the herbs. As you direct your energy, recite the following:

    "I bless my dreams by the power of earth. So mote it be."

9. Place the herbs into the sachet and tie it closed with the silver ribbon.

10. Close the sacred circle.

11. Sleep with the mojo bag under your pillow to vanquish your nightmares and enjoy a good night of sleep.

ELEMENTAL HEALING - WATER

The four natural elements are extremely important in healing spells. Each element has specific healing qualities ascribed to it and ways to efficiently direct those qualities. Although each of the following elemental healing spells are written in self-healing language, they can easily be converted to heal others either locally or remotely.

Water is considered the gentle element of healers. The fact that our bodies consist mostly of water may explain why water is so strongly associated with healing across a wide range of ailments. Physically, water is used to heal diseases of the blood and lymphatic symptoms. It is also the element used to assist in pregnancy issues. Psychologically, water is used to help with symptoms of depression, mood swings, and sleep disorders.

The drinking of wine within a sacred circle is also a way to specifically incorporate the element of water into your magick.

You will need:

- Fresh, clean water in a goblet

- Rose incense

Instructions:

1. Cast a sacred circle.

2. Holding the goblet of water, describe your intention and invoke the power of the element of water to aid in your healing.

3. Speak to the water in the goblet. Gather the energy from around and within you and focus it into the water. Touch the water, allow yourself to feel absorbed by the element.

4.   Pour the water over yourself. Be sure to get water on any specific parts of your body which need healing.

5.   Focus and "feel" the water soaking and incorporating itself into you, feel the power of the element changing and healing you from the inside.

6.   End the spell by reciting the following:

"So mote it be."

7.   Close the sacred circle.

ELEMENTAL HEALING - AIR

The element of air is used in the physical healing of ailments of the lungs, which makes sense. When it comes to the more emotional side of healing, the element of air is used to provide a clear mind, to call upon inspiration, and to encourage logical thought patterns.

One often overlooked aspect of the healing power of air is the representation of the element through speech. The use of the spoken word is, after all, a manipulation of the air. As such, healing of ailments or the calming of fears related to speech or public speaking can be addressed through the element of air.

Because air is constantly present all around us (hopefully) at all times, we do tend to become desensitized to its presence. A daily routine of meditation and mindfulness can help us to pay more attention to the air around us. However, in the meantime, or if you are not interested in developing this type of daily routine, the use of a hand fan can bring the air to the forefront of our consciousness.

You will need:

- A hand fan

- Incense associated with the element of air (i.e., lavender, sage, lemongrass, meadowsweet, etc.)

Instructions:

1.   Cast a sacred circle.

2.	Announce your intention and invoke the power of the element of air to aid in your healing, by reciting as follows:

"I invoke the power of the air, the element of the body, and of the mind, to heal the suffering being caused by the {ailment}."

3.	Light the incense. Breathe deeply. Gather the energy from round and within you, as the air you take in becomes a part of you.

4.	As you feel the air dissipate within you, recite the following:

"Air, power of creation and destruction, I bring you in."

5.	Fan the incense smoke over yourself, from head to toe.

6.	End the spell by reciting the following: *"So mote it be."*

7.	Close the sacred circle.

ELEMENTAL HEALING - FIRE

The element of fire is associated with healing neurological and autoimmune disorders, issues with libido and a failing spiritual energy. It is useful for raising your life force. When doing spell or healing work using the element of fire, bring as much energy into the sacred circle as you can muster. It is also helpful to add the crystals of amber or tiger's eye, extra candles, and incense representative of fire such as basil or rosemary.

There are instances when calling on the element of fire can be detrimental to the healing process, even if the list of symptoms calls for this type of healing. Because fire *is* energy (both physically and spiritually speaking), and is extremely powerful, some individuals may be too weak or in too delicate a state to treat with the fire element immediately. In these instances, it is recommended that the first round of healing be performed through the element of water in order to bolster and prepare the energy and spirit of the individual seeking the healing.

You will need:

- A grouping of 9 red candles bound together using orange ribbon

Instructions:

1. Cast a sacred circle.

2. Light the grouping of red candles.

3. Gaze into the flames of the grouping. Much like when using fire for divination, allow your eyes to lose focus and allow your consciousness to melt into the flame.

4. Bring the fire close to you mentally and physically. Recite the following:

   "I invoke the power and energy of healing fire."

5. Hold the candle grouping near the portion of the body which needs healing. If an emotional healing is being requested, hold the candle grouping near the third eye.

6. Focus on the heat and move the feeling of that heat throughout your body. Allow the heat to fill your entire body and being until you can imagine being lit, aglow, from the inside.

7. As you feel the warmth envelop and begin healing you, recite the following: *"Fire, heal me."* Repeat this incantation 9 times.

8. End the spell by reciting the following: *"So mote it be."*

9. Close the sacred circle.

ELEMENTAL HEALING - EARTH

The element of earth rules the physical body (or your "meat suit", as I have called it). As such, it is vital in the healing of muscle, bone, tissue, and organs. Earth is also associated with appetite and eating disorders, both anorexia and morbid obesity.

Emotionally, earth is a stabilizing, strengthening, and grounding element. It roots us in the here and now, in the current moment, which can be very helpful in the treatment of Post-Traumatic Stress Disorder.

You can bring additional earth elements into your spell work by including salt, the consumption of bread, milk, limestone, granite, and organic potting soil or organic gardening soil.

You will need:

- Limestone or granite rocks (enough to surround your workspace within the sacred circle

- A brown candle

- A small amount of Mugwort

- A small amount of olive oil

- A small amount of salt

- A small bowl of organic potting soil

Instructions:

1. Dress the brown candle by rubbing it with the olive oil and rolling the candle in crushed Mugwort.

2. Cast a sacred circle.

3. Use the limestone or granite rocks to create a small circle around what will be your healing workspace.

4. Light the brown candle.

5. Announce your intention and invoke the power of the element of earth to aid in your healing, by reciting as follows:

    "I invoke the power of the earth, the grounding root of my physical form. Earth! Heal me! Earth! Heal me! Earth! Heal me!"

6. End the spell by reciting the following: *"So mote it be."*

7. Allow the brown candle to burn itself out and bury the remnants.

8. Close the sacred circle.

SPELL FOR LONG-DISTANCE HEALING

There may be times when we need to heal someone who is too far away for us to lay our hands on. This spell will work for a wide variety of different types of healing. It can be modified to fit the ailment(s) from which your client or loved one is suffering, or even combined with elemental healing if so desired.

The sacred circle that is cast at the beginning of a spell work session or ritual serves a number of protective purposes. However, it also serves as the gateway between our plane and the spiritual plane. On the spiritual plane, distance does not exist in the same way it does on the physical plane. It is this property of the spiritual plane which allows for healings, spells, astral projections, etc. to take place over what would be excessive distance here on the physical plane.

This spell includes a slight modification in the casting of your sacred circle in order to highlight the "black hole" style property. In step one, when you have finished your regular casting of the sacred circle, recite the following:

> *"This is a circle between worlds, sacred, protected, a source of power and a gateway of manifestation. Here all things are possible. This is a location without location, existing in two planes and in all places at once. So mote it be."*

You will need:

- A photograph of the person being healed

- A personal item of the person being healed (this can be a snip of their hair, a button from their clothing, etc.)

- Incense of frankincense & myrrh

- A small amount of saltwater

- A small amount of mint oil

Instructions:

1. Dress the white candle with the mint oil.

2. Cast a sacred circle using the modified language from above.

3. Light the incense.

4. Cense the photo and personal item through the incense smoke and recite as follows:

"By air and fire, this is {Name of person to be healed}. {Name} is here in this circle. This is {Name} and {Name} is here!"

5. Wet the photograph and personal item with saltwater and recite as follows:

"By water and earth, this is {Name}. {Name} is here in this circle. This is {Name} and {Name} is here!"

6. Lift the photo and personal item towards the Goddess and God and recite as follows:

"Lady and Lord, see that this is {Name}. See that {Name} is here. Beloved Goddess and God, lend your aid as I heal {Name} in this circle. So mote it be!"

7. Focus all of your energy and stare at the photograph of the person to be healed. Repeat the phrase, *"You are healed"* as you send the healing energy to the individual. You can repeat this phrase for as long as you can maintain your focus on the photo.

8. Close the sacred circle.

9. Keep the photograph and the personal item in a safe and secure place.

HEALING SALVE

This is a witchy salve that is something I keep on hand at all times. It is handy for a large range of small wounds and pains - cuts, bruises, dry skin, chapped lips, headaches, insect bites, and bee stings.

You will need to infuse extra virgin olive oil with the herbs and flowers listed prior to making the salve. To infuse the oil, place the herbs and flowers in a large glass jar; pour the olive oil into the jar, keep the jar in a sunlit window, flip the jar every day for 30 days. After 30 days, strain out the herbs and flowers using cheesecloth and discard them. The oil is what you will be keeping for use in the preparation of the salve.

This salve is very protective and healing. It also contains properties of travel magick, so it is perfect for taking on vacation!

You will need:

- Equal parts of Comfrey Leaf, Calendula Flowers, Plantain, and St. Johns's Wort

- 1 cup of extra virgin olive oil

- 1 piece of cheesecloth (for straining)

- A chunk of beeswax (approximately 1 once)

- A small amount of lavender essential oil

- A small amount of tea tree essential oil

- A small amount of Vitamin E oil

Instructions:

1. Infuse the extra virgin olive oil with the herbs and flowers as explained above.

2. Melt the beeswax over low heat. Be sure not to burn it, just melt it.

3. Once the beeswax has melted, pour in your infused olive oil. Let the mixture warm up while stirring with a wooden spoon until it is fully combined.

4. Take the pan off the heat and add 6 or 7 drops of lavender essential oil, 6 or 7 drops of tea tree oil, and 6 or 7 drops of Vitamin E oil. Give the mixture a quick stir.

5. Pour your salve into small glass jars or aluminum tins and let it harden. The salve will remain antiseptic and safe for use for up to a year (although with small children, I usually run low in about 6 months).

CANDLE SPELL FOR QUICK HEALING

This is a classic-style candle healing spell. The goal of the spell is to aid in lessening the effects of an illness and speeding up recovery.

The size of the candle you choose should reflect the severity of the illness and length of recovery time you are manifesting. A votive or a small taper candle may be enough for a short-term illness, while a more serious malady may require a large seven-day candle for instance.

You will need:

- A white candle

- A small amount of healing salve

- A small amount of dried motherwort

- A glass candle holder appropriate for the candle chosen

Instructions:

1. Dress the white candle with the healing salve and dried motherwort.

2. Place the dressed candle in the candle holder.

3. Light the candle for 5-10 minutes per day in the room with he individual who needs to be healed. Upon lighting the candle, and **each** time you light the candle, recite the following:

    "The Lady and Lord shall watch over you and grant you the gifts of health and comfort. So mote it be."

4. Day by day, burn the candle until either the candle no longer lights (in which case, repeat the spell), or until the individual is fully healed and recovered.

5. When the spell is complete, dispose of the remains of the candle in the trash to rid the afflicted and the home of the illness for good.

Third Eye Opening - Psychic Spells

Remember the section on Psychic Abilities and Divination? Well, this is where the proverbial rubber meets the road. The "Third Eye" is the name ascribed to the portion of our brain which sees the unseeable. The third eye is a part of us which only some choose to acknowledge and develop. The third eye is the key to our psychic abilities. However, although often described only in esoteric terms, the third eye does go by another much more familiar biological name - the pineal gland.

The pineal gland was the last intracranial gland to be discovered. In 1640, Renee Descartes identified and named the gland nestled deep in the center of the brain, referring to it as the "seat of the soul". However, it would take another 318 years before an American dermatologist, Aaron Lerner, in 1958, discovered that the pineal gland exclusively produced a molecule he dubbed "melatonin".

The pineal gland is a tiny, pine-cone-shaped organ seated on the bridge between the right and left hemispheres of the brain. It is located approximately 1/2 inch above the center point between your eyes and straight back to the center of your brain.

What does any of this have to do with the third eye? Well, the pineal gland (located *inside* the center of our brain and in no way connected to the optic nerve which feeds signals from our eyes) is photosensitive! Melatonin is the molecule that regulates our circadian rhythm (making us tired at night and awake during the day). So somehow, the pineal gland releases melatonin when there is a lack of sunlight even though it is not linked to the optic nerve. That's right. The pineal gland is very literally a "Third Eye" and is located exactly where the third eye chakra has been depicted since the time of the ancient Sumerians!

The belief that the pineal gland is just the modern term for the rediscovered third eye organ known about for centuries past just shows how much wisdom has been lost and regained throughout the ages. Perhaps Descartes was exactly on point with his "seat of the soul" description.

There are ways for us to open our third eye and begin to develop our abilities to access the spiritual plane, including a meditation routine, the use of some herbs and plants, and of course through the use of spells and rituals.

Part of the journey of practicing Wicca or witchcraft is to open yourself to your psychic abilities. The more open you are, the better you will be able to communicate with the energies around you and the more power your intentions will hold.

You will need:

- A small amount of as many of the following dried herbs as possible: Mugwort, acacia, honeysuckle, peppermint, rosemary, thyme, cloves, yarrow, dandelion, lilac, lavender, and calendula

- A purple sachet

- A silver marker or paint pen

- A silver candle

Instructions:

1. Cast a sacred circle.

2. Using the silver marker or paint pen, draw an eye on the purple sachet.

3. Place the herbs into the sachet.

4. Light the silver candle. As you light the candle, recite as follows:

> *"I open my third eye, for the better to see.*
> *May these herbs awaken me.*
> *By the power of 3 times 3,*
> *My third eye open. So mote it be!"*

5. Touch the sachet to your third eye.

6. Repeat the incantation, touch the sachet to your third eye, twice more.

7. Allow the candles to burn themselves out.

8. Close the sacred circle.

9. Store the sachet under your bed or beneath your pillow.

There are herbs and essential oils which can assist you in the opening and clarifying of your third eye and psychic abilities. These herbs and oils should be respected. Some may be safely topically applied, some may be safely ingested, and some are only safe in aromatic form. It is, as always, important to speak with a reputable herbalist to know exactly how safe an herb or oil may be for topical use or ingestion.

- Angelica Root

- Cypress

- Elemi

- Frankincense

- Helichrysum

- Juniper

- Marjoram

- Patchouli

- Rosemary

- Sandalwood

- Vetiver

There are also a number of crystals that can aid us in our attempts to open and clarify our third eye and psychic abilities. For our purposes, placing a crystal or a few crystals on a table at our bedside can help to open our third eye as we sleep. Also, placing some of these crystals on your body, including one crystal in the center of your forehead over your third eye, during meditation can open your psychic center.

- Amethyst

- Angelite

- Axinite

- Azurite Sun

- Blue Aventurine

- Blue Tourmaline

- Celestite

- Chiastolite

- Dumortierite

- Fluorite

- Labradorite

- Lapis Lazuli

- Moonstone

- Phenacite

- Pietersite

- Purple Sapphire

- Purple Tourmaline

- Rhodonite

- Shungite

- Sodalite

- Sugilite

- Quartz

Please understand that when you open your third eye, you are opening a link between your spirit and other dimensions, other planes of existence. As you begin to open your third eye, you will experience some visions and other physical effects. Imagine having been blind since birth and then beginning to see for the first time ever. How confusing, strange, and frightening the sensation of vision would initially be! That is exactly what you ARE doing. You could begin to sense shadows or see other-worldly beings. Remain calm and rest assured that what you are sensing is real and is natural. You are not causing the sensations, you are just now able to see what has always been around you. Stretch your atrophied psychic muscles and begin to develop your abilities.

Personal Power Spells

If there was one word to summarize the draw, the feeling, of practicing Wicca and performing witchcraft it would be: EMPOWERMENT. Witchcraft allows an individual to perform magick, on the spiritual plane, in direct contact with all of the ancient wisdom contained in the universe, without the need of an intermediary priest or other religious leader. Witchcraft is about our power to function on separate planes. Witchcraft is a display of our power.

To be able to display our powers, it is necessary for us to be able to enhance our power, to gather our power from around us in order to direct it into our spell work.

Spells to enhance and gather our personal power can be as individualized as we are. There really is no wrong way to empower yourself, as long as you are respectful and do so without ill intent. So, you can feel free to use these spells as a framework for your own spells or rites, but they do not need to be strictly followed.

You will need:

- A quartz crystal

- A black tourmaline crystal

- A white candle

- A bundle of dried sage

- A cauldron or metal bowl

Instructions:

1. Cast a sacred circle.

2. Place the black tourmaline crystal in front of you.

3. Light the white candle. Use the flame of the candle to light the sage bundle.

4. Once the sage is smoking, place it in the cauldron or metal bowl.

5. Pick up the quartz crystal and cense it using the sage.

6. While holding the quartz, close your physical eyes and open your third eye. Visualize energy being gathered from all around you, swirling into you through your third eye. Energy flows up from the ground and into you. Visualize your aura growing stronger and brighter with each wave of energy that enters you.

7. Recite the following: *"I am magickal. I am powerful. I am compassionate. I am loved. I am strong."*

8. Repeat the affirmation 6 additional times.

9. As you begin to feel more and more powerful, as you feel magick surging through you, recite the following:

    "Magick running through me, help me see with clarity. Power that I have summoned here, protect me and I will have no fear."

10. Repeat the incantation 6 additional times.

11. When ready, end the spell with *"So mote it be."*

12. Quench the white candle and close the sacred circle.

Spell To Perpetuate Energy And Power

This spell is best performed during a new moon. As the moon's light increases night by night, so will your gathering energy and power.

You will need:

- A small amount of bay leaf essential oil

- A small amount of frankincense essential oil

- A small amount of jasmine essential oil

- A small amount of eucalyptus essential oil

- 1 yellow candle in a candle holder

- 1 red candle in a candle holder

- 1 blue candle in a candle holder

- 1 green candle in a candle holder

Instructions:

1. Dress the yellow candle with bay leaf essential oil.

2. Dress the red candle with the frankincense essential oil.

3. Dress the blue candle with the jasmine essential oil.

4. Dress the green candle with the eucalyptus essential oil.

5. Cast a sacred circle.

6. At the center of the circle, place the yellow candle to the North, the red candle to the east, the blue candle to the South, and the green candle to the west. You will be standing in the center of this secondary circle.

7. Light the candles in moonwise order, beginning with the yellow candle.

8. Recite the following:

    "I enter the flow of all that is. I am filled with loving-kindness. I release all negative and unbalanced energies. And I draw the best of power to me. So mote it be."

9. Relax and center yourself. Visualize a continuous flow of energy passing from each of the four candles and

entering into you through your feet and emanating up into your body. Feel the unlimited power fill you.

10.   When you feel that you have been filled with as much power as you are able to take, visualize the energy flow stopping.

11.   Extinguish the candles in counter-moonwise order.

12.   Close the sacred circle.

13.   With a clean cloth, wipe the remainder of the candles. Carry the cloth with you and, whenever you feel your powers begin to falter, smell the cloth for a quick recharge.

Cleansing Rituals

Being a practitioner of Wicca and witchcraft means that we are opening ourselves to the spirit world. As a result, we enjoy the ability to use our magickal power to affect change on the physical plane. However, it also means that we are accessible to a wide range of negative and/or evil entities. These entities exist for no reason other than to cause pain, distress, confusion, and havoc. And, as witches, we are seen as prime real estate for these destructive energies. These negative entities also find their way to unprepared and unsuspecting individuals. These individuals then become affected, oppressed, or even possessed by these evil entities. Unless, of course, they find their way to us first and we are able to cleanse them of their attachments. The removal of negative or evil entities from a space or an attached individual is called "cleansing".

Performing cleansing rituals is a vital task in sweeping away bits of negativity and darkness that may be present in a space or attached to an individual after breaking a curse or any type of psychic attack. Picture it this way, you had been shackled to darkness, chained to evil. When you break or explode from a chain, there are tiny bits or shards of metal that go flying off. They may be too tiny to see with your eyes, but if you walk around in bare feet you are guaranteed to end up with a sliver. Breaking a curse or a psychic attack tends to leave behind tiny shards of that negativity and evil. If you allow it to remain in your space, your soul is guaranteed to end up with a sliver. When you get free - stay free.

There are many thought processes and beliefs surrounding cleansing rituals. Every religion from Catholicism to Hinduism to Rosicrucianism has their "own". However, the truth is that, when viewed as a whole, they share more similarities than differences. As a result, there is really no harm to be done by trying one, two, or even all of the ritual examples which follow. All are designed to do the same thing: rid the space (and thus the people within the space) of negative energy and ward against the re-emergence of evil. So, explore. Find what works best for you, your space, and your lifestyle.

Unlike the majority of tasks in the spiritual realm, a successful cleansing will result in **immediate** relief. Oftentimes, although not always, when there is a negative presence or evil remnants are left from the breaking of a curse or spell, a general feeling of heaviness or unease will pervade a space. The stronger the negativity, the stronger the feeling. When you are able to rid your space of the negativity, the feeling of unease and the heavy atmosphere will disappear along with it. You will know that it worked because you will feel that it worked.

It is extremely important to continue cleansing until all of the evil and negativity has been removed. An evil or negative entity can be further enraged and empowered by a half-hearted attempt at cleansing it. The cleansing rituals quite literally hurt and weaken the entity. If the cleansing is not carried through, the entity will resume its prior actions with a much greater resolve and a newfound revenge-filled rage. Remember, we are making things better, not worse.

1. Smudging

Smudging is probably the most widely accepted and practiced cleansing ritual. Smudging is the burning and smoldering of herbs wherein the smoke is used as the cleansing agent. The most commonly used herb for smudging is a bundle of sage, specifically white sage. Sage is the kryptonite of dark entities (whether they be demons or restless spirits). However, a variety of different herbs have actually proven equally effective, including basil, lavender, and clove.

I personally use a mixture of dried herbs consisting of Mugwort, white sage, and lavender when performing a smudging session. I have found that Mugwort works as an excellent boost to my psychic abilities during the smudging session, allowing me to better sense the presence of the negativity or evil; while the sage and lavender work together to rid the space of the offending entities.

The "ritual" is actually extremely simple. It is one of the few rituals to preferably be performed during the daylight hours.

A smudging session should begin with a prayer or call for protection for anyone who will be in the home during the session. Next, the aura and body of each person present for the session should be cleansed. This is done by lighting the herb bundle and, once it is smoldering, tracing the outline of the person with the bundle, allowing the smoke to rid the aura and individual of any attachments they may be carrying.

Be sure to have at least one window or door open on each floor of the home. The negativity must be given a way to escape or it will be trapped and further enflamed.

Next, the smudging bundle should be carried into each corner of each room and public space in the home. Carry something to catch any of the smudge bundle ashes that may drop off (I use an abalone shell). Do not forget closets, basements, attics, side rooms, enclosed porches, etc. Once each and every space has been cleansed, you have finished the ritual.

There really are not any specific words that must be said during a smudging session. It is really up to those present to use visualization to help the smoke guide the negativity out of the home. However, some tend to give a short incantation within each room. If you choose to speak, commit to it being in each space and keep it simple. Perhaps something like,

> *"In the name of the Lady and the Lord, I implore all negativity and evil to leave this space. You have no right here and shall hold no power here."*

or

> *"Through the power of the Spirit, no negativity or evil shall remain in this home."*

Smudging is not even a ritual that should be used only to cleanse from a brush with evil. I smudge myself and my aura once every two weeks, and my home 3-4 times per year. It is a great way to maintain a clean aura and stay free of unguided attachments by evil entities, and to keep my home clear of pockets of negativity.

2. Salting

Salting is a widespread practice in eastern cultures, but it is quickly becoming accepted by the west as well. Salt has long been known as a purifier. Like quartz, salt's crystalline structure has the ability to hold and trap negative energies. It is a passive way of cleansing your environment of darkness.

There are a few different ways of deploying salt as a cleansing agent.

- A bowl of salt beside the front door (perhaps on a foyer table) can be used to attract and trap negativity or evil from individuals entering your home.

- Salt can be sprinkled in the corners of rooms in order to draw the negativity. Be sure not to touch the salt while it is deployed as a cleanser. After 4-5 days, vacuum or sweep up the salt and dispose of it.

- Salt can be used to encircle the outside of a home as a protective measure against the invasion of evil.

- Lastly, salt can be added to bathwater to create a cleansing soak for the individual working with the spirit realm.

It is important to note that I am not referring to common table salt. Table salt has been processed with iodine. Iodine affects the structure and clarity of the salt crystals. You will want to use whole or shaved pieces of unrefined sea salt or unrefined mineral salt. Don't worry, it is not as difficult to find as it sounds! A simple Google search will bring up many inexpensive suppliers.

3. Incense

The use of incense began, as far as we can tell, with the Egyptians who used it in healing rituals and the Babylonians who relied upon it when conferring with their divine oracles. The use of incense arrived in Japan in the sixth century - where it was used in purification rituals for the emperor and his court.

Today, incense can be found in a large number of scents and forms. Not to mention incense holders ranging from simple to amazingly intricate.

Incense is best used for personal and small area cleansing. Much like smudging, the smoke is the cleansing agent. However, unlike smudging, incense remains situated in one room. Just light the tip, blow out the flame and place the incense in the holder.

Among the best incense to burn for a cleansing ritual are:

- Sage

- Sandalwood

- Lavender

- Frankincense

- Palo Santo

- Linden Flower

- Juniper

- Hibiscus

4. Tuning Fork

Sound and music have been used in healing rituals for thousands of years. Early civilizations used singing bowls for sound therapy and Greek physicians used instruments and vibration to treat sickness and combat insomnia. Using a tuning fork for cleansing is merely an extension of the same idea. Tuning forks vibrate at specific frequencies. The frequency of 417 Hz is known as a "Solfeggio frequency" and has been found to rid the body, mind, and physical space of negative energy. It is not an absolute "must", but a fork tuned to the frequency of 417 Hz would undoubtedly be the most useful.

Find a comfortable spot within each room of your home. Set your intention for a cleared, renewed space. Lightly tap the tuning fork against something solid. Close your eyes and let the sound vibrate around and through you, allow it to clean all of the negativity and evil out of the room and you. Move on to the next room and repeat the process.

Unhexing, Banishing, and Eradicating Curses

The powers of evil and personal destruction that accompany a curse or a hex can be extremely strong and grow like a cancer, embedding themselves deep in our lives and psyche. It may, and most likely will, take more than one spell to free ourselves from this type of darkness.

This is not a one-and-done situation. I visualize curses and the other types of psychic attacks much like a mangrove tree. What appears on the surface to be a large swath of mangrove trees of many acres, or even an entire swamp, can actually be only one large mangrove tree. As the roots of a mangrove grow, they spread in all directions, not just down into the earth, and produce periodic shoots back above the surface. These become what appear to be separate and distinct trees, but are actually part of the original root system.

So it is with curses and darkness in our lives. What might appear to be unconnected traits or instances of negativity may, in fact, all be fed by the same curse. Just as you would not expect to kill a 4-acre wide mangrove system by chopping down one of the trees on the surface, we cannot expect to break a widespread curse or hex which has pervaded many aspects of our lives by performing one spell one time and then moving on.

That is why we need to see the fight against darkness as an ongoing war and not just a single battle. We need to be willing to fight for ourselves, our destiny, and for our bloodline. It may take repeating the same incantation once per day, or once per week, over an extended period of time to finally dig out the last effects of a curse in our lives. It may take performing the same ritual on successive new moons for a number of months to break a strong hex. It may even take a combination of the two! But please know that we are on the side of good, of light, of love, and of righteousness. We WILL prevail.

When you should utilize these prayers is completely up to you and your needs. A witch's link to the spiritual plane is always available. That is the beautiful thing about incantations, they take very little preparation and there is never a bad time to perform them. It is important to focus and calm your spirit, open your heart and mind. When you perform an incantation, whether inside or outside of a sacred circle, put your all into it.

Spell work is normally performed at night, under the light of the moon. Unless otherwise noted within the spell, it is safe to assume that the spells and rituals are meant to be performed at the time of the waxing moon. Also, there is a specific way to maximize the power you are putting out into the universe - try to perform your ritual near running water (i.e., a creek, a river, an underground spring, etc.). The electromagnetic energy created by running water is a natural, measurable fact. It is electromagnetic energy that powers our intentions into the universe and into the spiritual plane. Therefore, if you are able to be near a source of electromagnetic energy, your intention will gain strength merely by being in the location. As you are preparing yourself for the ritual, focus your intention and calm your spirit, cast your sacred circle, and make your intentions known clearly.

SPELL TO BREAK A MULTI-GENERATIONAL CURSE

It is an extremely important portion of this spell work that you be as cleansed as possible prior to performing this ritual. You should bathe in saltwater, cleanse your energetic aura with incense, focus your intention and calm your mind.

This spell should be performed on the night of a full moon.

What you will need:

- A small sachet or locket-style necklace

- Sea or Mineral Salt

- Coriander (Cilantro)

- A small drop of your blood (to be harvested during ritual)

- A black candle

- A Selenite crystal

Instructions:

1. Cast your protective circle.

2. Light the black candle. Use the flame to calm your spirit and set your intention - you will be undoing powerful dark magic that is transferred through generations.

3. When you feel focused, place a small amount (a pinch) of the sea salt into the sachet or locket.

4. Harvest the small drop of blood and put the blood onto the salt.

5. Add the coriander (cilantro).

6. Pick up the Selenite crystal. Slowly moving the crystal above the sachet or locket, recite the following:

> *"A darkness has followed*
> *in the blood of rich and poor.*
> *I purify with salt and fire*
> *to be accursed nevermore."*

7. Add one drop of the wax from the candle.

8. Tie the bag closed or close the locket.

9. Close the sacred circle.

10. Keep this sachet or necklace on your person every day until the next full moon. At that time, you may decide whether to dispose of the sachet/locket or to keep it.

It is most assuredly odd to include blood into a white magick spell. The reason blood is included in this spell is due to the type of curse (multi-generational). The power of the curse and the negativity is transferred and travels through the bloodline from generation to generation. Therefore, the only way to break the curse is to cleanse the blood of the curse. That is done through the purifying salt and the Selenite crystal. The cilantro is meant to contain the curse within the sachet or locket. There are times when the necessity of using bodily fluids in white magick does come up, but as you read other spell books or Books of Shadows, be aware that most uses of blood or bodily fluids are linked to the dark uses of black magick.

SPELL TO BREAK A CURSE AND REVERSE THE EVIL

Sometimes just breaking a curse is not enough and doesn't give you closure on the attack. Instead, we aim to break the curse and send the negativity back to the cursing witch. When you have been attacked spiritually by another witch or Wiccan practitioner, you are absolutely justified in returning whatever was released upon you.

You Will Need:

- A mirror

- A piece of paper

- A black pen

- A white candle

- A piece of white fabric

Instructions:

1. Cast a sacred circle.

2. Light the white candle.

3. Lay the mirror on the altar, reflection side up.

4. On the piece of paper, write all of the symptoms you are experiencing from the curse.

5. Lay the paper upside down on the mirror and cover it all with the fabric.

6. Recite the following:

> *"Your magick delivered*
> *A curse unto me.*
> *I remove and return*
> *Your curse back to thee."*

7. Press on the mirror through the fabric until it breaks (or smash it with a tool).

8. Gather all of the pieces of the mirror for disposal. Be careful not to either cut yourself on the shards, or see your reflection in any of the shards.

9. Close the sacred circle.

10. The mirror shards can be disposed of simply in the trash.

BREAK A CURSE USING A TALISMAN

With this ritual, you will create a talisman to absorb the negative energy of a curse and then destroy it, taking the negativity with it. This spell should be performed during a new moon.

You will need:

- Air drying clay

- Water charged with sun's energy (solar water)

- A slip of paper and pen

- Bay leaf

- Black candle

- Cauldron or metal bowl

- Toothpick

Instructions:

1. Cast a sacred circle.

2. Sprinkle some of the solar water within the circle and on yourself.

3. Light the black candle.

4. Write down on the slip of paper all of the effects that the curse has had on you (be thorough and specific).

5. Fold the paper around the bay leaf. Set the bundle on fire and place it in the cauldron or metal bowl.

6. When the ashes are finished smoldering, set them aside.

7. Take a portion of clay and anoint it with a drop of solar water. Mix the ashes into the clay thoroughly. Roll the clay into a ball and then flatten it into a disk shape.

8. On one side of the disk, use the toothpick to inscribe a symbol to represent the curse (it can either be a sigil or just a simple doodle that represents the curse to YOU).

9. Close your sacred circle.

10. Extinguish the black candle and allow the talisman to dry.

11. Once the talisman is dry, allow it to sit and charge in the sun.

12. Carry the talisman with you constantly to allow it to absorb the energy from the curse.

13. On the next new moon, take the talisman and smash it, rendering the curse that the talisman has absorbed broken.

14. Dispose of the shards outside of your home. Be sure that no residue of the talisman remains in your home or on your person.

QUICK INCANTATION FOR PROTECTION OF BODY AND SPIRIT

This quick incantation and visualization allow you to protect yourself when an unexpected threat appears. The greatest way to stay safe during a curse or hex is to not be hexed or cursed in the first place! So this incantation and visualization is a wonderful way to protect yourself from even being in a negative situation.

Instructions:

1. Recite the following incantation (even if under your breath):

> *"Power of the Goddess (or Goddess, Universe, Angels, Spirit,*
>
> *Ascended Masters, Protectors, etc.).*
>
> *Power of the God (or Goddess, Universe, Angels, Spirit,*

Ascended Masters, Protectors, etc.).

Cool as a breeze.

Warm as a stove.

Flowing like a stream.

Solid as a stone.

So mote it be!"

2.	Repeat the incantation a total of seven times.

3.	During each incantation, visualize an electric blue ring of flame encircling you until you have a seven-ring spiral from head to toe.

THE WITCH'S BOTTLE

Witch bottles have been used for at least 400 years to protect the home and its inhabitants from curses, hexes, and evil by creating a magickal double of yourself. The supplies needed are a bit odd, but this is ancient magick after all.

The idea behind a Witch's Bottle is that the evil spirits are drawn to the bottle instead of you, and then get trapped by the nails, pins, and knotted string and confused by the broken glass/mirror (like a funhouse mirror maze).

You will need:

- A glass bottle with a tight cork or cap

- Nails and pins (preferably bent)

- Broken glass pieces and/or broken mirror pieces

- Pieces of string, knotted multiple times

- Your own nail, hair clippings, and bodily fluids (i.e., urine)

- A red or black candle (just to seal the bottle cap)

Instructions:

1. Put all solid materials into the bottle while reciting the following: *"Harm be bound away from me"*.

2. Add the liquid ingredient(s). Close the bottle and seal it with the wax.

3. Bury the bottle upside down outside the front door of the home, or under the floorboards, or hidden in a remote corner of the lowest point of your home.

CREATING A JAMAICAN DUPPIE BAG

A "duppie" is the Jamaican term for an evil spirit or ghost. This sachet functions in a very similar way as the more familiar "mojo bag", however the Jamaican Duppie Bag is specifically geared toward ceremonial magick for protection and the banishing of freshly evoked evil spirits.

There is an ingredient in this preparation which you may not be familiar with - asafoetida. Asafoetida is an herb produced in Southern Iran, used in Indian cuisine, and integral to the Jamaican Duppie Bag. How is that for a multicultural plant! But don't panic because it can be found in most grocery stores and online in many forms.

You will need:

- A black sachet

- A black ribbon

- Asafoetida

- Camphor

- Garlic

Instructions:

1. As you fill the sachet with the asafetida, camphor, and garlic, recite the following:

"My Lady and Lord, of both moonlight and sun. See me safe, free of evil. Cause the darkness to run. So mote it be."

2. Tie the sachet closed with the ribbon.

3. Carry the Duppie Bag with you whenever you feel you may need protection from darkness or evil.

As an aside, I personally keep my Duppie Bag hanging from the rearview mirror of my vehicle so I can put it in my pocket at any time. We just never know when evil may try to gain a foothold.

SPELL TO BANISH EVIL AND NEGATIVITY

This is a simple ritual to banish harmful influences from your home and the bodies within. The red apple is seen as a symbol of purity, beauty, and rebirth in the Wiccan pantheon. This ritual should be performed on a Friday during a waning moon.

You will need:

- 1 red apple

- 1 bay leaf (this should be a fresh leaf)

- A piece of red string

Instructions:

1. Cast a sacred circle.

2. Place the apple in front of you.

3. Take a moment to focus your intent. Focus your mind on sending away all negativity and evil.

4.   Visualize a protective layer around you, like the skin of the apple, which makes all negative energies bounce off. Keep this image firmly in mind.

5.   Use your athame to cut the apple vertically into two halves. Lay the halves in front of you and cut sides up.

6.   Place the bay leaf on one of the cut halves.

7.   Recite the following:

"With red and green, I form a banishing dome. Cast all evil from within my home."

8.   Repeat the incantation two additional times, finishing with *"So mote it be."*

9.   Put the two halves of apple back together (leaving the bay leaf inside) and secure them with the red string.

10. Close the sacred circle.

11. Bury the apple on your property, the closer to your home the better.

UNCROSSING RITUAL

An "uncrossing" means to get rid of unwanted and unneeded energies and attachments that may have found their way or been thrust upon you. Perhaps you are suffering from a hex-related illness or you feel as if you have unintentionally been saddled with an oppressive negative entity, an uncrossing ritual may be exactly what you need to heal or free yourself.

You will need:

- 7 Bay Leaves (fresh or dried)

- 2 sticks of frankincense incense

- A small amount of ground cinnamon

- 1 white candle

- 1 plate (not made of plastic or paper)

Instructions:

1. Cast a sacred circle.

2. Light the white candle.

3. Place the Bay Leaves on the plate.

4. Sprinkle the ground cinnamon onto the bay leaves. While you do this, recite as follows:

> *"In the name of the great and victorious elements, I invoke the ancient forces. To crush and remove all negative entities, all curses and crosses. Break and dissolve. Bless and set free. As it is now, so mote it be."*

5. Cross the two sticks of incense on the plate over the bay leaves and cinnamon. Light them.

6. Allow the white candle and the incense to burn themselves out.

7. Close the sacred circle.

8. Any remains of the incense sticks, bay leaves, cinnamon, and the white candle can be disposed of in your trash. They do not need to be buried.

BULLY BANISHMENT JAR

As much as we hate to admit it, bullying and mean-spirited behavior is as much a part of the adult working world as it was when we were in school. Young, unconfident, spiteful children often grow up to become older, unconfident, spiteful adults. They may be in our personal lives in the form of neighbors or in our professional lives in the form of coworkers, but the realities are the same. Nobody likes a bully. We may not be able to banish these individuals from our lives, however we can banish the negative effects that their words and actions have on us. With a little help from a pickle jar. You won't need to cast a sacred circle at all for this ritual and it is perfect for your kitchen right at home!

You will need:

- A glass jar with a screw-type lid (I use pickle jars)

- 1/4 cup of apple cider vinegar

- A small amount of dried mint

Instructions:

1. Take the jar into your hands. Visualize the individual doing you no harm and simply leaving you in peace. Hold this image in your mind.

2. Recite the following:

    "{Person's name}, you will bully and intimidate me no more."

3. Add the vinegar to the jar.

4. Add the dried mint to the jar.

5. Screw the lid tightly onto the jar and shake vigorously as you recite the following 9 times:

    "Venom, viciousness, and vileness be gone!"

6. Open the lid and pour the contents down the drain under hot running tap water. Visualize all of the mean-spirited, vile, nasty remarks and behavior of the bully being washed down the drain and out of your life.

7. Rinse the inside of the jar and recite as follows:

    "{Person's name}, your power over me is gone. I am safe

    from harm. I am no longer troubled by you and I am free. No

    more will you distress me. I am stronger than you. So mote it be."

8. Dispose of the jar in the trash. You wouldn't want any of the energy from that jar being carried over into the next spell or use for the jar.

Chapter 4

Maintenance & Disclaimer for Professional Assistance

How to Know if Your Magick is Working

Once we have done all of our research, gathered ingredients, and performed our spell or ritual, how do we know if what we have done is having any type of effect on the physical plane? How are we to monitor whether the power and effort we pour into our magick is having the desired manifestations? It seems like it would be so simple. In our modern world, we have become accustomed to easily drawing conclusions between cause and effect, to understanding how "Action A" will change the state of matter around us. However, just like the majority of magickal practices, the spiritual plane does not function under the same rules as our day-to-day, physical plane.

That means that we need to be looking, and feeling, in different ways to monitor our spell efficacy. So, let's jump in and take a look at a few of the ways we can tell if our magick is working.

1. Signs from The Universe

As Wiccans or practitioners of witchcraft, we need to be cognizant and mindful of signs and signals from the Universe at all times. However, perhaps no time is more important than following the casting of a spell or performance of a ritual. The Universe is constantly sending us all kinds of signals, but we need to be ready to receive them. Signs can come in the form of weather changes, cloud formations, actions of wildlife, or many other types of seemingly "natural" occurrences.

2. *Mood Changes*

Perhaps some of the most common signs that any spell is working is how the spell caster is feeling. A successful spell should lead to a feeling of happiness, of clarity, of satisfaction, and of confidence. When you have given your all to a spell or ritual, when you believe in your personal power and your magick, you *should* believe that what you have done will result in the manifestation you have desired. Often, we notice this change as an instinctive feeling in our surroundings. We simply "feel" that our spell is working, we just "know" that our magick is making the required change to our world. Your subconscious will certainly make you aware if you have been true to yourself and true to the Universe, either through manipulation of your mood or through manipulation of your dreams.

3. *Messages in Dreams*

Dreams are not just random images as your brain runs a "defrag" program. All of our dreams have meaning. Being able to interpret that meaning can be very enriching and can allow us to receive signals from our subconscious which will help us to know if a spell is working.

4. *"Coincidences"*

I put coincidences in quotes because I truly do not believe that coincidences exist. What many see as a coincidence is actually a signal from the Universe. We need to be open to seeing signs in coincidences, even if the message is not immediately clear or understandable. Have you ever found yourself thinking about a friend or family member you haven't spoken with in quite some time, only to have that person contact you within the next few hours? The world would consider that a coincidence. However, we may recognize this moment as a signal from the Universe. The message being relayed is for the practicing witch to decipher, as only he or she can be aware of all of the intricacies, feelings, and spell work performed.

Further, it is important to remember that the spiritual plane does not function on your time, which is a good reason to avoid spell work that has a hard deadline. Even if a spell is completed perfectly and with enough power the first time it is performed, just because you want to see the completed manifestation within the first week, there is no guarantee that the Universe will comply with your timeline. In the same vein, just because you do not see the completed manifestation within the first week, does not necessarily mean that the spell was not successful.

We work on a plane outside of the known laws of physics, including those governing space and time. We are able to take advantage of this fact during some of our spiritual activities, like astral projection. But the seeming disregard to timing can be a rather frustrating difference with which to come to terms. Practitioners of witchcraft need to be patient, watch for signals and remain open to receiving confirmation of efficacy through non-traditional channels and not necessarily on cue.

Where Do You Go From Here?

Great job on getting this far! Now you have learned how to craft and cast spells on a wide array of subjects. And, best of all, you have trained your mind and discovered how to identify and develop your innate power to manifest effects on the physical plane. So you may be wondering, "Now what? Is this it? I am officially a witch, so I guess I just wait until I need something." No! You are just now beginning to scratch the surface of Wicca, of witchcraft, and of the spiritual journey that you have embarked upon. So, let's discuss taking the next steps!

First and foremost, LEARN! The world of magick is vast and deep. No matter how much you know, read, and learn, there will always be something new to explore, something new to learn. Perhaps you have already found a spiritual and magickal path that resonates with you. Perhaps you are still searching for your place in the universe. Either way, you should familiarize yourself with as many different schools of magick (and as many different schools of thought) as you possibly can. Each has something special to offer you. Each can lead you to new personal discoveries. And one of the exciting facets of witchcraft is that you are free to mix-n-match! Find the ideas, the spells, the theories, etc. that make sense and resonate with you and incorporate them into your own practice.

Learn about tangential fields of study like astrology, numerology, feng shui, tarot, demonology, etc. All of these ancient subjects have something to lend you and your spell work or may open doors into fascinating additional studies and expand your understanding of yourself and the world around you.

I am going to make a confession that you will not see from many authors: I do not know everything about any subject. That is why there is a "Resources" page at the end of this book. Yikes. But I have no fear in making that statement because the dirty little secret is that **nobody** knows everything about any subject! There is no shame in admitting that there is more to learn. Never run from knowledge.

Secondly, you need to PRACTICE! Any athlete or musician will tell you that in order to develop their talent they had to commit to an enormous amount of practice. And those same athletes or musicians will also tell you that to maintain and improve their talent they have committed to an unending cycle of practicing. Magick is simply not a spectator sport. You will never become a powerful, comfortable practitioner of Wicca or witchcraft by just reading about it. The more spells and rituals you perform, the easier they will become and the more confident you will become in your own ability.

So, meditate regularly, practice sensing energy, perform spells, try alternate forms of spells, practice working with various components, pay attention to your dreams, and keep a journal. These are all important factors to incorporate into practice. Do not give up on your magick. Your power is in there, it is a part of you. Putting your knowledge into practice is how you can release it. Just keep going.

Third, maintain a deep connection with NATURE. Try disconnecting from our technologically-laden world for long periods. Developing a rapport with the natural world will serve you in three ways: the majority of the ingredients used in spell work can be found in the natural world (herbs, flowers, stones, and crystals), you will give yourself an opportunity to become more in tune with the cycles of the earth, and nothing nourishes the soul more than time spent with Mother Earth. A happy witch is a naturally balanced witch.

Fourth and finally, consider practicing with OTHER PEOPLE. If you have been practicing your craft solo, consider looking around your area for like-minded individuals with which to practice some of your spell work. Yoga centers, health food co-ops, and New Age or occult supply stores can all be good places to start asking around. There are advantages and disadvantages to practicing with other individuals. It is something to consider, but not something I would necessarily recommend everyone try. It really just comes down to a matter of personal preference. Some advantages can be:

- It can be fun to share ideas and spend time with "kindred spirits";

- You can learn a lot from other people's experiences and perspectives; and

- Combining your energy with someone else's can ramp up the power of a spell significantly.

However, there are also disadvantages to consider, such as:

- If your energies or intentions are not compatible with those of the others in a group, your spells can get confused and murky;

- If you are working with people who tend to be domineering, or if you are insecure about your own abilities, you can end up being unduly influenced by another witch. No matter how long they have been practicing, and no matter how powerful they profess to be, they are just human like you. Never allow anyone to control your magick or to make you do anything with which you do not 100% agree.

Spiritual Activities Requiring Professional Assistance

I cannot possibly be the only one to have had this happen. You are driving down the highway when your vehicle decides to make some sort of horrific sound, kind of a whining and simultaneous grinding sound. Immediately you pull over to the shoulder and pop the hood. You find yourself staring under the hood of your vehicle, pretty much just hoping that whatever is wrong would start to glow or you would find something completely obvious that would get you back up and running. But, alas, you are doing little more than perusing your engine compartment and silently nodding to yourself like, "Yep. The engine is still there." Do you know what we needed in that situation? Help from a professional! And there is nothing wrong with that!

What can be even more dangerous is when we are staring at ourselves or a loved one in a spiritual crisis while we nod to ourselves like, "Yep. Gonna need to fix this on my own because I do not want anyone else to know about it." That is the kind of thought pattern that has pervaded far too much of society today. There is no need to save face when it comes to crises of the soul. They are a condition of being human and literally every human goes through them at some point. Just as we have been speaking and discovering ways over the previous chapters and sections to manifest our desires and manipulate spiritual energies on alternate planes of existence, we must also take into consideration that sometimes our knowledge is not enough, and it is time to garner the help of a professional.

We can, and should, feel empowered to explore our own spirituality at our own speed and in our own time. However, there are specific situations when we require more than our own power and knowledge. Some of those instances are:

1. **Yoga**

Yoga is far more than just a set of stretching exercises. Actually, yoga is a group of physical, mental, and spiritual disciplines originating in India over 5,000 years ago. It is based on an extremely subtle blend of art and science focusing on healthy living.

The word "Yoga" comes from the Sanskrit word for "to unite". Yogic scriptures state that the aim of the practice is to unite the individual consciousness with the Universal Consciousness, harmony between mind and body, between man and nature. This state is known as "nirvana".

The practice of Yoga involves training of both the body and the spirit. Make no mistake, Yoga is a spiritual practice… a religion… with its own set of scriptures (The Vedas) and its own leadership (gurus and yogis).

Although it can be difficult today to find even a small town in America without a Yoga studio or a Namaste t-shirt, it is important to remember that respecting the religious beliefs of others is a foundation of Wicca and witchcraft. The physical aspect of Yoga is a wonderful workout and is something that can be learned online or by many other methods. If you want to join a Yoga group in the park, try hot Yoga, or see what the big deal is with goat Yoga - go right ahead and have fun.

However, the spiritual side of Yoga is extremely complex. When it comes to learning the beliefs associated with Yoga and the union of humans and nature, I recommend seeking the assistance and the teachings of a professional yogi or guru.

2. **Demonology**

As a practitioner of white magick, we turn ourselves into targets, willingly. Over years of practice and study, an example of how a negative spirit experiences a white witch has become more and more clear.

Picture yourself in complete darkness, the type of inky blackness that does not allow you to see your own hand in front of your face. Nothing to see, nothing to feel, no way of orienting yourself in space (are you facing up or down), no way of being sure whether your eyes are even open or closed… for hundreds of years. The only thoughts in your head are of anger, panic and confusion. And then, suddenly, there appears a tiny ball of light. Your mind rushes to decipher whether the light is close but tiny, or large but far away. Since you can block the tiny light with your hand, it must be off in the distance. You rush toward it. As the light begins to grow in size and clarity, you realize for the first time in far too long that you are not alone in the darkness. You can suddenly sense other beings around you, seemingly drawn toward the same light as you. Some feel as though they have been there longer, some feel as though they are relatively new, and others feel like nothing you can put into such a category. These "others" do not even feel like people to you. They have no human energy, they have no residual spirit, they have no memories that they are giving off. More or less, you experience them in waves of hatred and repulsion. And the "others" are far faster than you, making you feel small and insignificant. You get the distinct impression for the first time in your existence that you are in the presence of a predator and that you are prey. These are demons. They are drawn toward the glow of the presence of light in the darkness, just like every other malevolent spirit, except they are well aware of what they are chasing. They want the white witch. They want to extinguish the light and exist in the darkness. Their only reason for being is to cause harm, pain, distress, fear, destruction, and death to all creatures of light.

There is no need to believe in the concept of a "heaven" or "hell" to believe in demons. Frame the idea in whatever context you wish, but the reality stays the same. There are entities that exist both in our physical plane and on the spiritual plane that consist purely of evil. I refer to these entities as "demons", although that is merely a label that I use because it is one with which I am comfortable and accustomed. You can feel free to use any word you desire.

Demons are evil entities, not spirits, who have never walked the earth as a human. They were never born in a meat suit, lived a life, died, and had their energy released back into the Universe. They have always existed in the form of negativity and are able to pass through dimensional planes only when a portal is opened from our side. Witches open such a portal any time they cast a sacred circle, the link to the spiritual plane, although their space is protected by the properly cast circle. However, there are many other unsuspecting individuals opening portals who are completely unprotected; and even leaving the portals open between dimensions allowing for free travel of spirits and demons alike.

One way of "accidentally" inviting a demonic entity is by the use of a spirit board (or Ouija Board). When an individual opens themselves to be entered and manipulated by the spirit of their dead grandfather, there is absolutely no way of guaranteeing that is the spirit that responds… if it is a spirit at all. This complete lack of control is why I never agree to the use of a spirit board, regardless of the skill level of the individual or witch involved.

Another manner of coming into contact with the demonic is through black magick. As we have discussed, white magick is used for good and pure manifestations only. Any magickal spell that injures, causes pain, causes misfortune, causes sickness, or causes harm to another is considered "black magick". The use of black magick should be strictly avoided for two reasons. First, the Wiccan Rede (which we discussed earlier) states:

> *"Bide the Wiccan law ye must, in perfect love and perfect trust.*
>
> *Eight words the Wiccan Rede fulfill: If ye harm none, do what ye will.*
>
> *What ye send forth comes back to thee, so ever mind the Rule of Three.*
>
> *Follow this with mind and heart,*
>
> *Merry ye meet and merry ye part."*

In other words, any black magick you perform, the universe will return to you three-fold. Not good folks. Not good. Black magick relies on the demonic to fulfill the desires of the witch. Witches who practice black magick do not worship demons or "the devil", however they do call upon demons (often by name) to assist them in their curses, hexes, and other dark rituals.

Demons are extremely malicious, destructive, ancient, and intelligent. There is a huge difference between the ability of a white witch (new or experienced) being able to banish negative energy, banish a negative spirit, clear a chakra, or bless a home and banish a demon from a residence or, worse yet, from an individual. Yes. I am referring to exorcism, though by another name. "Exorcism" is a Catholic ritual. "Banishment" is a spiritual boot in the ass of evil without the trappings of Catholicism.

Banishing or exorcising a demon is not a practice that should be undertaken by a single witch, regardless of their skill level. When we encounter the demonic, it is time to seek professional, specialized, help.

Where the help comes from is a matter of personal choice. It can be a Catholic priest, a non-denominational Christian priest, a Shaman, a Reiki Master, a practitioner of black magick may even be able to help, or a seasoned coven of white witches. Just DO NOT ATTEMPT TO BANISH A DEMON BY YOURSELF. Demonic attachment, oppression, and possession are a reality even in our technologically driven, shiny, plastic world.

3. Modern Medicine

Please let me make this very clear. Nothing within the belief system of Wicca, nor the practice of witchcraft, precludes or even dissuades one from seeking assistance from a medical professional. To be frank, modern medical practice and the practice of witchcraft work quite well hand-in-hand, although you would be hard-pressed to find a doctor to admit such. Modern medicine is, at its most basic, a re-introduction of age-old herbal remedies. The majority of today's wonder drugs are rooted in known herbal and pharmacological processes and properties. Today's doctors would have been persecuted as witches in previous centuries. They may call their healing "science" and we call our healing "magick", but truthfully, we are not using knowledge that is all that different.

So when we are sick, when we are in pain, or when we experience a physically traumatic event, we treat ourselves AND we seek professional help.

The same concept relied upon in the medical field above also applies to the psychological field. There have been psychological issues that I have been able to discover through meditation and self-reflection, come to terms with, and overcome without the need for any external assistance. But there have also been instances wherein I needed help with an emotional issue and have sought out assistance from a trained professional. Psychologists and psychiatrists use tactics not unlike those found in guided meditation to reach the root of an emotional issue. There is no shame in asking for help when delving into a place in our own minds which has been locked away for our protection. Sometimes the issue is simply too painful or deeply guarded for us to reach on our own. Find a professional to help guide you safely to your realization.

Conclusion

Congratulations! You have taken a huge step toward becoming a knowledgeable, practicing witch and/or Wiccan! Hopefully, you feel informed and empowered to work on the spiritual plane and to see your desires manifested in your life.

This is the comprehensive, vetted, and plain-language reference guide that all beginning witches and practitioners of Wicca have longed for. Within these pages, you have a reference guide for all of the basics you need to be a successful white witch or practicing Wiccan. We have discussed:

- The history of witchcraft;

- The basic principles, beliefs, and practices of Wicca;

- The yearly Sabbats and Wiccan calendar;

- The different types of magic and witchcraft;

- Do's and Don'ts of witchcraft;

- Psychic Abilities

- Divination

- Grounding and drawing your energy

- Ritual preparation

- Creating an altar and a safe space for your practice

- The basic tools you will need (your toolkit)

- Herbs and their uses

- Crystals and their uses

- Candles and their uses

- Over 45 basic spells

- Signs and signals that your magick is working

- The next steps on your journey

- Instances when you should seek professional assistance

I would love to be able to boil all of this information down into a tidy little sentence that you can simply carry off with you as you begin your practice. But, as we discussed, witchcraft is a lifelong journey of learning and exploring. Any bite-sized soundbite I could offer would never encapsulate the powerful and truly amazing spiritual enlightenment which Wicca and witchcraft offer each of us.

If I can leave you with one parting thought, let it be this: The Universe is infinitely more vast and remarkable than we could ever possibly grasp while tethered to our meat suits. There are planes of existence within planes of existence. And yet something about being human allows us an all-access pass to the wonder. Something about being human draws our consciousness towards the heavens and out into the vast unknown. Something about being human allows us to be one with nature and in control of nature simultaneously. Perhaps there is something unique about being human within the Universe and its dimensions. Perhaps we are all somehow part of a much greater whole. Perhaps miracles are not random at all. Perhaps it is all magick.

Do not fail to venture out into the Universe, my fellow witches. This is our workspace. If ye harm none, do what ye will. Walk ahead as witches. Walk ahead in confidence. Walk ahead not in fear, but with respect.

Last Message and small request from the Magickal Witches team:

We wish you nothing but magickal success and health on your journey of being a powerful witch! If you've enjoyed this book or found that it has been exactly what you've needed, please consider leaving the book a review <u>here</u> where you can find the book in Glinda Porter's author profile. You will also find all her other literature that you'd love to check out. We're sure of it!

All feedback is extremely important to us because it helps us deliver exactly what you want and it also helps other readers make a decision when deciding on the best books to purchase. We would greatly appreciate it if you could take 60 seconds to leave the book a quick review. You can also reach out via email to leave any feedback.

Email: magick@magickalwitches.com

Website: www.magickalwitches.com

Author Profile: https://www.amazon.com/author/glindaporter

Lastly, don't forget to claim the "Survival and Wellness Kit for Magickal Witches" where you will receive:

- 10 Elixirs For Detoxification and Aura Cleansing
- 12 Spell Jar Recipes For Protection
- Guide For Talisman Preparation For Use Outside Home
- 20 Daily Detox Tips To Keep Your Vessel Clear
- Master Ingredient Shopping List

Resources

Cunningham, J. *Witchcraft For Beginners: A Basic Guide For Modern Witches For Find Their Own Path and Start Practicing To Learn Spells And Magic Rituals Using Esoteric And Occult Elements Like Herbs And Crystals.* 2019

Nietzsche, F. *Beyond Good and Evil: Prelude to a Philosophy of the Future.* 1886. Chapter IV. Apophthegms and Interludes. Section 146

Lipp, D. *The Complete Book of Spells: Wiccan Spells For Healing, Protection, and Celebration.* Rockridge Press 2020
Phillips, G. Open Your Eyes-All 3 Of Them.

Retrieved from https://musingsfromtheuniverse.com/2021/03/08/open-your-eyes-all-3-of-them

Phillips, G. Something Wiccan This Way Comes-Part 1 of 2. Retrieved from https://musingsfromtheuniverse.com/2021/04/09/something-wiccan-this-way-comes-part-1-of-2

Shakespeare, W., & Gibson, R. (2005). Macbeth.

Cambridge, UK: Cambridge University Press

Vanderbeck, P. *Green Witchcraft: A Practical Guide to Discovering the Magic of Plants, Herbs, Crystals, and Beyond.* Rockridge Press 2020

Whitehorn, M.L. Why Earth Is Closest To Sun in the Dead of Winter.
Retrieved from https://space.com

Wigington, P. (2020, August 26). 7 Ways To Develop Your Psychic Abilities. Retrieved from https://www.learnreligions.com/ways-to-develop-your-psychic-abilities-2561759

Wigington, P. (2020, August 28). Methods of Divination. Retrieved from https://www.learnreligions.com/methods-of-divination-2561764

BOOK 2

Beginners Witch Guide to Hoodoo & Folk Magick

Gain Mastery in Rootwork, Conjure, and Spells with Roots, Herbs, Candles & Oils to Rid Negativity and Manifest Anything You Desire

Introduction

Like nature and the four elements, magick is all around us. We use it every day in ways we're not even conscious of. A cup of tea that helps you to feel calm is a form of magic. Same with telling yourself the same stories over and over again or wearing the color red to entice arousal in a mate.

Think I'm exaggerating? Take a look at the advertisements on Instagram or YouTube. Corporations that advertise on these platforms work very hard to occupy space in your mind.

Everything these companies do is done with intent (which will be an important word, as we'll cover in later chapters); from the music they use to colors and fonts.

If you want clearer evidence of magick in everyday life, look no further than some of their logos. In the magical realm, symbolism is considered a graphic depiction of what the magician wants. Logos are symbols, in some cases they are sigils.

They act as a graphical way for a company or organization to remain present in the minds of the people.

This is one way magick is used on us, though most people remain unaware. You may be surprised to know that you are also using magick on yourself. You use intent every day, even if that intent is not conscious.

This is why I believe it is important to study magic. With knowledge you can better use your power to create the life you want, not do what a corporation wants you to do or be subject to your old habits.

There are countless magical traditions, but by picking this book, you've clearly shown an interest in hoodoo. And hopefully, that budding interest comes with an open mind.

One of the first things you should know is this tradition has many different names: aka rootwork, folk magick or magick, or simply work. Practitioners will describe what they do as 'working', 'a working', or 'doing work'.

A simpler (and perhaps controversial) way to put it is 'casting a spell', however this isn't all hoodoo is. We'll get into that in the next chapter. For the sake of simplicity, we'll refer to this practice as either conjure or hoodoo.

You might be wondering what the term 'rootwork' has to do with hoodoo. In short, roots are *extremely* important, not just in magic, but in hoodoo specifically.

This is a tradition that has its source in spiritual practices from African cultures that were ravaged by the slave trade. It is in these cultures that we discover the source of many of the things hoodoo practitioners do, for example, divination, chanting (or reciting mantras), and channeling.

If you think of roots as a metaphor, the connection becomes clear. Rootwork is a way for the millions of people whose ancestors were displaced by slavery to stay connected to their roots.

Over time, hoodoo evolved to incorporate practices from Native American and European cultures, as well as Christianity and Judaism. In some aspects, there were similarities between African cultures and Christianity. In many cases, disguising rootwork practices in Christianity became a matter of life and death for slaves.

The reason for the development of hoodoo was a desire to change one's life, specifically in the face of being enslaved. It came out of a need to survive, to have autonomy.

In short, this *work* is about putting your power back in your hands, literally.

In this book, we'll cover the basics—what conjure is and what it is not; the balance, history, core elements and principles. These first chapters are short, compared to what we could cover, but they're meant to give you information so you can start your research—this book is not meant to be a complete survey of the origins of conjure.

Of course, you don't *have* to study the basics. You are free to flip to the chapter on spells for attraction and start buying your materials right away, but you would just be doing yourself a disservice.

Often, this is why people gravitate towards a magical tradition like hoodoo. They need a job or want a way to create peace in the home and discover a spell that can help. But without knowing what they're really doing, they often experience results that are different than expected.

They get a job with a boss who is impossible to work with, for example. But instead of leaving and finding another job, they stick it out and try to force things to change because this was the job they *worked* (in the hoodoo sense) for.

Moreover, because hoodoo worked the first time, they'll be convinced of its effectiveness, and then stuck on a path of going back, again and again, to try to change a situation that is doomed.

Without knowing the core concepts -- or *root*s of root magick -- you set yourself up for going down a path of anger and frustration that may last years.

Introduction

Your roots are perhaps the most important to consider as you embark on incorporating hoodoo into your life. Yes, I do mean your ancestors, but I am also using the word as a metaphor. Again, I use roots here to mean the roots in your mind, in your thinking.

If you think of your life as a plant, you've got the part that you can see; your experience in life, the money you make, your job, and relationships. Then you have your roots. The subconscious part of your mind that is creating your experience every day, moment by moment.

When you use hoodoo without understanding your roots, you can get what you want but your subconscious mind will often produce results that may be completely different than what you expect.

Everyone talks about examples of people who have won the lottery and lose all of their money within a couple years. Often the culprit is a scarcity mindset.

The same thing could be said of the person from the previous example, the one who got a job they won't quit. If they have the mindset that they won't be able to find another job (another example of scarcity thinking), they will be more inclined to stay in a situation that is unhealthy.

There are many practitioners who believe hoodoo is about you and your spirituality. It is a spiritual practice, not a religious one. This means you are free to worship according to your religion, if you so choose.

A spiritual practice is what will help you tend to your mental roots and get the results you expect with hoodoo.

To be successful, you need faith. Any fear, especially related to money or love, will mess with your results.

My intent with this book is to give you a basis upon which to begin your own journey in hoodoo. You'll quickly discover as you read that, same with the work of improving yourself, the research never ends.

This is why having what's called a 'beginner's mind' would do you well, especially after years have passed and you gain more and more knowledge. That's one of the great things about being an actual beginner–you have this covered.

Quick Recommendation from the Magickal Witches team: We would like to make the magickal journey you are about to embark on as smooth as possible. As with any journey, preparations need to be made, and there are tools fit for each witch, new or experienced. In our case, we'd like to recommend the "Survival and Wellness Kit for Magickal Witches", which is completely free. Not using these tools is like making a trip to a rainforest and not taking any sort of tool to protect yourself from mosquitoes. You can do it, but the experience won't be quite as seamless as it could have been. It's discomfort that's not necessary and can even be risky. This analogy fits perfectly; if you don't have the right tools to go through with this process, it can be uncomfortable, and there is even a risk of not having a practice full of magick.

Please access the following link here or scan the code below: https://magickalwitches.gr8.com/

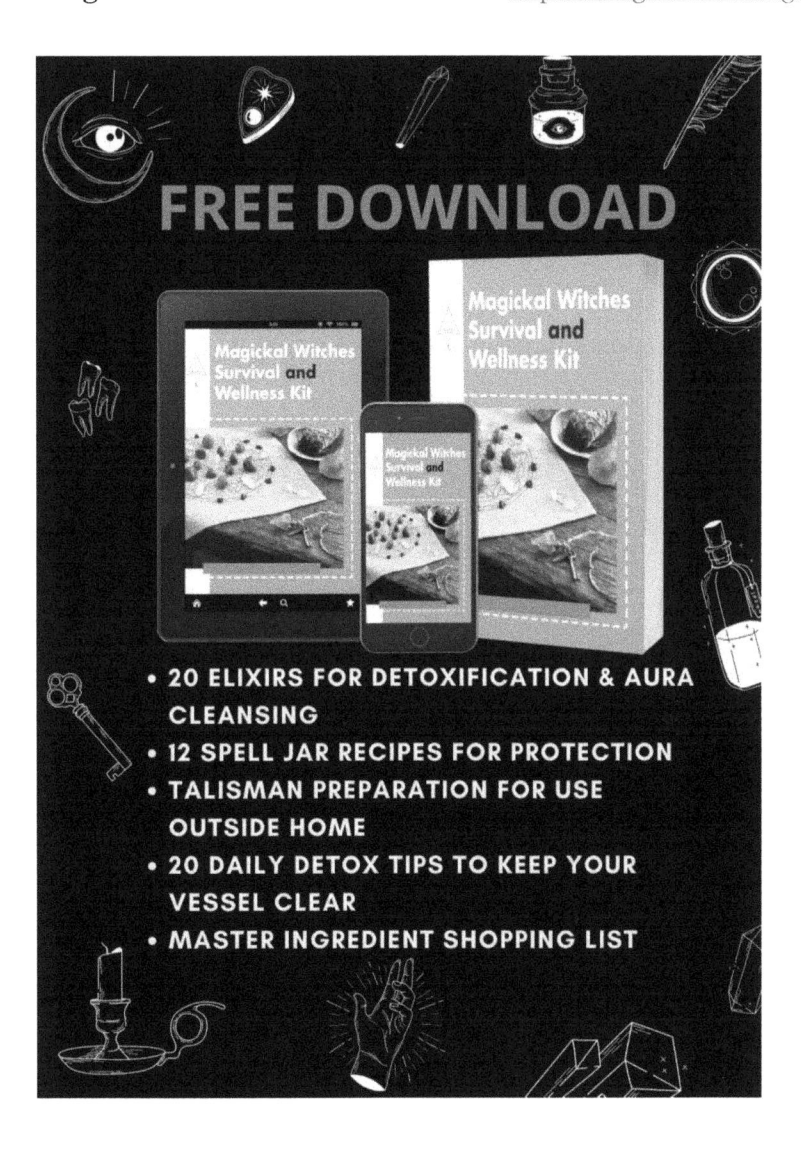

It may not be completely clear why these components are essential quite yet, but in further chapters, you will notice that this information will be very helpful. When you actually begin the practical side of the magickal work, you will come to understand. These tools are meant to alleviate some stress and obstacles that may show up along the way. For the time being, let's dive into understanding some theories that are meant to enhance the magickal journey you're here for.

PART I

Understanding the Basics

Many of our everyday practices can have magical uses. Taking a shower, organizing your files and workspace, cooking, working, exercising, even using the bathroom. Anything and everything can have a hoodoo application, if you're willing to get creative and open your mind.

You could say hoodoo is everywhere. A basic concept in hoodoo is paying respect to the things we can and cannot see. It is a way to connect, work with, and respect the powerful natural forces and world around us, and the forces that remain unseen to the naked eye.

By natural forces, I mean the earth: plants, trees, herbs, and dirt. More specifically, actual roots from plants, trees, and herbs. Common roots you will hear of are: High John the Conqueror, Mandrake, Licorice, and Angelica.

Unseen forces are exactly that: unseen. The air is often mentioned as an example of a force that we can't see but one we know exists. The same could be said of WIFI.

When it comes to hoodoo, we're talking about forces that are a little easier to deny. What our ancestors knew was (and is) that the spirit world is just as "real" as our 3D world. Colonizers saw how they lived, how close they were to Spirit, and immediately labeled it as evil.

Unfortunately, this mindset spread and eventually it wasn't the colonizer saying working with spirits was 'evil'; it was the descendants of our ancestors.

You may have encountered people who think like this in your life. If you want to build your practice, you have to give yourself permission to see things differently.

What is Hoodoo?

In simple terms, hoodoo is a magical and spiritual practice that emerged out of a need. 'Work' is an important word. You do work, and you find what works to achieve what you want.

Hoodoo is a practice that is about creating a change in our internal and external worlds. This is done through a series of methods that have been passed down for centuries.

Later on in this book we'll cover specifics, but for now know that these changes are signaled by using items such as oils, mojo bags, altars, (actual) roots, lights, candles, waters, colognes, herbs, and much, much more.

One thing that trips up many who are new to the practice is the use of biblical concepts and verses in conjure. This goes back to the influence of Christianity, as I mentioned in the introduction. This influence cannot be understated. To disguise what they were doing, many African slaves were able to practice their magick as long as slave owners thought they were practicing Christianity.

This goes back to hoodoo being about a balance between physical and non-physical worlds. When working with spirits, we approach from the perspective that we're working with the people who paved the way for us, often from hundreds and thousands of years back.

When we engage with hoodoo, we are engaging with ancestors whose lives centered around the church, whether Christian or Catholic.

This isn't to say that you need to memorize your bible verses in order to practice hoodoo, but it is a component that shouldn't come as a surprise to you when you come across a prosperity working that requires you to recite Psalms 72, for example.

If you have negative perceptions when it comes to the bible or talking about God, it's at this point when you have to decide if you're willing to put them aside so you can get serious about this practice.

This goes back to what I said earlier about respecting forces that are seen and unseen. We may not be able to understand the significance of the bible in this practice, but reverence to our ancestors is more important here than our personal preferences or histories.

For some, knowing this is all it takes. They're able to throw out all of their old ideas about Christianity. It's beautiful to see their relationship with God transform through a new perspective. None of this can happen, however, without willingness. Only you can decide if the sacrifice is worth it.

Let's look at a simple spell a beginning hoodoo practitioner may use to draw in money.

They work from home, in an apartment building, so this becomes the obvious place to focus on when doing the working. They start with a cleanse, during the waning moon, by removing items that they haven't used for years. Over this process, they tell themselves that they're cleaning out all of the old ideas they have about money and wealth.

As a last step to the cleaning, they use a floor wash that is made with things they have on hand: thyme, licorice root, Florida Water, frankincense essential oil, and holy water (that they made themselves, their belief being the most important ingredient).

After cleansing they bury nine coins in a plant on their balcony and cover it with dirt from a local bank. Throughout the working, she's praying and repeating her petition. She's also keeping her vibration high by *knowing* that what she's doing will produce results. After she's done, she watches her mindset for leftovers from the old ideas she'd cleansed out.

The physical things she used included the herbs and roots, the oil, the holy water, coins, the plant, and dirt.

The nonphysical things she used were the spirits of each item. The spirit of the thyme, licorice root, Florida Water, frankincense, and the holy water. Make no mistake: these spirits are where the power is contained. This is where hoodoo works.

In addition to recognizing the spirit of the roots and plants, the conjurer in our example made a point to pay attention to the unseen forces within *herself*. She didn't just do the working and go back to the same thoughts and ideas about money she had before. She could use the physical act of cleaning her space to stand in as a metaphor for a non-physical act, cleansing her mind of poverty thinking. This is another example of how magick blends the physical and non-physical worlds to create change in a person's life.

Before you put a list together of items to buy and whip out a credit card, there are some basics when it comes to hoodoo that you must have secured prior to doing your first working. We'll cover this in the coming chapters.

Striking a Balance

We know what some say about magick already: that it's evil, that it spawns from the devil, it's a sin, and it should be abolished. On the other side of that, what is considered being 'good'? It doesn't take much to imagine what that is like. Many of us know this intimately.

Maybe you made the mistake of sharing your enthusiasm with the wrong person.

It doesn't have to even be magic, unfortunately too many of us know the pain that comes with sharing our happiness with someone else who lashes out in anger, thereby making us and the things we love "wrong".

Ironically, this negative mindset was responsible for eradicating the same practices that many of us are now trying to reconnect with, via conjure.

If you have experienced negative reactions to your spirituality, you may have already learned an important lesson about secrecy. As you build your practice and gather your materials, you'll know to keep your work to yourself. Or another way to put it: you'll know who you can talk to and who to keep your work secret from.

This is one of the many truths of conjure. In this world, you will find support and scorn, depending on where you look. You can share your enthusiasm for the abilities you always knew you had with someone else, maybe another person reading this book, and you will find someone else who is also discovering their power and is just as excited as you are.

However, tell the wrong person that you are reading this book, and get a very different reaction. This is the reason I kept my tarot cards and candles hidden as a teenager.

It's also the reason why the best response when encountering people who have negative things to say about your practice is silence.

I am using this fact of magick to make a point about balance in the world of conjure. We have this idea that there is "good" magick and "bad" magic, thanks to Hollywood. People who work bad magick wear a lot of black and dark colors. They are evil, hungry for power, or acting out some lifelong revenge plot.

In reality, the concept of 'good vs. evil' has no real place in magic. It depends on how *you* look at it. Once you decide there's a type of magick or intent that is 'good', you've created 'bad' magic. But these rules are your own. Even if they are passed on to you by someone who claims to have some expertise that you don't have, their ideas aren't real for you unless you decide to make them real. If this sounds like the law of attraction, that's because it is.

Thinking of magick in terms of good and evil will *not* keep "evil" magic away from you. It will do the opposite. You will see evidence of 'evil' magic. You'll also be more likely to criticize or label other people's practices. Keep in mind, this labeling of what others do is no different than how colonizers criticized traditional African cultures and spirituality.

So, what does balance mean when we're talking hoodoo?

Many things.

The reason why it's important to remove any thoughts of 'good' vs. 'evil' magick is because these ideas only cause you harm. We all have light and dark within us. What we tend to label 'evil' is that dark side, our shadow self.

This is the part of us that we try to hide from ourselves and from the world. I keep mentioning money and lack mindsets, but the truth is this is where a lot of people struggle with their shadow.

Let's look at an example people may be familiar with: hating wealthy people. What some will not admit is that their hate for rich people stems from jealousy at not being able to live the life they want to live. What's underneath that is deep pain and feelings of despair and fear.

One of the reasons many workers will tell new conjurers to do shadow work is because you can curse yourself with these unexamined emotions of fear, jealousy, envy, or hate.

Even if you do all of your shadow work, you will still have a shadow. That is the nature of being a human. If you accept that your shadow is always there. Within you light and dark both exist and owning this opens you up to your full power.

The truth is, you have the ability to bless and to curse. This is what practitioners call being able to work with both hands, or being a 'two-headed worker'.

Think of what happens in nature when a plant is uprooted, or a weed is pulled: new growth happens in its place. Everything in nature, in life, happens in balance. Seeing evidence of a world you create in your mind is a form of this balance. Another way to put that is, as within so without.

When we as conjurers use plants and roots for our magic, we're taking and using the energy and spirits of that plant for our own purposes. You could use these powers without any reverence at all, but then you are not practicing hoodoo to its full power. When we talk about balance in conjure or hoodoo, we're talking about a give and take relationship.

You might read that and think: *what do I have to give to spirit?*

Approaching hoodoo from the perspective that you don't have anything to offer is another example of poverty thinking. Do everything you can to wipe that idea from your mind because it is simply false. Many of us think that what we have to offer is limited by the money in our bank account. This is another example.

Every thought you have, every place you put your energy in now, whether that is in studying to improve your craft or scrolling through Instagram, is a "payment" of sorts.

Of course, actual money is a form of payment as well, and some spirits will accept this as an offering, but I'm willing to bet that if you were able to get your hands on this book, you already have an abundance of ways you can give back to spirit to show your gratitude.

You might be wondering who your thoughts pay. The answer goes back to unseen forces, or the presence of spirit in our lives, and the idea that we are helped in countless ways by these forces. What many fail to see is how poverty thinking results in more poverty thinking. What's really happening is, the spirits fed by a poverty mindset grow; much like the wolf in the Cherokee legend. This spirit grows in balance to how much you feed the mindset.

This same concept is applied to roots, and if we want to work with roots to change our lives, then we must work to give as much as we take.

We also want to provide a clear channel for change to happen by doing the work on ourselves to remove blockages. Shadow work never ends. Healing is a journey that continues even after death, so there is no being 'done' with your dark side. You use your awareness to work with your shadow.

Principles

Respect for Ancestors

Who are we working with when we practice? Who are the spirits that help us on the other side? Who helps us in ways we can't see or recognize?

Our ancestors.

You might not know who your ancestors are by name, but they know who you are. Reverence to those who have worked hard so we can live the way we live is a core principle of hoodoo practice.

We've talked a bit about respecting the herbs and roots you use for workings. I bring it up here to emphasize a core principle of respecting the natural forces in and around your environment.

You personally have countless ancestors, in the thousands. The spirit of the men and women who came before you are with you now, in your blood and bones.

Each person you are connected to had to survive the physical harshness of life. They had to live in societies that tried to wipe out their livelihoods and beat their spirit down. They fought in wars. They worked and worked just to get the opportunity to pursue a better life in another country and had to make decisions that you and I could never fathom.

Somewhere deep down, you know all of these stories because a part of you *lived* these stories. And I'm not just talking about past lives.

When I think about everything my ancestors went through, I take all of the hurt, anger, and despair and commit to living my life in peace, love, joy, and abundance in hard and in easy times.

In my personal relationship with those who have paved my way, I know that this is what they want for my life.

It took some time for me to be able to listen to the voice of my ancestors, and to be confident that they were with me in the first place. I'm guessing that you weren't raised in a home where it was common to talk to ancestors, and if my guess is correct, then you and I have this in common.

I started my relationship with three things: an open heart, a sincere desire that went beyond curiosity, and respect.

Respect for Environment

Hoodoo is a practice that looks different, depending on which region you are in. New Orleans is probably the most notable example of this. You might not have a hoodoo practice specific to where you live, but what I want you to take from this is you and your environment come first.

You might find a working online that asks for Angelica root, but if this is hard to find in your region, this is something you need to be aware of at least. Most of us are lucky to live in countries where anything we want is accessible, if we're willing to pay the shipping.

You'll also want to be mindful of going out and picking fresh flowers and plants. This is knowing what plants grow natively in your region, what trees and plants are endangered and which ones thrive. This might require getting another book to research botanicals, but if you're serious about this practice then you don't need much convincing.

Pine is easy enough to find, depending on where you are. If the working you're preparing for calls for this plant, it's always better to go out and find it in nature rather than buying it. Keeping the principle of respect in mind, you want to know the specific varieties of pine growing close to you and information about the plant if you're going to use it in a spell.

Before ripping a branch off of a tree, speak to the tree, the roots, and show your gratitude. One of the ways I do this is by cleaning up any garbage I find in wooded areas in my neighborhood. However, you don't have to do this just when you're looking for something for a working.

For example, pine trees are a resilient plant species that can survive through harsh winters. It's commonly used for cleansing, protection, healing, and in some cases exorcisms. Because this tree is native to North America, it is likely that you'll find some use for it in your workings. What kind of pine grows in your neighborhood?

A bit of research will tell you Sugar Pine, for example, is considered 'king', and has a sap that was used by some Native Americans as a sweetener. This is information you can find on Wikipedia. Knowing this, you might pray to the Sugar Pine plant and ask that it add its sweetness to a cleansing, a nice touch if you're using it in a wash for your home.

Louisa was ready to start working conjure, but knew she had some work to do. As a child, she witnessed domestic violence in the home and even though those years were long gone, it was difficult for her to release some of the patterns she'd learned.

Somewhere in her late teens she started to believe that her life was an aberration.

Thinking this way didn't feel right, but it helped her to stay small, and in that it helped her to survive. As she got older, the idea became less about survival and more about staying inside the small life she'd created in her mind.

Initially, Louisa came to hoodoo for money problems. As you can probably guess, she was heavy in debt and never seemed to make enough to get by. But in our consultation, I told her that if she continued with this mindset, she would never be released from her struggles.

Even if we found a working that drew in the money she was looking for, without tending to her roots she would be stuck in a cycle. It would be better for her to deal with what she thought and felt about herself first.

The good thing about my meeting with Louisa (and I have changed her name to protect her identity) is that she had awareness of what her issue was and had a strong desire to be honest. This is a power, one that she had to acknowledge was sharpened like a knife over her childhood.

As an adult, she has learned to accept her own darkness for what it is. She also had to accept how uncomfortable she was with the concept of having power. Her ego was wrapped up in the idea that she was weak and powerless to change her life.

But to change her financial condition, she had to accept the power she had over her experience of love, security, and money.

She also had to accept that the thoughts she had would show up in both her physical and spiritual worlds. Otherwise, the workings done would be out of balance, she would be working with spirits that serve her old mindset.

Nothing can happen in the physical world that doesn't appear in the spiritual. Balance is one of the core principles of hoodoo.

A Relationship with Your Ancestors

Get into your history; who your people are. This is the place that you need to start at the beginning of your hoodoo practice.

Q: What if my ancestors didn't believe in magic?

This is a great question. If you've heard negative things about magick from your parents or grandparents, it's reasonable to deduce that these ideas were passed down to them. It follows, then, that your ancestors may not appreciate your efforts to become better at a practice they didn't believe in.

Here's what I would say: first, when a person passes on, they leave behind their physical body and other aspects of the human experience. They literally get to see life for what it truly is (if they want to).

Have you ever visited or seen a medium speak to someone who has passed on? More often, these spirits send messages to their loved ones that demonstrate that after passing, their perspective on life and the things that happened while they were on earth has changed.

The way we think is one of the things that we can leave behind once our spirit goes beyond this plane of existence.

This isn't to say that your ancestors gained a new perspective of magick once they died. I can't say that, I don't know you and I don't know your people. The only way you can begin to figure out what they felt is to ask them.

There is a chance that once they passed on, their perspective changed. This is one of the reasons it is important for you, in your home and in your practice, to build a relationship with your ancestors.

Here's where your prayers and inner knowing come in. What do I mean by this? All-day, every day, if you wake up and have life in you, you are repeating things to yourself. They might not be full sentences, but you're feeling some kind of emotion. You are creating a vibration. This vibration is a form of prayer or talking to yourself.

Rev. Ike (who could have been a hoodoo practitioner, we will never know) says it best: *God is thought*. We all know the sayings: 'thoughts are things' and 'life and death lie in the power of your own tongue'.

If your mood has ever changed because of what someone else said or did, that is a demonstration of this power.

You can use this power to communicate with your ancestors right now by thanking them for everything they've done to bring you to this point in your life.

Connecting with Your Benevolent Ancestors

Here's another truth: we all have ancestors in our bloodline who would not be supportive of what we're doing to improve our lives. They are just like the people we encounter every day. By the same token, we all have ancestors who are eager to support us in whatever we want to do.

The way to connect with these ancestors is to simply ask, using the power of your thought and your words.

A simple prayer might include the following:

1. A statement of gratitude to your ancestors for bringing you to this point in your life, and for the things they do that you may not be aware of.

2. Affirming your overall intent; what you're looking to do. With this, you may want to state that you will keep your heart and mind open to their messages.

3. What you need help with, or why you're approaching your ancestors.

4. Acknowledgment of the things you're looking to sacrifice or banish in your life now (if applicable).

5. A request that your benevolent ancestors come to your aid and show you the way.

You can close this prayer the same way it was opened: with thanks. After praying, it's up to you to stay open to their communication. I'm going to assume that this listening is something you're somewhat familiar with, even as a beginner. It's the same kind of listening you do when dancing or creating art, it's hearing with your "good" ear.

Listening

Many feel some confusion when practicing this kind of listening because it is easy to block it out and think you are making it all up by yourself.

It might help for me to share what it feels like when I'm listening, especially when I was just starting out on my hoodoo journey. My mind was overrun with negative thinking, even in the smallest ways. So, whenever something very positive or uplifting came to me, I knew that was the voice of God speaking through my higher self.

This is where communication with my ancestors started. The channel was open, you could say. The more I was able to hear the voice of God, the more I could attune myself to the voice of my ancestors. The differences are very slight, but subtlety is the nature of communication with God.

It might be the same for you or slightly different, depending on your openness, and how comfortable you are with receiving communication.

As you open up, you'll also improve at hearing your own voice; the voice of your ego. Maybe on reading those last few sentences you thought that I must be "better" at communicating with God than you are. A Course in Miracles would call this a 'trick of the ego'.

Once you start to listen, you cannot avoid hearing. You are strengthening your sensitivity and attuning yourself to more and more subtle forms of communication. I struggled with this myself: the more I got quiet and listened, the more I heard things I didn't want to hear.

Hearing the Ego

The more you learn to listen to the voice of your own ego, the more you'll hear it speak to you in patterns. One common pattern that all of us know is statements around an idea that sounds like "I'm not good enough". Thinking someone else is "better" than you at something, like talking to spirit, is an example of this type of thinking.

The benevolent ancestors you call on can help with hearing their voice over your own as well. Again, the only thing you need to do is ask. If it sounds like I'm talking about capital-s Spirit, that is on purpose. Your benevolent ancestors are connected with Spirit, with Infinite Love, Infinite Abundance, Infinite Wisdom.

It's this connection that will help you live in balance and maintain that balance in your hoodoo and conjure work.

Another mindset that we're quick to shift to, especially as we consider solving our problems with magic, is that we are stupid for having the problems we have in the first place, that the minor things we're dealing with are too small or insignificant for these mighty powers.

You guessed it: this is another trick!

'Big' vs. 'Small' Problems

Even if you don't know how they're going to help you or you feel like your problems are too small, take them to your ancestors.

I would say that as a beginner, you *want* to take the problems you think are small to your ancestors. Chances are you'll find those small problems are connected to bigger ones, so doing this is a way to ease into your practice.

And eventually, you will discover there are no 'big' problems and 'small' problems when it comes to Spirit.

Like dividing magick into 'good' and 'evil', this concept of complicated problems is self-made. Thinking a problem is big gives you a reason to feel like it cannot be solved, and that way of thinking curses you to continuously search for answers and solutions outside of yourself.

This might be the reason you decided to begin practicing hoodoo for yourself. If you've gone to practitioners over and over again, you already know what it feels like to think your problems are bigger than you are. It's a trap many have fallen into.

The problems you are approaching hoodoo to solve were created by you. As big as you think they are, you are bigger. Before working, you *must* know this and believe it.

You must believe in the power of your ancestors. You must know the power of your ancestors flows through you and contributes to your power. Use this thought to replace any belief you have in the power of your problems.

You might wonder why you have to change your perspective on your problems if you're taking them to your ancestors. The question really is: where is your faith? In some ways, having faith in yourself and in your ancestors (by way of God) is the same. In a way, this goes back to the section on hoodoo Principles: Respect for Self.

You have to believe God exists inside of you, so that the work you do can take effect because it is by your hands that you do this work. The work starts with you. If you don't believe in yourself, how can you believe your work is going to do what you want it to do?

If this isn't an idea you are comfortable with, then you can just focus on having faith in God and your ancestors. As your work becomes more and more successful, your faith in yourself will grow in proportion to your faith in God. In other words, your ancestors can take care of your lack of faith in yourself (as long as you remain open and willing)!

Building Your Altar

How great is it to know that all of your problems can be solved with the help of Spirit?

If you're beginning to feel some gratitude in knowing this, try to bottle up this feeling. Gratitude is the vibration you want to conjure and maintain when building your altar.

An altar is the physical manifestation of your relationship with your ancestors, and a non-negotiable for the serious hoodoo practitioner.

This is a place for you to speak to and receive messages from your ancestors, a place to present your offerings and to do your work. It is a kind of a spiritual center for your home. You can also keep specific types of altars in your space for your working.

Some practitioners have multiple altars; they keep one specifically for their ancestors, another for working (which we'll get into later). An altar for money, one for love, the list goes on.

Do not worry if you don't have the space for all of this. The point is to have a dedicated area for your work. Altars can take different forms, but a basic altar set up usually has:

- a bible,

- at least one candle,

- water in a wine glass or other glass,

- images of your ancestors, and

- items belonging to your ancestors, such as jewelry.

Usually, this is set up with a white tablecloth atop a table. You will find altars as different and varied as there are homes.

Other basics include food. This is usually cooked or baked, it's always better if you know what foods your ancestors preferred and take the time to prepare and offer what you know they like. You can also include your tarot cards or anything you use for divination, images, or any depictions you have of deities that mean something to you.

You don't want to keep food on your altar for too long. When drinks or food get cold, dispose of it. If you were to offer your ancestors an afternoon cup of tea, for example, in the evening you dispose of it at your front door. Or if you don't want to make a mess of your hallway, find a tree and pour it out there. This is how you dispose of food left on your altar as well; never throw out or put food in the compost.

Offerings can be left as often as you like, but try to ritualize this, for example leaving food once a week.

The table in your home can take any form. It might be built-in, like by a bay window or shelf. If you have more space, you can go bigger and use a small desk or table that has a dedicated spot in your home.

It's most important to set up an altar that works for you. This might mean creating an altar that doesn't *appear* like one at first glance. Or it might mean that you use a smaller table that can fit perfectly in a corner.

This space is and will become sacred. It should be out of the way of anyone touching it, other than you. Do not feel obligated to tell anyone what it is or why any of the items are on it. If it seems too many people are interacting with the space, you may want to move it to somewhere more private.

Once the altar is built, do a small ritual where you call on your ancestors. The main purpose of this is to present your altar space to them so that they know this is their physical home in your life, a representation of the home they have in your heart and mind.

Getting Prepared

You need a way to get calm and centered. Not just for this ritual, but for everything. You do not want to begin this ritual with *any* anxiety at all. Maybe you've never done this before, but remove any jitters or feelings of being 'freaked out'. Unsure is fine, but try to convert that unsure feeling to reverence.

Do something that tells your mind this is a special moment. One simple way to do this is to get dressed up; wear all white or something that marks what you're doing.

Prepare what you are going to present as offerings to your ancestors. A few ideas: coins, warm food, a drink you know they liked (though wine, rum, or whiskey will suffice), fresh flowers, coffee or tea (with sugar), coins, bread or fruit that has been cut and is ready to eat. If you leave a food, like nuts or seeds, leave it open (i.e. not in a bottle or jar that's closed).

The last thing you want to have on hand is your prayers and a bible, either physical or digital to read from (unless you have what you want to recite memorized).

Your prayers will require some thought beforehand, depending on how formal you want to be. If you're more comfortable just talking to your ancestors like a friend, do that.

Opening the Ritual

Open the ritual by anointing yourself and your space with a hoodoo oil. There are many ways to anoint yourself, but here's a simple method using your body's pressure points and third eye.

1. Set your intention (i.e. Say aloud something like: *Thank you, [your name for God] for facilitating my connection to my ancestors.*). Continue to repeat your intention throughout as you apply oil to your pressure points:

2. Apply a drop of the oil to one wrist and rub your wrists together, then apply oil (take more as needed):

    a. The upper shell of your ear.

    b. Behind your shoulders.

    c. Your third eye.

Alternatively, if you don't have an oil or prefer not to use them on your skin, you can anoint with a spray or a cologne.

Do not worry about buying an oil or spray. These can be made with water and a few ingredients you probably already have in your kitchen. These instructions will be covered in Part 2, under Cleaning Rituals and Spirit Washes.

With sprays, you set and state your intention while spraying the air at least once. Three times is more than sufficient. The number of times you spray is important. Three represents a holy trinity.

After you've anointed, get the fire started: light your candle(s) and/or incense.

Make Your Offerings

If you're using smoke, run the items you're offering over and through the smoke to cleanse them and then 'present' them to your ancestors. This can be done by holding the item and then lifting it, as if you were giving a gift to someone much taller than you.

Do this act with your whole being. Imagine your benevolent ancestors coming around and graciously accepting what you offer.

Dial In

Read Psalms 23. If you don't have a bible, look the prayer up online. There are also many bible apps available for free and with no ads.

Call on your ancestors. Here's an example of what you might want to say. Feel free to edit or change according to your needs: *I now call on the benevolent and honored spirits of my lineage, every man and woman who sired and birthed the men and women who now live through me.*

I invite you into my home and into my life. This altar is where we will meet, and where I will offer my deep gratitude for the sacrifices you've made, and the work you continue to do on my behalf.

I offer you [name the items you've offered in the form of food, scents, items, etc.] with honor, love, and thanks. I hope they are pleasing to you.

You don't have to make the call super formal. I would actually recommend telling your ancestors that you're just starting on this journey, that this is the first time you are working with them (though there's a good chance they know already). You can also ask for guidance on your relationship with them. Be open to even the smallest ways that they speak to you.

Once you say that your altar is the place where you will meet and offer gratitude, you have to actually use your altar to meet your ancestors and offer gratitude when you get there. This ritual is about making a commitment to a relationship. What you say in this meeting is important, so take note.

Get Comfortable

Spend some time in silence, just listening. You may receive guidance on things you're dealing with right now. Or you may just feel feelings, like love, peace, or just a general good You Are Blessed feeling. Sit as long as you like. You will intuitively feel when your time at the altar is complete.

You don't just have to sit and listen, however. You can sing, read, and talk to your ancestors as if they were there with you. Share what is going on in your life right now. Be open to getting answers to questions you've been asking for years. This has happened to me and is not uncommon.

However, keep your expectations checked and clear. You may not get the answer you're looking for right away, but this might be because you are not ready for the answer. The most important thing to do here is stay open.

Close

I keep the closings very simple at my altar. I simply clasp my hands, close my eyes, and feel gratitude throughout my body. This is my everyday practice, and since you're doing a first-time ritual at your altar, you may want to do something more formal.

Express gratitude. Even if you didn't "feel" anything, tell your ancestors that you're grateful for their presence.

Some practitioners will end rituals by putting out a candle or clapping once. These acts read more 'sending spirits away' to me. I prefer to use a large candle that I can burn for as long as I am at home.

As mentioned previously, food should not be kept on your altar for more than a week. And once you're ready to dispose of it, put it outside. Do not throw the food away.

In your practice, you'll come across countless more altar and ritual ideas, some you'll work, and others you'll let go by.

Working Altars

An ancestor altar is very common in hoodoo practice. In addition to this, you may want to create an altar specifically for a certain aspect of your life or something you want.

Here, I go over a few of these types of altars, and some ways you can get creative. With each, you want to think about

how you can invite the presence of God and/or the Goddess (or Solar Light, whichever deity speaks to you). Your ancestor altar may have God in every aspect. Or you may use a candle to represent Solar Light.

Some altars are permanent, but if there's something specific you're working on, you could use a temporary altar.

The Self-Love Altar

If you've struggled with self-image issues or come from a childhood home where you witnessed violence, a self-love altar is a space to center and heal.

It's a place where you can take everything you love about yourself and honor it. This might require some creativity as you're taking intangible aspects and making them physical.

A candle on this altar could represent your inner light. And with the countless different types of candles you can get, you can really find something that speaks to *you* on a deep level.

The four elements are thought to stand in for aspects of life and living: earth honors your foundation, water your emotions and intuition, wind your thinking, and fire your willpower. These are common elements in all altars. You can use things that you like to represent these elements.

For example, if you love frogs, you could create a self-love altar that is heavy on the frog decor. If you're an artist, you could paint your self-love altar on a massive canvas. The advantage of this is it saves space in your home.

Small statues, trinkets, and figurines are great for altars in general, but especially for tapping into your personality and attributes. Animal and mystical symbolism is great for this. A horse, for example, could represent freedom, strength of spirit, triumph, and courage. A fairy could represent a sense of wonder and magic.

A trinket like a pair of glasses or binoculars could represent foresight. Jewelry, abundance and beauty. Crystals like rose quartz are great to represent love.

A figurine of a small Oscar award can be immensely powerful if you one day want to win an Oscar.

As you can tell, the possibilities for this kind of altar are endless. Searching options on Google is a great option, but you can also use tarot cards or think of things that just mean something to *you*. However, don't deny the power in common symbols, like stars. Many times, you can go to a local dollar store and find lots of usable stuff. Or you may already have something at home.

You are a strong spirit. A self-love altar is a space where you can honor your true spirit, regardless of how you've had to shift and bend to exist in the world.

The Money Altar

What's your relationship with money? How do you feel when you look at people who have more money than you? A money altar is a space to heal your relationship with money, if you need to, or honor the strong relationship you already have.

Many of us have the misperception that "no one will pay us the money we want". A money altar is an ideal place to heal this idea.

You can be creative with this altar, creativity is the channel through which money and abundance flows. The only rule is to keep the intent of the altar focused. Putting a random object on your money altar will muddy up the lines of communication.

Money is one of the first things you want on this type of altar. If you have any dollar bills or coins hanging around, especially if they're different denominations, use these. It doesn't matter how much or what denomination you have, even monopoly money will work if you want it to.

Old checks hanging around are *great* for a money altar. This is an idea from The Secret, but applies here. You might have a check from a closed bank account. Use these to start writing checks to yourself with amounts that you want. Write an infinity check!

The usual items for most altars apply for this type as well: crystals, candles, herbs, roots, and other items like money, oils, and dirt that we have and will cover.

Statues of deities that are associated with wealth and money are ideal for a money altar, for example, Oshun, or Fortuna.

Tarot cards work as well, though you may want to purchase a deck that is separate from the one you use for readings, or you can print out an image from online.

You want to think about things that mean something to you for your money altar. A growing plant can be a symbol of expansion. Watering a plant on your money altar every day can be important symbolism, same with pruning the plant and removing dead leaves (removing old ideas).

Pinecones or double samaras (those things that fall from trees in a pinwheel motion) are a symbol of abundance, if you live in an area where these things are everywhere.

The Deity Altar

Before building a deity altar, you want to have a clear idea of the deity you're building for. This seems like it goes without saying but having a deep relationship with a deity is key.

If you respect more than one deity, then you'll know whether you can use one altar for every deity or if you need one altar for each deity.

Some deities require their own space, so sharing their sacred space in your home is not an option.

You'll also want to know what the deity you're honoring likes to receive. Money is one example. It means something to us, and can work on your money altar, but some deities may not care for money at all.

One of the basics you'll want on the altar is a statue or some representation of the deity that the altar is being built for. Some altars will even include more than one statue or depiction. You want these visual elements to represent the deity for you, items that as soon as you come into contact with them, you connect with your deity.

Creating an Altar in Your Mind

This is an option to consider if you don't have space for an altar or aren't really interested in creating a physical space in your home, as described.

To Spirit, everything is energy. Our physical world helps us humans with that, but for spirit, these physical things don't mean much. This is why intent is so important. You can (and do) create a whole world in your mind and without intention, you can create a lot without being aware.

Creating an altar in your mind uses visualization, an important skill that some people find easier than others.

You can create a whole castle in your mind that is an altar, then speak to your ancestors and the spirits you are calling to let them know that space is for them. If you are unable to purchase or find the items for your altar, you can just imagine them. Or better yet, create them in your mind and place them in your mind altar.

Whereas there are specific rules for ancestors, you can create an altar for whatever you want to draw into your life. Remember how everything has a spirit? Creating an altar is basically honoring these spirits.

The Choose Your Adventure Altar

You can create an altar for style, peace, and serenity, beauty, a season, a career you want, good health, education, a s port, a craft, for a loving family, cooking, the elements, even a place, maybe somewhere you want to live, like a cottage or a farm.

Your Practice + the Elements of Hoodoo

Dipping your toes into hoodoo can seem daunting. With no familiarity with what it is and how it works, just finding a spell for you can be a challenge, especially when you are new to the practice.

If you have to work in secret from nosy friends and family, getting a package of 7-day candles, Florida water, and holy oils might not be so easy.

And that's not to mention the costs. There are the costs of buying what you need for a working and possibly the costs of setting up an altar.

As with everything, part of respecting your ancestors, your environment, and yourself, means doing your research and knowing what works for you. Copying spells from someone else is fine, but with your knowledge and knowing the core elements of hoodoo, you are better equipped to create your own workings.

If you know the core elements of hoodoo, this becomes easier with time. This is where we incorporate many of the topics we've covered already. In hoodoo, Spirit is at the core of everything. Practitioners think about the spirit of everything they work with, what is at the core or root.

1. Working with Spirit.

2. Working with Nature: Roots, plants, herbs.

3. Working with Water: Cleansing, purification, protection.

4. Working with Place: Graveyards, banks, churches, crossroads.

5. Working with the Mind: Balance and containment.

As mentioned, hoodoo exists to make your life easier. Do not burden yourself with getting supplies and materials that someone else says you need for a spell.

There is a way to practice with what's readily available to you. The things you already touch and experience every day can be used in your hoodoo. Plus, you probably already have some powerful herbs in your kitchen cabinets. Often items you have just hanging around as decor, like candles and seashells, can be used in your working.

Working with Spirit

Your day might start with a prayer acknowledging the ancestors and reconnecting with the work you're doing in your life. A practice could begin with acknowledging those who went before you and the power they lend to you.

If you don't have an image or any idea of who your ancestors are, this might seem like a challenge. This is one of the painful consequences of the slave trade; many descendants of ancestors living in North America don't have any connection to those who came before them.

Many of my clients know this pain intimately. Some of them come from families who just do not seem to care about their lineage, so their questions and quest for knowledge are met with indifference, if not anger.

Their blood still runs through your veins, and in this way, you will stay connected to them for as long as you are alive. Use the power of prayer and your words that we discussed in the previous chapter to start building the connection. You might not have names, but a desire and deep respect are all you need.

Keep going back to your altar and keep working at building these relationships. Here are some methods you can start using immediately as part of your practice:

1. Visit your altar every morning and say *good morning!* to your ancestors. In The hoodoo Altar, I'll talk about how you can create an altar in your mind if you don't have access to your physical space.

2. Make offerings every week of food, flowers, jewelry, money, or other 'special' items. Do not half-step with this. Give full bottles of alcohol if you choose to give alcohol, clean money, fresh flowers, and fresh food.

3. Clean your altar regularly. Add cleaning your altar to your regular home cleanings. Or align cleanings with moon cycles.

4. Go to your altar throughout the day to offer your own energy; sing if you can, offer gratitude, say a prayer, some thanks. Go to your altar throughout the day if something troubles you or you have questions. Get into the habit of going to your altar, even if you don't have something physical to give.

Working with Nature

The term 'rootwork' is interchangeable with hoodoo. Other than roots, natural elements, such as herbs, plants, seeds, leaves, peels, and dirt play an important role in hoodoo practice. Take any vegetable or plant you have or that grows around you.

An orange can feed your body, but the peel can also be used in working for luck and money. Same with fennel seeds and bay leaves.

Each of the natural powers we use in hoodoo pulled their power in from the earth. Not only does the earth power the growth of the plants and herbs you use, but it also powers our own growth. It feeds us every day and grounds us in place, even as we run around and get distracted with living life.

Often, we get so enthusiastic about a spell, we're looking around to find a store that sells everything in one place. Before buying roots and herbs was a possibility, conjurers either grew what they used on their own, or got what they needed straight from the source: the earth.

If you can, try to forage what you need or grow it on your own. This might mean doing a few substitutions here and there, and if you choose to use an alternate ingredient, be careful to understand what results you might get with what you're using.

Working with Waters

I'm using 'waters' here as a metaphor for cleansing and purification. Your energy is affected by countless things on any given day. Our world continuously bombards us with all types of ideas that can either zap our energy or empower us.

Let's be honest, we're more likely to be drawn to the things that zap our energy.

Need I list examples? The news, social media, gossip YouTube channels, reality television, trauma fiction. Going out and having a negative interaction with someone on the street or in a grocery store is a prime example of the kind of interaction that can muck up your energy.

Of course, we'd all like to think we're immune to the energy of others, but even with a strong mental and vibrational shield, most people need to continuously keep their field maintained.

In this way, your spirit is a lot like your physical body. It requires work to keep healthy and in tune. As sensitive people, we are open to absorbing negative energies that need to be removed regularly.

We'll talk more about cleansing in another section, but for now, know that within hoodoo there are various liquids; oils, colognes, perfumes, spiritual waters, and vinegars that are used for multiple purposes. There are money drawing oils, two types of Florida Water, war and peace water, and Four Thieves Vinegar, for example.

Working with Place

Spirit is everywhere. Have you ever walked into a place and noticed that it just *felt* different? Some would call this a "vibe", short for vibration. You feel this when you walk into someone's home, but types of places have the same effect.

Think about what it feels to walk into a school, a library, or a bodega. Each of these places has a distinct vibe to it that you know but don't think about too much.

Graveyards and crossroads are two important places in hoodoo because of the energy they carry. Other places that you'll often hear or read about in your research are banks and churches.

Specifically, you'll most often work with the spirit of a place like a bank by using the dirt from the land around where it is located (if it's surrounded by concrete, that is another story). You could really get creative with this but using dirt from just anywhere could produce unintended results.

The symbolism of crossroads is also big in conjure. The crossroads represent many things. In our plane of existence, we live in a world where we can experience both 3D life and the spirit world.

Working with the Mind

Just like the spaces in our 'real' world that have special meanings in hoodoo, there are some mental concepts that conjurers give reverence to. Another way to put it, is there are definite hoodoo laws.

One example we've touched on previously is the law of *balance*. You could say this is a law that rules our lives, but, as we know, in hoodoo this concept is respected on a different level.

Look around your life and within right now. Can you find examples of places where there is perfect balance? What does that look and feel like? What does it look and feel like when things are out of balance?

It's easy enough to pick these out because the situations that you came to hoodoo for are probably the same ones that are out of balance. This is how we know that things are out of balance: we feel it. It's obvious in many ways, and it's often very uncomfortable. You see this often in the workplace.

There always seems to be one person who is less than qualified for the job they're doing, which means the other people on their team (if we're honest, it's usually one person) is left picking up the slack.

The person or people who have to work more than what they usually would are then out of balance within themselves: they're working more than they're being paid for. This is fertile ground to trigger emotional imbalance as well. Often when we see the words 'emotional imbalance', we go straight to depression, but here I'm talking about emotions like resentment, anger, and jealousy.

Imbalance also highlights the next concept, *containment*. When things get out of balance, it tends to affect other areas that most times are never even considered. In the example above, co-workers are less effective in their own work because they're distracted by the extra weight they have to carry.

This is a simple example of the concept of containment in action. In the above example, we're explicitly talking about boundaries. But many magical traditions use this concept. In the hoodoo tradition, one example of containment is in workings like mojo bags or nation sacks.

Here, the power of spirit is concentrated and contained within a vessel for use in whatever way directed by the working.

Before planning your spell, you want to understand exactly what is out of balance so the work you do is applied (or contained) with specificity.

Mind practices:

1. Take a moment each day to practice stillness. Some people would call this 'meditation' and if that works for you, then work it.

2. Say 'I don't know' more. This might sound or seem simplistic, but don't think of this as pretending to be stupid. Our egos like to convince us we know everything. This practice is about opening up and working your beginner's mind.

Hoodoo Roots

In its earliest days, hoodoo was called many different things. One of the terms for healing that the first conjurers practiced was called 'rootwork', 'mojo', 'conjure', 'folk magick', or 'mojo'.

There are also different names for magickal practices similar to hoodoo. For example, what's known as hoodoo in the United States would be called 'obeah' in Jamaica.

Rootwork

We used to use plants for healing. Many indigenous cultures still do. One of the more common ways plants are still used in this way is with teas. You probably have a selection of teas in your kitchen cabinet right now that can be used for one purpose or another.

Take some time to research the different dried flowers in your teas and what their magical correspondences are. Having tea is really having dried flowers, which are dried plants. As we know, there is a lot of power in these plants.

You may discover that you already have a plant that will work for what you need, in the form of a tea.

To practice seriously, you'll need to do more than spend a few minutes researching. Smell the plants, herbs, and roots you have. Feel them. Look at them to know how they appear so you can tell one dried or fresh plant from the next.

You may already know the taste from cooking and drinking, but ideally you get to a point where you can tell a plant (and know its properties useful for your work) by looking at it.

Often beginning practitioners have a list of things they go out and buy for their first spell. While this is fine when it comes to working, hoodoo is about being connected to plants, roots, and herbs. It is the root in rootwork.

This might mean a lot of research and time for you at first, but really what you're doing is connecting yourself to the spirit of the earth. You don't want to rush this just for the sake of getting to whatever spell you want to work. The relationship you develop is a lifelong one and will serve you for years to come.

After your teas, do some research on the spices you have, the plants and flowers growing in your backyard or in pots. Next, you may want to look into how you can grow more herbs on your own. Eventually getting to the point where you don't have to buy a plant for a working.

The Power of the Root

"[W]e wouldn't ask why a rose that grew from the concrete for having damaged petals, in turn, we would all celebrate its tenacity, we would all love its will to reach the sun, well, we are the roses, this is the concrete, and these are my damaged petals, don't ask me why, thank god, and ask me how."

This Tupac Shakur quote speaks to the strength of the human spirit, but we also know that it speaks to the power hoodoo taps into: the power of roots.

We can use roses as an example of this; it's one many of us are already very familiar with in many cases. The roots of a rose pull energy from the earth to create a plant that is unique. Its smell is distinct, same with its petals.

We also know roses have thorns. It's as if in creating a rose, the Universe knew how popular it would be and built in a level of protection. Now, when we approach a rose, we do so with care.

These aspects of the rose aren't just things we made up, they contribute to the plant's power, contained in its spirit.

Rose has the power to attract, which is why they are so popular in love and attraction spells (and on Valentine's Day), specifically in drawing these things to the person doing the work, or the person who the work is being done for.

Without roots, however, the rose wouldn't exist. Roots survive, even with no sunlight, even under concrete. They do their work in the dark, away from what we can see and feel. They represent the work that happens in the spirit world, or unseen places.

If you're using a plant to keep negative energy away from your home, for example. You might be drawn to purchase or use mandrake root, a versatile part of the plant that it is said can be used in any working.

However, it's careless to buy a sachet of this root and just throw it in your working. Not only do you want to have your intent for your spell, but you also want to have an intent for why you're using the mandrake. You would also want to know whether or not this plant is right for your working based on its profile, and your relationship with the root.

Yes, your relationship.

Much like the spirit of your ancestors, you want to start and grow a relationship with the herbs, plants, and roots you're working with. You can start by getting still and introducing yourself to the spirit of the plant.

It's normal for this to seem odd at first, but this kind of respect is one hoodoo practitioners have built and cultivated for years.

The Power of Dirt

Just like you wouldn't throw any plant inside of a working without knowing what the plant is and why you're using it, you wouldn't collect and use dirt from just anywhere.

Especially not a graveyard.

As discussed in the section Working with Place, dirt from different locations can help with our magic. Aside from graveyards, these are commonly:

- Hospitals,
- Churches,

- Banks,

- Colleges or Universities,

- Courthouses,

- Casinos, and

- Rivers.

Folks definitely get creative when it comes to collecting dirt. Any place you come across has a spirit, and that spirit gets into the soil around and underneath. With the right process, you could technically collect dirt from anywhere, not just the ones listed above.

If you're in or around a major city, there's dirt from districts, like financial or fashion. You could potentially get dirt from a neighborhood, a beach, park, zoo, airport or bus terminal, community center, city hall, soccer or sports field, club, animal shelter, even an adult store.

There is dirt and dust used in hoodoo that doesn't come from a specific place but is tied to a circumstance or situation. One example is anvil dust, which is commonly substituted with magnetic dust in many spells. These two things are not the same.

Anvil dust is specifically collected from what is leftover in a blacksmith's shop, where hard work happens, and direct focus is necessary. Anvil dust is infused with that spirit.

Taking dirt from a place is taking some of the power for your own purposes, so before going out to collect dirt, you want to know why you're taking dirt and what you plan to do with it.

You also want to take with you something to leave in place of whatever you took. Coins are a common offering, as is rum or whisky. If you don't want to leave anything or disturb the roots, you can clean up any garbage left in the area and leave the space better than you found it.

Collecting graveyard dirt isn't for the novice practitioner, but if you do venture out, you want to ensure to collect at the right time. Take note of the cycle of the moon and time of day. As a general guide, collecting after midnight and in the early morning hours is best.

Another consideration is the exact location of the dirt collected, again, this is especially true when collecting graveyard dirt. Depending on your spell, you may want to collect dirt underneath a shadow, at the entrance or the four corners of the graveyard.

In this case, it is definitely safer to purchase from someone who is more experienced at collecting graveyard dirt, rather than collecting yourself. If you feel anything negative *at all*, leave the graveyard and do not collect any dirt.

Practitioners will also be sure to leave something in exchange for the dirt they collect.

Seeds, Roots, Barks, Leaves, and Herbs

A list of *some* common roots, barks and wood, leaves, and herbs that are commonly used in hoodoo.

Just because an item is listed here doesn't mean it will be available in your area. Note the roots you're interested in using, research what they are, and what they're used for before purchasing. In all cases, try to either find the plant yourself in nature, or purchase from a supplier that grows these plants for magical purposes, specifically.

I've tried to go with some of the more common natural elements, hopefully some that you can find easily or already have. You'll also want to research where a plant has a root and leaves that are used for different things, as in the case of Comfrey.

There are a few different ways these can be used in your magic.

As an offering to your ancestors or to deities. Many of the seeds, plants, roots, and herbs we use regularly were also used by our ancestors. Usually about half a teaspoon of herbs or seeds can be added onto a small plate and left on the altar once offered.

Burned as an incense. It's much easier to do this with some herbs and roots than others. Burning can heighten the vibration of a space and prepare an environment before a ritual or spell.

Added to your working. One of the easiest ways to use the power of seeds, roots, barks, leaves, and herbs is by adding them to a mojo bag, hoodoo lamp, or jar or bottle.

Dressing candles. In rituals or prior to meditation, some hoodoo spells require dressing of a candle, though you can also dress any candle that you're getting ready to use. If you've set an intention for the day, for example looking for a job, you can dress a candle with herbs that can help and let it burn while you're going about your day.

There are many other places that you can use. Dried leaves and herbs can be infused in water, for example, and in workings like hoodoo lamps and washes.

Keeping Note

When you start your practice, you'll soon discover it can be hard to keep track of what you have in your hoodoo pantry. Here's where keeping a magical record is useful. Some traditions would call this a 'book of shadows'.

There isn't really a hoodoo equivalent to a book of shadows, and it doesn't take long to figure out why. Keeping a diary of magick is something people who have the privilege of privacy do. This is why, in starting your hoodoo practice, you want to recognize that you can read a book like this or keep notes and not be in trouble should someone else discover what you're doing.

All this to say, if you're reading this, I'm pretty sure you can get a binder or some other notebook to write down how you're progressing in your practice.

Section out a few pages to keep track of what herbs you have in stock and if you'll need to resupply soon. Alternatively, you can keep a digital list of some sort. These can help with marking which items you need to get and when your stock is running low.

The point is to find a system that works. You don't want to go out to buy something only to get home and find you already had it.

Seeds

Caraway. Can be used to stop someone you love from straying away, also helpful for increasing mental powers, bringing in love, passion, and is said to be anti-theft. Offer on a love altar or add some seeds to a mojo bag.

Cardamom. For increasing the love in your life. Particularly useful to soothe your own heart if you've been hurt or in pain. Can help with your luck in love, and fidelity.

Celery. If placed under a pillow, it can encourage prophetic dreams while sleeping, also increases psychic abilities and helps with concentration.

Chia. Not much is known about the magical properties of this seed, but if you have it in your pantry, some say it can be used to help stop gossip against you. Burn on a charcoal disc or use them to dress a candle for a ritual.

Coriander. Commonly used in love spells, for lust, can be added to wine in ground form (though be careful with this). Can be used to ease the pain of a breakup. Great for mojo bags or dressing candles ahead of love rituals.

Cumin. Can be used to keep evil away, cursing enemies, or increase fidelity in your relationships. Can also be used to prevent theft and for protection. Can be burned on a charcoal disc and used in workings.

Fennel. Use these if you are going through hard times and need some extra support. Good for healing spells. Also works in purification, strength, and protection. Tie in a satchel and hang in your home to protect your space from evil and unwanted energies.

Fenugreek. Commonly used for drawing in money. One way to use it is to keep some seeds in an open container on a kitchen counter or table, and add seeds to it over time. Can also be used in the home by adding seeds to floor washes.

Flax. Can help to ward off any harsh or angry energies. Used in spells for healing and drawing in money. Also called Linseed. Combine with a few coins and place them on an altar for financial stability.

Mustard. Different types have different uses. White or yellow seeds are usually associated with faith, as the bible verse says. Yellow mustard seeds can be carried in a small bottle or amulet for faith and success.

Poppy. The highly potent drug opium is extracted from these seeds, which aligns with how it can be used in magic: to help with getting rest and feeling pleasure. Can also be used to confuse enemies or people who are in your way. Carry some seeds in a mojo bag or satchel.

Star Anise. Can increase your psychic ability and awareness. Carried to increase your luck and is said to be able to keep the evil eye away. Also used in money magic. Excellent for container spells or carried for luck, protection, and divination.

Roots

Adam & Eve Root. Available in two; one root is shaped like a large marble with a flat side and the other shaped like a large nail. Together, these roots can be used to attract love to you. If you're in a relationship, each partner can carry one of the roots to keep your union strong. These roots come from orchid plants, which are endangered in many parts of the United States.

Althaea. A protective healer. Use in your spells when you or someone else needs to ease a broken heart or any emotional discord. It is said to draw spirits to you that will help in whatever you need. Can be burned on a charcoal disc.

Angelica. The root of angels. This is often said to help women with feeling strong and protected. Add to a bath or personal skincare products, grow in a garden or balcony to protect your home.

Arrowroot. A multi-purpose plant that is often used in baking when converted to a powder. In magic, the powder is most often used for luck. Often used as a substitute for graveyard dust.

Marsh mallow. These look and feel nothing like marshmallows, rather very light pieces of grey paper. Used for psychic protection and to enhance your intuitive abilities. An ideal addition for mojo bags but can also be consumed as a tea. Also known as Althaea Officinalis.

Bat's Head. Also called Devil Pod, Vampire Root, Cat's Claw. This is an actual pod that appears to have eyes and a mouth. It looks a little scary but is considered a favorite among hoodoo workers. Used primarily for protection, but also has powers in granting wishes.

Dandelion. For strengthening psychic abilities. A plant that can aid in transformation and abundance. If you live in an area where there are many of these plants, forage for your own instead of buying from a supplier. Be aware, dandelion leaves have slightly different uses than the root.

Calamus. To gain control over yourself, or to get the upper hand in situations where you need it. Also great for protection. Often used in work that has to do with domination; casting a spell or added to oils.

Comfrey. If you are planning to travel anytime soon, this root may be good to keep on hand. *Note that Comfrey leaves have different magical correspondences than the roots. Keep in the home or vehicle, any place where you want to protect things from being lost or stolen.

Culver's. A major purifier. Other names for this root are: Bowman's Root, Brinton Root, Culver's Physic, and Physic Root (yes, that's physic, and not psychic). If you need spiritual purification beyond what you can do on your own, an experienced practitioner may use this root.

Ginger. A root that is amazing for building confidence and going out into a brave new world. Next time you're in the market for ginger root, look for one that is shaped like a human--this is said to be a powerful magical tool. Use to add fire and speed to spells.

Ginseng. Used for various magical purposes, including protection, healing, love, sex, and general luck. Famously used to boost male virility. Burn to keep evil spirits away or carry to draw luck to you.

Gravel Root. For help in getting and maintaining a job. Additionally, it can be used to ease distress, so if you are having trouble at work, this root may be an ideal option. Best used when carried, especially while working.

Jezebel. Said to be used by sex workers to draw clients who are submissive and give good tips. Can be used equally well for cursing an enemy. Use in a money-drawing mojo bag or honey jar.

John the Conqueror. One of the most popular roots used in hoodoo. Used as an all-purpose root for confidence, strength, success, health, protection, and money. As your practice advances, you'll want to have this one handy. Used in any magick you need, to be carried or used in baths and washes.

Licorice. Generally used in spells about love and relationships. However, it is also often used for spells with the intent of gaining control. Can be carried to attract love or chewed to build confidence.

Mandrake. Another common all-purpose root used for wealth, health, love, and protection. As its name suggests, this root is shaped like a man and said to 'scream' when it is harvested. Keep in your home, on a mantel or altar, for protection. Place on top of money for financial abundance.

Valerian. For peace, harmony, love, and protection. May be helpful in situations where there's discord in a relationship. Also known as 'Vandal'. Can be burned, to hex, or burned with a yellow candle to clear a hex cast on you.

Verbena. An all-purpose. Noted to help with all of the usual life situations: money, love, protection, healing, and peace. Additionally, helpful with maintaining youth, helping with low vibrations and increasing creativity. Also known as 'Vervain'. Include in prosperity spells or carry with you when you need to be creative.

From Trees

Cedar. There's some disagreement on how this wood can help with your magic, but it's generally said to be protective and helpful with matters of the home. Available as wood chips, but branches are also used in incense. Can be burned for cleansing in the same way as sage and palo santo.

Frankincense. A massively powerful resin used in nearly all types of spells to boost their power. Usually burned on a charcoal disc to clear a space and to heighten vibration, so excellent to use ahead of rituals where you need extra power. Resin can also be offered to ancestors and deities on your altar.

Myrrh. Another powerful resin that can be used in the same way as Frankincense. Associated with Isis. Used for spiritual healing, to raise vibrations ahead of meditation or rituals. Excellent for blessing your space and magical tools and is a connector to the dead.

Palo Santo. This wood is sacred to Indigenous cultures in North America, and, as of 2019, was on the watch list for becoming endangered because of its popularity. It is generally burned and used for cleansing, but there are thousands of options for this, which is why I recommend steering clear of this wood for your use.

Pine Needles. An alternative to palo santo, if you're in the need of spiritual cleansing. In addition, it is said to attract prosperity. Pine trees survive in harsh conditions and are worth a try if you need some of that resilience in you, or your magic.

Leaves

Acacia. Used in spiritual practices and rites for thousands of years, in cultures around the world. A masculine all-purpose plant that can be used to clean and consecrate your magical tools. Burn, or use in washes.

Agrimony. A spell reverser. If you think or know someone has hexed you, this leaf can help and dissolve the things that can get in your way: depression, anger, sadness, fear, impatience, etc. Use in body washes and in oils.

Alfalfa. A leaf commonly used for money and financial abundance. In addition, it's also said to keep away poverty and hunger. Dispersing under a carpet in your home may help with attracting clients and customers for your at-home business,

Basil. All-purpose: love, cleansing, protection, attracting money, love, and abundance, must-have for any serious practitioner. Widely available in North America, considered sacred in some cultures. To use for blessing your home with prosperity and happiness, soak some dried herb in water for three days. Strain and sprinkle the water by your door.

Bay. Another all-purpose leaf that many practitioners across many different magical practices use regularly. Particularly effective at keeping evil away, specifically when dealing in hexes and curses. Write what you want on a leaf and burn it to draw in your desires. Excellent to purify the air (by burning) if someone sick has been in a room.

Catnip. Used for love, particularly by women who want to attract a specific man. Can also be useful in mojo bags for physical attractiveness and self-love. Can be carried to attract someone to you. Hang dried over your door to draw in luck and good spiritual energy.

Damiana. Another leaf used for love, and lust specifically. Also used to increase psychic ability and to help align the chakras. Helps build the energy of other magical herbs. Use as an offering on a love altar, or in sachets, honey jars, mojo bags, or candle working to draw love to you.

Eucalyptus. For healing and purification. Is also available as an essential oil, which can work in spells just as well as the leaf. Is said to help keep evil away and cleanse after being around lingering vibrations that you don't want around. Can be used for protection and for health when carried in a mojo bag or sachet.

Holly. Used for protection and drawing luck. The same leaf is often associated with Christmas, so you'll find it hanging in practitioners' homes during Yule. It can draw protection for the home when burned with incense. Often used around Christmas time.

Lemon. Lemon leaves have similar magical properties to the fruit. Very effective for cleansing negative energy, especially from old or reused items. The leaves can be used for cleansing, either your body or home.

Marjoram. Can draw in wealth, protect, and dispel negativity. Is also considered good for the home. Good to carry around for money and for protection. Being placed under pillows may bring you revealing dreams. Can be carried or placed in the home to draw love.

Mint. All types of mint are good for magic. Good for protection and healing. Peppermint specifically helps with feeling peace and keeping vibrations high. Place the mint on your altar(s) to draw good energy and good spirits.

Mistletoe. Not considered a particularly strong leaf, but a good addition to boost your magic. A healer and protector. Can be hung in the home for protection or worn to prevent you from getting attention you don't want.

Oregano. An herb commonly used in food can also be protective and give your magick some added energy. Oregano leaves have been burned for centuries to keep negative energies away.

Passion Flower. Doesn't quite arouse passion but is useful in love spells and for building your social circle. Promotes sleep when placed under a pillow.

Patchouli. A masculine leaf that's useful for money and for love. Is also reported to be useful for breaking spells cast on you by someone else. Often used in spells, oils, and bags for love and for money. Can be placed in your wallet to draw money.

Pennyroyal. A protector against any negative vibrations, regardless of where they're coming from. Is useful to mend problems in the home, issues with family, or negative energy in the home. Can be worn or carried to keep negative vibrations away and help your business.

Rosemary. Another leaf used by many practitioners, particularly by women. Can both heal and protect. Also said to be useful in the home, particularly when hung dried over a window or door. Use to draw love or healing by creating a poppet of yourself and filling it with this herb.

Sage. Like Palo Santo, Sage is a leaf used for cleansing, blessing, and purification. Certain types of sage are specifically sacred to Native American cultures.

Thyme. A common spice in the kitchen, also used to draw money, and attract a positive reputation. It can be worn on the body or hung in the home to draw in protection and strength. If you tend to feel more mellow negative vibrations, like boredom, burn on a charcoal disc to change the energy and uplift.

Violet. Can be worn to keep a calm temperament and stay peaceful. May also help with drawing in love. Place leaves in a green mojo bag or sachet to heal physical and emotional wounds, and protect yourself when wounded.

Herbs

Allspice. Useful for boosting your luck in any situation. Can also help when it comes to finding treasure, or an added boost to any charms you already have. Berries that are available either dried, or as a powder. Burn for money and luck.

Asafetida. Said to help with repelling evil and can be used to bring difficulties to your enemies. Does not smell nice. Burn on charcoal and say your petition in the name of the devil to stop someone from bothering you.

Black Pepper. A common kitchen ingredient that can also be used to blast out and protect from negative energy. Can also keep positive energy away if used too much. Often used with other herbs in magick and rituals. Place it around your wallet to dispel negative energy.

Buckeye Nut. Generally used for luck, particularly when chance is involved. Also used in drawing in money and with male virility. Carried in your pocket, this nut is said to draw luck and money.

Calendula. A flower used for psychic and spiritual powers, boosting your luck, and getting help when it comes to legal matters. Can be placed in a garland on your door to keep evil away. Useful in love working or as an offering on a love altar.

Chamomile. Widely used for healing, to diminish stress and clean an environment of any hexes, curses or lingering energy. Also useful for luck, bringing in money, and attracting love. Use in a bath for love.

Cinnamon. A fiery spice that can be burned for heightened spiritual abilities, for prosperity, and to raise your vibration. Beneficial for drawing in money and success. If you have cinnamon-burn it! It can draw money and love, purify, and aid your psychic abilities.

Cinquefoil. Can be useful when you're dealing with legal bodies, since it helps with finding your words. Five points represent love, money, power, health, and wisdom, and it's said this herb will impart those on anyone who wears it.

Cloves. Can be used for any magick related to fire (i.e. your willpower). Helps with money, love, and protection. Burning cloves as incense can work to attract money and raise vibrations.

Elder. Roots, leaves, berries, and flowers are major for protection, but are also poisonous, so be careful. Can be used to guard your home and your money-making endeavors. Can be worn for protection.

Garlic. Widely used to protect against all forms of evil, including vampires (energetic or otherwise). Healing and great for exorcising negative energies or entities. Hanging in the home won't protect against vampires but will boost your willpower and strengthen family bonds.

Hops. This beer flower is excellent in magick to help induce sleep and pleasant dreams. Also beneficial in healing and money magic. Use in dream pillows or to help with inducing restful sleep.

Hyssop. A mint mentioned in the bible (Psalm 51) for spiritual purification. Highly popular in magick for cleansing, particularly for washes and baths. Soak in water for a few days, strain and use the water to cleanse your magical tools and objects.

Jasmine. A flower that is good for attracting a soul mate and generally being open to love. Also useful for divination, drawing wealth, and charging crystals (quartz specifically).

Juniper Berry. Used for attracting love and increasing attraction and lust. Keeps things you don't want away and has the ability to attract good vibrations and health.

Lavender. A flower used to attract love, heal from depression. Promotes sleep and can help with purification. Highly popular as an essential oil. Burning the flowers and spreading ashes can help with love spells and rituals.

Mugwort. Often used to cleanse and purify tools used for divination, such as scrying mirrors. Can also help with fertility. Create a Mugwort 'tea' (or infusion) by mixing one teaspoon of the herb with one cup of boiling water and using this to clean your altar and magical tools.

Nettle. Nature's 'Return to Sender'. Return any spells or hexes cast on you, build your will, strengthen yourself and your ability to handle emergencies.

Nutmeg. Whole, helps with luck and winning at games where luck is needed. Can also be used to attract prosperity, protection, and help to break a hex. Sprinkle on a green or white candle for use in prosperity spells, use in mojo bags, and satchels.

Red Pepper. Crushed or pods, have the same correspondence, cleansing and triggering a breakup of a relationship. Used for 'enemy' magic, to drive someone away or cause bad luck to someone else, often with other herbs like salt and black pepper.

Rose. The love flower. As a rose has its thorns, so does this flower's protective ability in magic. Can help with any matters of the heart, finding love, self-healing, and removing bad luck. Place roses on your love altar to honor Venus, goddess of love, beauty (and much more).

Skullcap. Used in money magic, also used to keep partners (usually the masculine energy) faithful in relationships. Can also be helpful in fostering peacefulness. Some of this herb in a lover's shoe is used to help keep them from being noticed by others.

Wormwood. Is said to be good for creating peace in war-like conditions. Also helpful in protection and assisting in receiving clairvoyant information. Can be carried or placed as protection from accidents, so in a satchel, bag, or car.

Yarrow. Popular in spells and workings for courage and self-confidence. Useful for healing and drawing love to anyone who wears it in a sachet. Rubbing over your eyes is said to help with clairvoyance.

Waters

Beware of applying waters, and the oils listed in the next section, on your skin or ingesting them. I do not recommend you put any of these on your skin or eat them, you have to know what is safe for you.

Florida Water. A widely popular in many magical practices, but hoodoo in particular. It is an all-purpose water that can be used across multiple purposes in your magic. Technically a cologne.

- Attract good spirits and repel negative ones.

- Cleanse your area before a working by using it in a spray.

- Add to your ancestor altar as an offering.

- Create a wipe for your altar and use for regular cleanings.

- Add to spiritual baths and scrubs. While Florida Water is considered safe for skin, you want to test this out first.

Kananga Water. Is a cologne used for spiritual cleansing and protection in the same way as Florida Water, though not as widely available.

Orange Water. Made with orange essential oil mixed in distilled water. Used topically, for those who are wishing to increase their luck or looking to get married. Offer on money and love altars. Use it as a wash in a bath or shower. Can also be added to your altar when doing rituals or prayers focused on love or fortune.

Peace Water. Like the name suggests, used to promote peace wherever it is used. Comes in an indigo blue color. Use on self-love or altars for the home. Sprinkle around your space after cleaning to encourage a peaceful environment.

Rose Water. Generally used on the body to attract love, also used in beautification rituals and spells. Can also be offered on love altars or to love goddesses. Add to baths and include it as an offering on your altar.

War Water. Used in witch wars and for hexing. Often contains an iron nail along with herbs and plants consistent with the purpose. *Definitely* not for drinking.

Willow Water. As a tree that grows near water and is often found in or around graveyards (usually in the South), willow water is good for healing, poured as an offering at gravesites. It's considered a natural remedy to physical ailments and can be offered on ancestor altars. Can also be presented as an offering to your herbs, plants, and roots.

Cleansing Oils

There are *many* different types of oils in the hoodoo practice. We're just going to list the cleansing oils here, but there is an oil for money and abundance, keeping your home peaceful, attracting love to you, hexing and blessing, breaking curses, and getting lucky.

To use the oils, you can anoint yourself, anoint any special paperwork you're using for a working or just in your life. You can anoint your altar or tools used on your altar, such as statues of deities. You can also use oils to bless your personal items, such as a wallet.

For this section of the book, we'll focus on just the oils for cleansing. As we'll cover in future chapters, cleansing and protection are very important when you're working with spirit.

Cut & Clear. An oil you'll find at almost any hoodoo shop. For cutting and clearing anything out of your life, such as habits, exes, and attachments. Anoint yourself, use in personal care products, wear on your body like a perfume.

Dragon's Blood. Considered a powerful all-purpose oil. Is red in color from Dragon's Blood, a deeply red-colored resin. Add some drops to your cleaning products or use to anoint your tools and altar.

Hindu Grass. An oil for cutting out things from your life. This could be a relationship or a pattern of thinking or behavior, tied to past events. An oil you can use on yourself, anointing and wearing.

Blessing. There's Blessing oil, *and* House Blessing oil. The first type is generally used for yourself, the second strictly for your home. These oils cleanse and are said to help bring favor from deities. Depending on the type of oil, you can use it on yourself or for your home. You could also offer this oil to your ancestors or deities you're working with by leaving some drops on a plate or leaving an open jar on your altar.

Psychic Cleansing. If you need a psychic cleansing of old energies weighing you down or getting in your way, try a psychic cleansing oil. Anoint yourself before meditating or offer some of the oil on a self-love altar.

Purification. A blaster of any blocks or energies that remain in your way. Not as available as the other oils, but an excellent option if you're just getting out of a bad relationship or attachment. Burn this oil on a charcoal disc or add it to a self-healing mojo bag.

PART II

Spells, Tricks, and Rituals

Now that you have some basic information about the basics of hoodoo, in this section of the book we'll be going over some specific spells, tricks, and rituals you can incorporate into your practice.

'Tricks' here are not about doing something to your friends to have a laugh. A 'trick' in hoodoo is another way to say 'spell'. The terminology you'll often hear is 'laying down a trick', 'fixing tricks', or 'laying down'.

This meaning is on purpose. If you think of the origins of hoodoo, using these terms sound more or less inconspicuous. Telling someone you're going to 'lay down' doesn't sound odd to most of us. But using this code was very important to earlier practitioners to avoid the punishment of being accused of engaging in hoodoo.

Preparing to Work with Roots

Buying roots from a supplier you trust is a convenient way to get what you're looking for without going outside and foraging or searching for what you need in your environment. However, every hoodoo practitioner I know would rather go out and forage.

Most of us are used to living around plants every day but we don't pay much attention to them aside from watering and watching out for bugs. A good practice to start now (if you're not doing it already) is to go outside and take note of what's growing in your neighborhood and region.

No matter what you're going through, there's probably a plant that grows in abundance in your backyard that can help. In this section, we'll cover what you'll need to successfully forage for roots.

Before you head out, you will have to do some research on what's available in your neighborhood and local wooded areas.

Root Reverence

It's best to go out with an intent, for example, if you know you want to find wild strawberries for a working, you'll know what it looks like and where it's most likely to grow. On the other hand, you can search around and take photos of what you find, whatever looks interesting, and then do your research at home.

Even if you're planning to purchase from a local retailer, you want to know if what they're selling is available to you locally. Not only could this potentially save you money, but you'll also know if what you're buying is endangered.

Hoodoo is where you get to really put your hands into the work. The plants you touch will have their own spirit, as we've discussed, and in preparing to work with plants, you want to honor these spirits.

When you're foraging, you are taking a plant from its natural habitat for your own purpose. This isn't wrong, the plants we use are given to us by mother nature for our use (everything in nature is created for the use of everything else), so foraging requires some respect and care.

Introduce yourself to the spirit of the plants and tell them what your intent is. While foraging, you want to stay open to communication from the plants you're touching. You do not have to speak out loud, you can do this all in your mind. Express gratitude for mother earth, to nature, for providing the materials we use to survive, and what you're taking for your working.

This reverence is part of the practice.

The Practice

The relationship you build with the roots, and all of the tools and materials you use for your magick is somewhat similar to the relationship you have with your ancestors. With all of the herbs you have in your home, or any plant you purchase, it does not work to bring it home and start casting a spell with it right away.

Once you have some privacy, it's time to consecrate the herbs and start building your connection.

Start by putting some of the roots in your palm and holding them. Take a moment to smell and get acquainted. saying a prayer of thanks. You can open your prayer by saying something like: "Mother Goddess, I come to you now in respect," and then continue with acknowledging the herb or seed you're holding.

Say that you are welcoming their spirit into your space. At some point, you can recite Psalm 23 over the roots in your palm (you'll probably want to have this one memorized).

Your prayer can include a reference to what work you intend to do with the root and what your highest intentions are. Speak slowly and take note of how you feel. Create in yourself a feeling of gratitude; you may be already feeling this as you pray.

Everything you have is there to help you, no matter what change you want to make in your life. Share your gratitude with the spirits you speak to; you're going to get what you want, and the spirits are ready and willing to help.

Bless your roots after your prayers. Breathe deeply and open yourself up to an experience of your own power. If you need some help with this, think of your own divine self. Choose to identify with the part of yourself that has no problems, breathe and connect with the part of you that knows all of the answers to your problems.

Then, as you're standing in your power, say: *I bless the spirit of [name the item]*. Continue to offer your thanks, acknowledge the specifics of *that* spirit.

For example, if you're connecting with the spirit of Fennel Seeds, acknowledge their strength, specifically through hard times, how they can heal and protect.

You may want to share how you can learn from this spirit, and how in your relationship you intend to keep your ears and heart open to their guidance. In case you're wondering, yes, Fennel Seed was very important to me in my own hard times.

In terms of offerings, you may see other practitioners blowing smoke on the roots or spilling alcohol like whiskey. These are offerings.

If you don't have whiskey or a cigar/cigarette, your words of praise, songs, or coins will suffice. Present these things the same way you would to your ancestors.

You want to regularly speak to and pray over your roots and make offerings in whatever form of your choosing.

You'll want to repeat this process (or something like it, with your modifications) over everything that has a spirit and that you intend to use for your working. This includes candles, crystals, waters, and oils.

Time and Space

A root burrowed deep into the ground is an admirable thing. Of course, for most plants we never see it happening. The only way to know for sure that a root exists is by what we do see.

It's work that is done and happens by the force of nature alone, and the deeper and thicker the roots, the more time it has taken for growth to happen.

Roots grow and do their thing with little human intervention. And even when humans do intervene, it's seldom necessary.

This is one of the reasons time is important. A plant needs to be given enough time to grow before it's pulled from the earth. Once it's been harvested, the growth process stops.

Yes, nature is abundant and regenerative, but that is exactly what it is that we deeply respect and are grateful for.

There are many considerations that will dictate when and where you forage: season, time of year, time of day, moon cycle, and location are a few.

Season

Not every plant can be picked in every season. Berries are probably the best way to demonstrate this. You can't pick a berry that isn't ripe. Depending on the berry, this could be Fall, as in with Elderberries. Or summer, as with cherries.

However, some plants and seeds can be foraged year-round, depending on where you live, like Acorns for example.

Time of Day

Another factor to consider when harvesting is the time of day you're out and picking plants for their roots.

Some plants would be best picked early in the morning, while dew is still on the leaves. Others, it would be better to pick at night. The only way to know for sure is to know what you're picking.

Moon Cycle

To get the highest magical potency from the roots, you'll also want to consider what cycle the moon is in.

If you're not familiar with how to do this, an online search for 'moon cycle' will show you where the moon is for the time of month. With most calendars you can also see when the moon will be full or new, which can help you plan your foraging day.

Gardening by the Moon says that the moon also determines the best times of year to plant, weed, prune, and harvest plants.

Time of Year

When the moon is in Aries, Leo, Sagittarius, Gemini, or Aquarius, it's considered the best time to harvest. For this information, you could buy an almanac, but these dates are also widely available online.

You may be able to find a calendar that tells you what phase the moon is in (i.e. waning crescent, new, waxing, full), and what sign it's in, but if not, you will have to look this information up separately.

Location

Unless you have a backyard where you can grow plants already, you'll most likely be out at a park or forested area nearby.

You could go out and take what you need in the moment, however many experts recommend watching the plant you're planning to harvest over some time, at least a month.

This might be more difficult if you're foraging at a local wooded area or park, but it's really not much more than going for a walk and checking in on your chosen plant.

If you're looking to do a spell quickly this might seem like an unnecessary wait, but as a beginner, you want to take your time with hoodoo, and foraging especially. Not having the right energy in the roots you find will impact your magic.

There are many reasons a spell may not work in the way you expected or intended, foraging with the wrong energy or at the wrong time could be the reason this happens, but you want to mitigate this as much as possible.

The only way to do that is to build a relationship with the plants you need before finding them in nature. Roots you take time to cultivate a relationship with will be more powerful as a part of your magic.

Equipment and Tools

When finding roots, you want to get as much of the root as possible. There will be small pieces left behind, but if you're harvesting for roots, you will be collecting whole plants.

You may not use the whole root in your working, so this way you can use what you need for your work, and replant what you don't use, either in your backyard or a pot in your home.

Does this mean you'll potentially have a house full of plants? Hopefully.

The tools you'll need to collect roots are simple: **gloves (the gardening type)** and something to dig the roots out with. This can be a type of **gardening knife called a 'Hori Hori'**, but you can also use a **garden fork**. To snip herbs or flowers, you'll need **scissors** to make a clean cut of the stem.

When it comes to carrying and storing what you forage, you'll want to have a bag handy just for what you collect. You may also want to have string on hand if you plan to hang dried herbs.

In the next section, we're covering some basic techniques for making extractions from the herbs and plants you forage or have on hand. You certainly do not have to know how to extract from plants, but it can be helpful if you want to conserve the essence of some of the herbs you have.

For extraction, you'll need some of the common tools most hoodoo practitioners have:

1. A mortar and pestle.

2. Alcohol (a high-quality rum can be used for extraction, and for offerings to your ancestors and to your roots and herbs).

3. Empty bottles. Try to get ones that are easy for you to clean. Some extracts may be sensitive to light. In this case, darkly colored bottles are recommended.

4. Something to filter with, like a sieve or some cheesecloth.

Often other common kitchen tools are used in extraction, like a small kitchen fan used to circulate air. You may also use pots and pans and a stove to bring substances to a boil.

Getting some **disposable gloves** is also a good idea, especially if you are dealing with more volatile substances or hoodoo powders. You probably already have a mask you can use to prevent yourself from breathing in any fumes, but these are also good to keep on hand.

Gathering and Drying Herbs

Another common practice among many practitioners is drying herbs that have been gathered, usually in a bunch hanging by a window or door, but there are a few methods to drying, such as sun drying or using a microwave-yes, microwave drying is possible!

You can hang any herb with a stem to dry. such as marjoram, basil, and mint. So, when gathering your herbs, make sure to give yourself lots of stem, especially if you're going to use the hang-drying method described below.

Herbs need to be completely dried before being stored, especially if you're planning to use jars or containers. If not, you'll be trapping your herbs in with water, which is great for creating mold (though fungi have been used in magic, so there's probably some use for mold as well).

After gathering your herbs, carefully wash them and remove any debris or dead material, if you see it. Adding water will, of course, mean your drying time will be longer, so if you don't see anything to wash off, feel free to skip this step.

Once your herbs are clean, gather them in a bunch by the stems. It should look like you have a small bouquet of herbs. Use string or a rubber band to secure the bunch. Once tied together, they can be hung from your roof or a drying rack. A tea towel or j-cloth underneath the herbs will catch any falling drops.

While it looks pretty, hanging your herbs to dry may not be the most effective, since these herbs will often collect dust and stuff floating in the air. Left too long, and you'll soon start to see dried leaves and flowers falling onto the ground.

To prevent this, you can secure the bunched herbs within a paper bag. Though this is optional. Many herbs can be magical just hanging to dry. It all depends on your intent.

With a few candles and some herbs hanging around, your space can really start to look and feel like a magical home.

If you'd prefer not to hang dry, you can use the sun or other heat sources. For sun drying, you'll need to put your clean herbs on a screen or other porous surfaces. Most people will use the screen from a door. This is to give the moisture already in the plant somewhere to go and to make it easier for air to circulate.

You'll also want to put something underneath where your herbs are sitting, again to catch water. As the name suggests, you'll set leaves on the screen and leave them in the sun until they're dry.

Keep in mind: this is sun drying, not moon. If you leave herbs out for a day and they aren't dry, you'll have to take them inside overnight. This way you keep the morning dew from slowing the process down.

The last alternative is microwave drying. You want to be careful with this method because left in the microwave for too long, and you can burn the herbs or worse, start a fire. This is also why it's important to remove any excess moisture from your leaves first.

Once the herbs are as dry as you can make them, place them in the microwave in a single layer, in between two sheets of paper towel. Set the microwave for a minute on high and check the leaves. Continue heating the leaves for 30 seconds at a time, checking each time.[1]

Storage

Your dried leaves can then be stored in an airtight container, in a cool, dry space away from direct sunlight and away from heat.

Air is not a friend to your dried herbs, so however you choose to store, make sure that the container is airtight. Humidity in the air can undo the work you put into drying your herbs.

Regarding a 'cool, dark place', most of the time a fridge is a fine spot, but if that's not available, any spot that is out of the sunlight will do.

Last, take note of the herbs you dried, which method you used, and the date you put the herbs into storage. This is good practice for your kitchen, so you might have a place to note these details down already.

Dried herbs don't necessarily expire, but as with most foods, they do have a 'best before' date. Generally, the time frame for dried herbs is two years, sometimes three. However, this doesn't mean that you can't use the herbs after that date.

Mojo Bags

A mojo bag is a very popular working in hoodoo. It is also one of the first things you want to create as you start your practice.

The hoodoo definition of mojo is spirit.

We talked about containment in a previous section. This is a concept specific to the Yoruba tradition, out of western Africa.

A mojo bag is about concentrating the energy of spirit in work towards whatever your intent.

---

[1] Herb Gardening: Harvesting, Drying and Storing Herbs. (2021). Herb Gardening: Harvesting, Drying and Storing Herbs. https://web.extension.illinois.edu/herbs/tips.cfm#:~:text=With%20proper%20storage%2C%20most%20herbs,the%20sides%20of%20the%20bags.

You generally can't go wrong when creating one of these for your personal use. You can find many, many spells for mojo bags online or in hoodoo books. It makes a great first spell for beginners because you are encouraged to get creative.

One practitioner I know used a name necklace that broke in such a way that their name was split almost in half. She wasn't interested in getting the piece fixed, but she also didn't care to throw it away because it meant something to her. The broken necklace made a perfect addition to her self-love mojo bag. Her intent in creating the bag was to heal a broken spirit.

Generally, the purpose of these bags is to draw love, money, success, or protection to you. You can use it while you're working to create a larger change in your life.

Let's say, for example, that you want to draw in real romantic love. Not just a new boyfriend or girlfriend (or boyfriends or girlfriends), but a true shift in your outlook on love.

You know, however, that this will require a change in your mindset and you're not sure about what this will look or feel like.

With a mojo bag, you can get help making this deeper shift so that when your love spell works, you don't block the love you deserve.

The rules for a mojo bag are simple:

1. No one but you is to touch, see, or use your mojo bag for any reason. We're all used to keeping things in secret, that applies here as well.

2. You can either keep it on you all the time, or every day over a period, like a week or lunar cycle, depending on what you're using it for.

Making a Mojo Bag

Traditionally, mojo bags are made out of flannel. Most people think of the plaid type of shirts when they hear that name, but flannel is a yarn or wool material, and is not specific to a pattern. You can get flannel cloth in any color you want. Which is good when it comes to working hoodoo.

In addition to carefully choosing the color, you want to get flannel in a material that feels good on your skin. This is especially true if you plan to wear your bag close to you over a period of months or weeks.

It might seem excessive to buy a whole yard of flannel online, just to create a relatively small item. Another option may be searching through your closet to see if you have any flannel that will work or checking with anyone who may want to donate some fabric to you.

However, most flannels are available cheaply, and if you enjoy making a mojo bag, with enough fabric you can make bags for your friends and family.

You want to create a mojo bag with intention, in the same way that you would create your altar.

You can also imagine that the items that go inside can include things you would put on an altar; curios (small items like figurines and symbols), herbs, oils (usually in small glass jars or container), crystals and energy stones, dried plants, petitions to spirit, hair or fingernails, coins and dollar bills, jewelry, and, of course, roots.

There are two different ways you can make one of these bags for yourself, depending on how comfortable you are with a needle and thread. For the mojo bags below, you will need your flannel and string, again, in a color that *speaks* to you and your working. However, the simple and effective choice in many cases may be to go with your favorites.

Before creating your mojo bag, you'll want to do a good cleanse and prayer over *everything* you'll be using to create and make your bag.

One thing I have not included in the ingredient lists below is *you*. In each mojo bag you create for yourself, you must include inside something that has your DNA, your energetic signature. This can be as simple as the breath.

After all of the ingredients, adding your breath can be saying your intention at the mouth of the bag or over the ingredients inside. You want your breath to come into contact with the ingredients you've put inside.

Other than your breath, you can include hair, toenails, fingernails, spit, blood; anything that comes from your body. Most practitioners would recommend adding some substance of yours, such as your toenails, and your breath.

You want to keep your mojo bag as close as possible to your body for at least a week.

The advantage of the sewing option is the ability to create a satchel that can hold more than the non-sewing option.

The Sewing Option

1. Cut a piece of flannel cloth, 4 inches wide by 12 inches long.

2. Fold the flannel in half on the "wrong" side so the bag is 4 inches wide by 6 inches long.

3. Sew inside about a quarter inch along the long edges, leaving the top open.

4. Flip inside out, and now you have a little bag.

5. Pray over and bless each item before putting it inside. As you fill your bag, you will start to feel the energy building.

6. Tie string around the closure or create a simple drawstring.

The Non-Sewing Option

This type of mojo bag is commonly called a 'flaming comet' because once tied closed, it looks like a comet.

You'll want to cut your flannel in the shape of a square; 5in. x 5in. is sufficient. The idea is to put all of your materials in the middle and then gather the ends and secure the string around, so everything is contained tightly inside.

Ingredient Lists

Now that you know how to make a basic mojo bag (you can, of course, get more elaborate if you have more advanced sewing skills), here are a few basic recipes for common workings. All of these are designed to be interchangeable; some of the items may be a little difficult to get, but if there's one you want to make, get creative and substitute anything you don't have for items you *do* have, or can get easily.

Each recipe has a few color options for your flannel. You'll also find most recipes include: a small symbolic object, a natural element (such as a root or dried herb), one or two crystals.

The reason I am not providing you with a specific recipe is because there is no way for me to know what speaks to you. Hopefully, upon reading the lists below, you'll have the materials you need to create your own mojo bag already. If not, at least the options will inspire you.

However, you need to know how the different elements you're using work together and how these elements will aid in your working. For example, let's say you have no problem attracting money, but you're creating a mojo bag to help with keeping money and growing your investments. You may not want to include a citrine stone in your mojo bag, since this stone is more about manifesting wealth.

Do not include anything in your mojo bag that you don't connect with, or that doesn't mean anything to you.

Speaking of energy, I would recommend not creating any of these mojo bags if you're in an agitated emotional state. This is especially true if you're creating a bag for money, inner peace, healing, or luck. You can purchase the most expensive materials from people who grow and create items for magick specifically, but your energy will change everything if you're not careful.

Another name for a mojo bag is a 'hand'. An apt name, since to make these bags, you use your hands. If your energy is off in any way, that is going to transfer through your body, through your hands, and go into the bag you're creating.

Before you begin praying and cleansing, get as calm as possible. If you can't get calm, choose another date or time to create the bag. Create a feeling of excitement. As you create your bag, keep in mind that you're getting everything you want, and the specific circumstances that led you to create this mojo bag! Think and agree with yourself that every item you're using to create your bag will *work for you*.

A few elements listed below are universal, meaning you can use them for any of the bags listed. Instead of going for a generic green, for example, choose a shade that aligns with your intent. For an inner peace or inner healing mojo bag you might go with a sage green, while for money you could use an emerald green.

In addition, often you'll find crystals that are molded into different shapes, for example, a rose quartz in the shape of a heart or a jade stone in the shape of a frog. These objects can do double or triple duty in your mojo bag, if used with intention.

I should note that while white is a universal shade for magic, a mojo bag is created to be carried with you all the time, which would mean it may show dirt easily. Consider using white for the items you place inside of your bag. Otherwise, be prepared to clean your bag constantly.

For Inner Peace

Flannel Color Options: Green, Blue, Yellow, Pink, Black.

Charm Options: Peace symbol, peace hand, dove, feather, or a charm with the word 'peace' engraved.

Crystal Options: Selenite, moonstone, pink opal, opalite, blue lace agate, rose quartz, alone or combined with amethyst, petrified wood, scolecite.

Herb and Nature Options: Chamomile, Lavender, skullcap, vervain, or verbena.

Place Options: Dirt from a church. Small seashells from a beach, smooth stones, like those found in a park or a wooded area.

For Money

Flannel Color Options: Green, purple, red.

Charm Options: Currency symbols, like a dollar sign, tree, acorn, infinity symbol, a cup (to represent your cup being full), sun and/or stars.

Crystal Options: Pyrite, citrine, red garnet, green aventurine and/or jade, clear quartz, tiger's eye, malachite, amazonite, tree + moss agate (combined), lapis lazuli.

Object Options: Dollar wrapped in white or green or gold thread, coins, specifically if you can find coins minted.

Herb and Nature Options: Bay leaf, alfalfa, bee pollen, catnip, star anise, sugar, peppermint, basil leaf, patchouli leaf.

Place Options: Dirt from a bank.

Roots: Licorice Root, Mandrake Root.

For the charm, you may want to include a trinket that represents anything you desire, for example, a small yacht, a model car, a home, even a beach umbrella. You may also want to use anything that symbolizes abundance or wealth in your culture. Salmon, for example (Native American).

For Luck

Flannel Color Options: Green, orange, red.

Charm Options: Four-leaf clover, elephant, horseshoe, a key, dice, ladybugs, a number 7, evil eye, sun and/or stars.

Crystal Options: Smoky or clear quartz, labradorite, amethyst, carnelian, tiger's eye.

Object Options: A penny or coin you've found.

Herb and Nature Options: Star anise, buckeye nuts.

Place Options: Dirt from a casino.

Roots: High John the Conqueror.

For Love

Flannel Color Options: Pink, red, green.

Charm Options: Heart, rose, cupid, swans, doves, (any animal that is said to mate for life), a Claddagh ring, ankh.

Crystal Options: Rose quartz, aventurine, malachite, moonstone, lapis lazuli, garnet, amazonite, citrine, rhodonite, hibiscus flower.

Object Options: An object from a wedding you've attended. An image of the person who is your love interest*.

Herb and Nature Options: Cardamom, fennel seeds, rosemary, rose petals, lavender petals, oregano, patchouli, yarrow, thyme, basil.

Place Options: Dirt from a church.

Roots: Mandrake.

The charm idea from the money mojo recipe above applies here as well. Any object that means love to you will work in your mojo bag. This could be a small music note, if you love music, a little spoon, a book, or a teddy bear.

About Love Spells in General

Here's where I address the little * on the object option above. Magic for love is a controversial topic.

Some practitioners refuse to do love spells for themselves, or for anyone else. They say that when it comes to love, they do not want to mess with another person's free will. They want to know that the person who is in love with them is making their own choice and is not manipulated by any outside forces. I am inclined to agree.

Often, when someone wants a love spell done on a person who is refusing to be with them, there are deeper self-love issues involved. Specifically, a lack of self-love.

Balance is *essential* when it comes to love spells. If you or a person who wants work done is 'stuck' on someone else for whatever reason, that points to an imbalance.

When it comes to love, what 'balance' means is often skewed. We can confuse getting what we want to mean balance, when this universal law has nothing to do with our desires. Often the best choice is to heal and move forward.

For Self-Love and Inner Healing

Flannel Color Options: Green, black.

Charm Options: Sun, yin-yang, lotus, cosmogram, rod of Asclepius (a snake coiled around a rod). Anything with silver.

Crystal Options: Amethyst, prehnite, ocean jasper, sunstone, pink opal, rhodochrosite.

Object Options: An image of yourself or some other object that represents you.

Herb and Nature Options: Yarrow, peppermint, rosemary, sage, chamomile, rose, lemon balm, honey, hibiscus, cinnamon, cardamom.

Place Options: (See above)

For Health and Physical Healing

Flannel Color Options: Green, red, orange, yellow, blue.

Charm Options: Rod of Asclepius (a snake coiled around a rod), a heart, mini-workout equipment, like a running shoe or dumbbell, a woman's or man's body.

Crystal Options: Red jasper, fuchsite, amazonite, seraphinite A+, golden healer quartz, fire agate.

Object Options: Your picture or a picture of the person you're creating this bag for. A petition for healing a specific issue.

Herb and Nature Options: Caraway, chia seeds, cinquefoil, coriander, ginger, ginseng, heal all, high john the conqueror, juniper berry, magnolia flowers, mandrake, pumpkin seed, rosemary, sage, sassafras, tansy, thyme.

Place Options: Dirt from a hospital or place of physical fitness.

For Success in Career

Flannel Color Options: Green, gold, purple, orange, brown, red.

Charm Options: A star (gold, specifically), small electronic devices, like a phone or computer, currency signs, a pen (to signify signing contracts), an award or trophy.

Crystal Options: Pyrite, citrine, fluorite, green aventurine, lapis lazuli, amazonite, carnelian, tiger's eye.

Object Options: A petition with the type of success you're looking for. Make it long-term, if this is a mojo bag you want to keep for a while.

Herb and Nature Options: Basil, bay leaf, bergamot, chamomile, cinnamon, clover, frankincense (a resin), ginger, high john the conqueror, hollyhock, honeysuckle, lo john the conqueror, lucky hand root, mustard seed, pecan, pennyroyal.

Place Options: Dirt from a bank or financial center in a city.

For Protection

Flannel Color Options: Black, blue, red, purple.

Charm Options: The eye of Horus, pentagram, arrow, scarab beetle, bear (or any animal that speaks 'protection' to you), dragon. The evil eye is a very common charm for protection.

Crystal Options: Black tourmaline, shungite, clear Lemurian crystal, quartz (clear or smoky), pyrite, turquoise, pink tourmaline.

Object Options: An image of yourself.

Herb and Nature Options: Acorn, African violet, angelica, asafoetida, basil, bay leaf, betel nut, black pepper, black pepper, calendula flower, chrysanthemum, cloves, dill, elderberry, eucalyptus, garlic, ginger, high john the conqueror, lavender, mandrake, marjoram, marshmallow root, peony, petitgrain, rice, salt (all types, but different colors have different energies. Pink salt, for example, for a more loving protective energy), vervain.

Place Options: Dirt from a bank or try dirt from a gated community.

Q: How do I put oil and dirt in my mojo bag without making a mess?

The mess isn't such a bad thing. Mojo bags aren't made with the position that the ingredients will be used again, so feel free to let all of the elements and energies mix about.

If you do want to keep some ingredients contained, you can reuse or find very small containers, especially the kind with a cork or porous closure.

A local dollar store is a great place for these, but any supply or arts and crafts shops usually have them.

Q: Can I create a mixed mojo bag? For example, luck and money?

It might be better to approach creating your mojo bag from the perspective of what you want and what you need. So instead of creating a 'luck and money' mojo bag, create a money mojo bag that includes elements that will bring you luck, for example, a penny or coin you found, an elephant, or clear quartz.

One combination you may want to consider making for yourself is a self-love mojo bag, as I mentioned above.

There are thousands of stones and crystals out there with different correspondences. A stone-like pink and green tourmaline, for example, is said to help with overcoming problems with father figures. If you're harboring pain from childhood related to your father, you might want to consider a stone like this for an inner healing mojo bag.

This said, I must caution you to not get too worried if you can't find a very specific stone for what you need.

Just like the thousands of crystals available from every corner of the world, there are countless ways you can combine elements to make a mojo bag that is just right for you. Don't distract yourself and waste energy looking for something you don't really need.

The herbs and items you have right now can contribute to a very powerful mojo bag because it will speak to *you* in a way that is unique to your energy.

Magic Candles

As you begin your hoodoo work, you'll quickly discover the importance of candles. When it comes to depicting magick this is one of the things Hollywood gets right.

Hoodoo candles aren't just the pretty pillars you can get at a dollar store or local home decor store, though the candles you can buy at these spots can work just as well as candles made with magical intention.

Your first hoodoo candle will probably be called a 7-day candle. These are available in a tall, glass cylinder, and as their name suggests, are built to last seven days. They are about 8 inches high and just over 2 inches in diameter.

You may have seen religious 7-day candles before. These are the ones with religious figures depicted on them, like Mother Mary, and may have a prayer printed on the back.

You can get plain candles, or ones in various colors. A 7-day candle may have seven different colors or two. These different colors can help you with blessing your candle, and with doing spells that require you to do a working every day for a week.

Some spells require you to bless a candle halfway up and halfway down. Two-colored 7-day candles show you easily where the halfway mark is.

One kind of candle you can purchase can have multiple colors, sometimes two, but you can find candles with up to seven colors in a column, as if each color is stacked one on another.

Another type of candle that is easier to use for spells that are not designed to last over a week, are smaller, thinner pillars in different colors. You could make these candles stand on something by melting the wax at the bottom and sticking the candle down on whatever you're working on.

Using a Lamp

In addition to candles, part of your practice can include the use of hoodoo lamps. If you have a traditional lamp at home, consider yourself lucky. You can use these lamps in your hoodoo.

More often, you'll find the kind of lamp that is created using a mason jar or other glass-type of container. Most of your magical items and ingredients will go inside of the jar with your oil. Your floating wick would then go on top of the oil and you can light it to activate your lamp.

What you're creating will look different from anything you may have seen in the past. Even in the hoodoo tradition, there aren't many people who create lamps. That said, it is not complicated.

At the end of your working, you'll most likely have your lamp sitting on a plate with different curios and items floating inside of the glass, with your flame or wick burning on top. On the plate, you may have more curios or items with the purpose of bolstering your working.

Generally, these floating wicks can last up to 24 hours, but you never want to leave an open flame by itself.

Foot Track Magick

We've covered how important hands are in hoodoo. Your hand has the power to create life, specifically the life you want to live by your work.

In hoodoo, the feet are arguably just as significant as hands, though in different ways. You'll see this in foot track magick, which is often used as a way to control or cause strife in another person's life.

If you think of what the foot means, literally and metaphorically, you'll see how many opportunities there are with a bit of hoodoo.

There's the path you walk in real life, and then the one you walk every day. You can 'step over' someone to get ahead in life, walk around obstacles in your way, or with someone else in a love relationship. You can walk out of someone's life, walk a mile in someone else's shoes, walk the straight and narrow, or walk right into something (usually a joke at your expense). I could go on, but you get the point.

Cursing and Hexing

One of the most popular ways foot track magick is used is to hex or curse someone else. The reason why this can be so effective is (if you'll allow me another metaphor) people often do not watch where they're going. Because of this, it can also be very easy to hex someone with foot track magick.

Most of the time, all you need to do is lay the trick down on a place where you know your target will walk, often by their front door. Once the person steps over or walks through the trick, the magick takes effect. In other words, they step in 'it'.

In life, where you're going determines what you do every day and how you live. Foot track magick, then, has the ability to affect others in some serious ways.

Most of these spells have the power to stop someone in their tracks and force them off of their life path. These spells usually work to confuse, deter, and distract the subject of the working.

These spells can also sometimes cause a wide range of physical symptoms.

Because this is dealing with negative spirits, who must be invited in for the work, often when someone wants to work a curse on someone else (and any type of curse, not just the foot track kind) a professional is hired. The bottom line is, doing something to impact someone else will return to you in some way.

Protection and Love

You can also work foot magick on yourself. For example, putting violet leaves in your shoes is said to attract love to you. Protection spells can also be cast on your shoes, or you can use knot magick on your shoelaces (though knot magick isn't considered hoodoo, specifically).

When it comes to love, foot track magick is often used to keep a lover in line. As mentioned in the herbs section, skullcaps can be placed in your lover's shoe to help with keeping them faithful.

Spiritual Cleansing

When we go outside or interact with people, we are constantly in touch with energy: other people's or the energy of an environment.

You've probably felt this when you walked into a room where there was a tense argument or came across someone you did not have a good feeling about.

There are more subtle ways energy affects us that can go unnoticed. Groups of people can have a certain energy that can affect you. This is one of the reasons awareness is so important.

And the effect energy can have on your aura is one of the reasons cleansing is so important.

You can carry stones or a mojo bag for protection but doing this alone will put a lot of stress on your mojo bag. Your own cleansing will assist greatly with staying centered and protected.

There are also more serious cases that warrant cleansing, but I will caution you to not get too wrapped up in the possibility that you've attracted negative entities. There are some common emotional states, however, that you need to be aware of so you know what's possible, and why cleansing is so important.

Feeling lonely, depressed, or sad for prolonged periods of time can lead to being visited by energies and entities that feed off of this type of energy.

The unfortunate thing here is that often a person who is depressed does not know if they're being visited by an entity. The thoughts they have every day seem like their own thoughts, not things they are being told by an entity.

Even a passing comment by a stranger or an awkward encounter can affect your energy. The encounter itself wouldn't necessarily leave you open to spiritual attack, it's how your energy is affected afterward.

Before getting into the details of cleansing rituals, one thing you need to know is: cleansing and protection go hand in hand when it comes to magick. After every cleansing ritual you do, always protect.

For these rituals, you can use many Psalms, but a few I'll call out are Psalms 10, 19, 22, and 74.

Before protection, you may want to bless your space and yourself as well. Some say to bless after cleansing, but I would recommend blessing after protection.

The choice of when (or if) you bless is optional. Cleansing and protection are not.

Q: What about being hexed or cursed?

Usually, more serious cases do not happen out of nowhere. If you've invited or engaged with negative entities in any way, often they will hang around as they've been 'invited'. You can unknowingly have an entity attached to you, but these things do not happen without some kind of request from you.

Just as you would take showers regularly, the aura and energy in yourself and your home must be cleansed and protected with similar regularity.

Often *thinking* you are hexed or cursed *is* the curse.

In this state of thinking, any issue in a person's life can be a potential symptom of a curse, instead of regular life. Not only that, being overly concerned about whether or not someone has hexed you will put you in a state of being afraid, angry, and suspicious. In other words, just thinking you're hexed can put you in a personal state of hell.

Even if someone has cursed you, by getting worked up about it you are falling into the hex that was set. You create a mental condition that can be as difficult to remedy as an actual curse.

If no one has cursed you, then you've effectively cursed yourself. The best (and only) remedy for this is to live the happiest, most joy-filled life possible. No one can do anything to you that you don't allow, so do not worry about it.

Q: How do I know when my energy has been affected?

This requires some level of awareness. You need to know what your energy is like on a regular basis. Once you know who you are, it's easier to pick up on changes in your energy.

These unexplained changes are one clue that your energy has been affected and that it might be time for a deeper cleansing. Prolonged periods of emotional unrest are very common in the western world, to the point where many of us, unfortunately, believe it is normal to be hateful or cynical.

Peace and serenity are your natural state.

Any time you do not feel peace or serenity, your energy has been affected. Even if the reason you are affected emotionally is justified, your energy is still affected. This is one of the reasons many people will take extra good care of themselves whenever they're going through something troubling.

The short answer is: You'll know if your energy has been affected if you *feel* like your energy has been affected. The only way to know this is by bringing yourself to a calm and serene state. If you can't do this, that is one clue.

Cleansing Rituals and Spirit Washes

Being in a state of anger creates more anger. We all know someone who is just an angry person.

They always seem to be angry about the same things, or just angry wherever they go. This energy is a spirit. When something happens that annoys you, carrying anger with you afterward leaves you open to this spirit, and then vulnerable to all kinds of entities as your defenses are lowered.

In this section, we'll discuss the washes and methods that can be used to keep your aura and energy cleansed and protected.

Spiritually Cleansing the Home

Regularly cleaning your home isn't just about dusting and mopping. This is a ritual that many people do every weekend without thinking about the spiritual effects, beyond how it feels to have a clean space afterward.

As a regular practice you want to keep your home clear of clutter. If you already have some clutter in your home, this might seem like a daunting task, but it is a necessary one. You can start by taking this one step at a time.

Go through each room and make a pile of things you haven't used for at least a year, and then get rid of it.

Once you've cleaned your home of clutter, you can start on your first house cleaning. It doesn't matter if you've just moved in or have lived in the space for ten years.

A traditional hoodoo cleansing of the home starts in the uppermost corner, furthest away from the door. The walls are cleansed and washed first, and then the floor in each room.

For your wall and floors, you'll want to use a mixture made specifically to spiritually cleanse your home, such as a Chinese Wash (also called a Chinese Floor Wash).

This can be purchased at most hoodoo shops and can be diluted with some water. It does not need to be rinsed away, like a typical floor cleanser.

If you do buy anything from a curio shop that sells waters, consider putting 'you' into it, your saliva, blood, or nails.

When doing this type of cleaning, you want to use new, or clean rags, mops, and cleaning supplies.

While cleaning you want to pray over your space. This can come from your heart or you can recite a prayer specifically for purification and cleansing.

While going through your home you want to continuously state your intention by asking God to remove the negativity from your home. As you throw out and refill the warm water, state that negativity is permanently leaving your home now.

After cleaning each room, you can go straight to a protection prayer or ritual, or bless the space first. Blessing is moving through your home, in the same order that it was cleansed, and inviting love, peace, serenity, and any other good vibrations you want in. You can also sprinkle House Blessing oil as you go around to each room.

While you're blessing the home, you can also ask that *God and your guides lend their power to protecting your space*. However, most protection takes the form of having items in your home with the purpose of keeping negative energies away.

For Home Protection

There are countless ways you can protect your home and space, some more obvious than others. Really this is about helping you to *feel* protected, so if one method doesn't help you to feel protected in your home, try another one until the energy is right.

You can, of course, recite another Psalm specifically for protection: 14, 24, 29, 64, or 101.

After reciting the Psalm, you would make a statement of intention. Something that says the space is now protected from harmful entities and negative energy.

Another method of protecting your space is using a spray. Florida water is perhaps the simplest and easiest form of spiritual protection for your home. You can create your own spray using Holy Water, if you're able to access or purchase it.

If Holy Water isn't available to you, or you'd prefer to create your own cleansing spray, you can make one with some water (you can convert it to holy water from home, if you want) and some common ingredients from your kitchen.

Salt is one of these ingredients. The reason practitioners love it so much is because salt can do anything. Salt is like the clear quartz of your spice rack. Try a mix of consecrated salt and basil with water to create a home protection spray.

Dried herbs are great for protecting your home. You can hang an herb like basil to dry, and at the same time use it for keeping unwanted energies out of your space. You can also hang satchels of already dried herbs, like hyssop.

There are a number of items you can have in the home that will serve to protect your place. First: your plants! Specifically, cacti, orchids, ferns, snake plants, and ivy.

Chances are you probably have one of these in the home already. You can actually watch your plant as it grows and changes over the seasons. Start talking to your plants and share with them that you'd like their help in protecting where you all live.

If you are open to keeping a flame burning while you are at home, you can use the fire as a way to protect your space. Speak over the flame your intention and offer gratitude.

As an added boost of protection, you can place some crystals around the candle, such as black obsidian. Himalayan salt candle holders are widely available, and excellent for this purpose.

As mentioned, salt is all-purpose. Pink salt, specifically, is beneficial for filling your space with loving vibrations. It's also great for bringing prosperity to you.

In addition, the most powerful protector of your space is you. It is easy to overdo it when it comes to protection, which then underestimates your faith and the same power available to you.

When I mentioned above that you need to feel protected in your space, this isn't about using a spray or keeping a row of cacti on your windowsill. You decide if you feel protected or not, not the things you have in your home or the Florida Water you spray around. Feeling protected is a choice, do what you can to choose it. All of these methods are supposed to help you feel that.

Regular Cleaning and Protecting

Cleansing and protection need to happen regularly. There are many different methods for each. One of the most popular includes using fire and smoke.

This is a very popular way to cleanse your space. If you've ever burned sage, you're already familiar with how to do this. Usually, dried sage is burned loose inside of something called an abalone shell and wafted around using a large feather.

These leaves will often be available as a bundle, which makes it easier to carry around and wave around your space. You don't have to use a sage bundle for cleansing, however. You can make your own bundles for cleansing your space using pine or herbs.

Incense can be used to do both cleaning and protecting, as long as you use it with the right intention. There are lots of different types of incense, but as long as you get a high-quality one that was made for what you need, you will be covered.

Resins like Frankincense and Myrrh are very popular for this purpose. These are burned on a charcoal disc, a round, black stone-looking thing that just needs a little fire to be lit. Usually, these are available in esoteric shops, or any place where you find incense.

Spiritually Cleansing the Body

It is very easy to carry negative energy with you in our current climate. As warped as it may sound, us living in the west are almost rewarded for living in fear, or by keeping our light hidden.

Many of the communities that make up life in our world are created around negativity; racism, homophobia, misogyny, misandry, transphobia, fatphobia, the list goes on. The truth is, in many cases these types of negative mindsets impact the people who think in these ways more than they affect the identified community.

This isn't all of it, there are seemingly a countless number of ways that your energy can be attacked. Mercury being in retrograde, for one.

Hoodoo Baths

If you were to see an experienced hoodoo practitioner, one of the first things they will most likely recommend to you (especially if you're not on a personal spiritual path) is a bath, but not the kind that we commonly see in commercials and on Instagram.

This kind of bath will usually involve collecting the tools and herbs we've discussed in the previous section. You may be asked to create a mixture with the intent of clearing your aura. If you're new to spiritual practices such as cleansing and protection, your spiritual body will be heavy *stuff* or baggage collected over your lifetime.

A mixture for cleansing will usually involve collecting a combination of roots like hyssop and rue, and Florida Water. There are mixtures (or 'dressings') that can be created for love, peace, healing, abundance, etc. They are often stirred around with each other, or literally cooked on a stove with prayers and petitions.

If you do have any allergies, test the ingredients on your skin individually prior to making the dressing and using it for a bath. The practitioner you're seeing will have more direction for you on this, depending on the working.

Once made, this dressing is usually rubbed on the body or put into a bath prepared for yourself. In the bath, you rub the roots and everything all over your body, into your skin and hair. Afterward, you'll most likely be instructed to keep the roots on your body as you air dry.

Baths like these can also be done outside, in a backyard for example if you are blessed enough to have access to one, or a space where you can be outside and have some privacy. In this case, you might take some of the mixture and rub it into your body, going from your toes to your head.

You might be tempted to get into the shower right away to rinse the debris off of you as in a typical bath or shower. It's important to follow the instructions of the practitioner you've hired exactly. It might feel awkward to have bits of rose petals in your nooks and crannies, but there's work happening. That's the important thing.

Will this make a mess? Yes. Will you get results? Definitely.

Hoodoo... Showers?

If you're not comfortable with the idea of a bath, a shower can be just as effective. Though, this isn't what's generally recommended in hoodoo, since with traditional baths, you're expected to really immerse yourself into the water with the prescribed ingredients you're using.

A shower version of a hoodoo bath can take place outside, as described above, or in your shower by just rubbing yourself down with the dressing. You would do the same thing as in a bath, just with a shower instead.

But your regular showers can serve double duty. Letting water run down your body isn't just an amazing experience, it can also take all of the things that you have collected and impacted your aura and wash them down the drain. You just have to speak it and make that intention known.

As with your home, after cleansing, you want to protect (and bless). Your form of protection may be using a lotion with an essential oil, like Frankincense. Blessing could be just anointing yourself with the oil by placing it on pressure points.

You'll also want to say a prayer or Psalms while you're blessing and protecting, a separate prayer for each, and then closing your blessing and protection with a statement of intention.

This is something that can be highly personal to you and your beliefs. If you're not sure how to do this or what to say at first, Psalms 23 is always a good option. You could also try: Psalms 19, 21, 24, 46, 65, 95, or 122.

You could also speak words over yourself. Remind yourself of your strength and power, your commitment to your path, or following inner guidance.

You might even be interested in my bother book called: "Prayers and Protection Magick to Destroy Witchcraft; Banish Curses, Negative Energy & Psychic Attacks; Break Spells, Evil Soul Ties & Covenants; Protect & Release Favors" -- as this book will give you many prayer options to recite and to add to your practice. You can find it at https://www.amazon.com/dp/B096W6J97R

For a deeper spiritual cleanse, you can use a number of common household items. Just like you can use salt to protect your home, you can use it for your body.

Mix some table or sea salt with coconut oil (though this can clog your drain, so be aware) for an in-shower scrub. Not only will you be able to get an exfoliation, a massage, and soft skin, but your energy will be clear. State your intention as you scrub and the dirt washes down the drain.

Soap

Many of the hoodoo oils you can find are also available as soaps, but there are some that are specific to the practice that are worth mentioning.

Sulfur soap is one example. If you're in need of a deep cleansing of negativity, washing with this soap every day will help. As with any product used on your skin, you'll want to test on a small section of your skin first.

Body Oil

There are many hoodoo oils created specifically to use on the body. These could be blessing oil, cut & clear, or psychic cleansing. These aren't the only oils you can use on your body, however. There are oils created specifically to attract love, abundance, good sex; almost anything you can think of.

You can use these oils to anoint yourself or add them to the washes and lotions you already use.

Body Powders

Some retailers offer hoodoo powders that can also be used in various ways. In most cases, these powders are used to hex someone else, by placing the powder in the path of the target.

However, you can find cleansing powders made from herbs that have been consecrated and prayed over. These powders can then be used as part of your cleansing rituals, so for example, you can use them to dress your candles. You can also add them to a mojo bag or add some onto a paper you've written a petition on.

Sweet Waters

As the name suggests, these waters can help to add some sweetness to your life or any of the situations that you want worked on.

These are made by using sweet substances, most often sweet herbs, sugar, and honey, but most ingredients with some sweetness will do, and of course the key ingredient: water. Baths with a sweet water can also typically include other ingredients like rose petals and holy water.

You'll most often find these used in spiritual baths, but they can also be used as offerings in rituals.

On the other hand, sour waters are made with sour ingredients such as vinegar and ammonia.

Fragrant Waters

These types of waters get their power from being used and *worked* with for many, many years. This means that many spirits have used and interacted with these waters before us, so by using them we create an association that spirits are familiar with.

These are also a common ingredient in baths, but you can also use them as a spray to cleanse and protect your aura or space.

Although Florida Water is a cologne, it is also considered a fragrant water. Other waters in this category include: Angel Water (also known as Portugal Water), Kananga Water, Rose Water.

Some of these types of waters are easy to make; you can also make substitutions. Rose Water is made using rose petals and enough distilled water to cover the petals (it's fine if some of them stay at the top of the water).

This combination is then boiled for about half an hour, and then strained to remove the petals.

If you don't have rose petals, you can use this same recipe to make other waters at home, such as lavender. If you don't have petals of any kind, an essential oil will do just fine, though be sure to use distilled water. Keep your homemade fragrant waters in the refrigerator.

Cleaning with Eggs and Crystals

A common method for cleaning in hoodoo is by using an egg, the same kind you might eat for breakfast. One egg is taken and rolled over the body. As this happens, it's said that the egg will absorb any negative energy. This can be done by going from the top of your head down to your feet.

Once this is complete, you can break the egg and flush it down a toilet. The egg would then have negative energy, and you don't want to keep those vibes hanging around.

Some crystals can be used in a way that is similar to the egg, but once cleansing is finished, your crystal needs to be cleared of the energy it absorbed. We'll go over this in Part III, Eradication and Getting Professional Help.

For Body Protection

Here's where you may want to carry a mojo bag, but as with home protection, there are *many* tactics you can use to protect yourself and your aura.

The simplest way to protect yourself, especially when you're out in public, is by carrying crystals. Many retailers on Etsy sell crystals as necklaces and bracelets. For most people, these pieces are sufficient for any and every situation.

If keeping crystals isn't your thing, try using a bay leaf. Charge it by praying to the leaf and asking for protection and carrying it on you.

Prayers are very effective in protecting your energy. Say one while you're at home in the same way you would bless yourself. You can also use protective prayers and mantras as you're out or whenever you feel like you need extra protection.

Repeating verses from Psalms can work for this, or by saying something like: *I claim divine protection as my birthright. I am now balanced and centered.*

On Knowing You Are Protected

In the same way that you have to claim protection over your home, you have to claim protection over yourself. Thinking that you are 'vulnerable' and 'in need of protection' will lead you to being vulnerable and in need of protection.

It can be difficult to trust that you are protected at first, because it doesn't feel like it should be that easy; to be protected by just claiming that you are protected. This goes back to your faith in God, and, by extension, your faith in yourself, the power of your word.

Things can always happen to you physically. This is just a fact of being human; our bodies are 3D and thereby frail. Your job, and my job, *our* job is to correctly identify who we are and what we are. What we are not, is these frail, itchy bodies.

You may have heard this line before, but it bears repeating: we are spiritual bodies in a physical experience. If you've never taken the time to think about what this means, consider this the moment.

You can cast spells for physical protection, but if you're not in a situation where there is immediate danger, I encourage you to not worry about the potential ways you can be physically hurt in the world.

It is *very* easy to undermine your own power when it comes to the concept of protection, especially of the body. Let's take two people who say in their morning prayer: *I claim divine protection over my mind, body, and spirit now.*

The first person says the statement and then charges a crystal necklace with those words and anoints their mojo bag. Throughout the day they repeat the statement and touch their mojo bag whenever they feel threatened. They touch the bag when it looks like a stranger is getting close to them, and in their car on the way to work.

At the end of the day, they may realize they were safe and protected, nothing happened that actually put them in danger, but then in their mind they negate that thought by thinking something could happen tomorrow and making a statement to themselves that sounds like "people are crazy".

The other person says that statement, takes a moment to actually claim it, and then goes about their day never thinking or wondering if they're protected. Their day looks a lot like the first person, but they know they are protected even when a barking dog rushes towards them on an afternoon walk.

To be clear: I am *not* saying one approach is "right" and one is "wrong". Both approaches are "right". The first person is doing amazing work to help themselves *feel* protected. This work must be recognized. Eventually, if they keep their practices up, they will have less of a need for them and may come to some awareness about how their own thoughts are creating their reality.

My point with this example is to demonstrate what it can look like when a person tells themselves one thing but contradicts that with their actions. The person who tells themselves they are protected but then throughout a day feels they need protection especially where there is no real "danger", proves to themselves the opposite. They prove to themselves that they are *not* protected.

Likewise, the person who says *I am protected* and then behaves as such is training themselves to believe their own word. They effectively are protected simply because they claim that for themselves as truth.

What we're talking about here is the power of your tongue. As Proverbs 18:21 says: *The tongue has the power of life and death*. If you're trying to create a condition in your experience, you are trying to bring something 'to life'.

You might be trying to bring love into your life, or more money, or luck ahead of a game. On the other hand, there are probably conditions in your life that you are trying to wipe away or banish. If you want love, the thing you want to banish might be loneliness.

This verse from Proverbs means that the words you use can either make these things happen or leave you in a life where you're constantly searching for what you want. The person who believes themselves when they say *I am divinely protected* has brought protection to life in their experience using their words.

The person who says they are divinely protected, but then says things in contradiction with that statement, brings to life a conflicted experience. They feel protected when they pray or touch their mojo bag, but then they say something to themselves that causes them to feel vulnerable (like "people are crazy").

I see this often with new practitioners who have been victims of physical abuse or violence. Growing up in a violent household can leave us scarred for life, and constantly worrying about when the next attack is going to come is one of the ways these scars can show up.

This worrying, as we've covered, is another spell--a curse, specifically, one that you can cast on yourself.

This is one of the reasons self-love and self-respect are so important. You have to love yourself enough to not tolerate any self-bullying.

Your spiritual practice and hoodoo can help you to heal these scars. You do have to be willing to give up the pain. It is hard work, but it's harder to live in fear and pain, in my opinion. So, if you're going to have a difficult time, why not just put your effort towards believing in your own power?

Chance is a natural part of the human experience. At the same time, it *is* natural for you to be at peace, healthy, and wealthy at all times. You can claim protection just by claiming your birthright as a peaceful, healthy, and prosperous human being.

Staying Protected

Connect with your divinity now. Say to yourself: *I connect with my higher self and divine spirit now*, and then give yourself a few moments to actually connect.

Then check in with how you feel.

Do you feel like you need protection in this state? If the answer is yes, then you know that protection is yours without needing anything else. The crystals and mojo you use to that end are to *help* you maintain this feeling.

You feeling protected is the key ingredient here. Without this, nothing you buy or create will work for you. If you can imagine that you're not safe, you can also imagine that the powerful tools at your disposal can't or won't work.

From that you have created a curse on yourself, and if you're constantly in fear or anger. One of the ways this 'self-curse' can show up in your life is through sickness or illness. At the very least, claiming protection as your birthright protects you from the assault on your immune system that can result from a fear-based idea or thoughtform.

Fires, Candles, and Incense Rites

Fire is cleansing. It has the power to shed light on everything and burn it all away-the good and the bad. Which means handling fire requires extra care. There are multiple ways you can use fires and candles in your daily practice.

You can simply talk to a candle. If there's anything that is troubling you or heavy on your mind, go to your altar and just make a practice of talking to the candle. Bring any problems or issues you have to the flame and then when you leave, imagine your problem has been burned away.

Don't forget to express your gratitude to the spirit of the fire.

Fire can also be used to protect, if used carefully.

A rite, in hoodoo, is a simple practice that is not quite a spell and not quite a ritual. It can be done every day, once over a week, or any other regular interval. An example of a simple fire rite is burning cloves in your home to remove your space of negative or harmful energies.

Rites are also often accompanied by a repeated prayer or affirmation.

Smoke cleansing is very popular in many Indigenous cultures around the world. Smoke was also used to summon spirits and to heighten the energy in a space.

This is taking the herbs or leaves that you are burning and lighting them in a heatproof dish. Many practitioners use an abalone shell, but any heat-resistant dish will do, but it has to be one that you can carry if you're going to smudge an area with different rooms, like your home.

Walk around with the smoking leaves and incense and use a feather to gently waft the smoke around the area.

As you're doing this, you can recite a Psalms or state what you want. This might sound something like: *I invite God's light into this space right now. Cleanse this space of any negative entities or energies.*

You can continue going back and forth in the space until whatever your burning has gone out, or until you feel like the space is cleared. Your intuition will tell you when this is.

We're a little more accustomed to using fire as a form of magick in everyday life. This is what it means to blow out candles on a birthday cake! But we also light candles to change the energy in a space, such as creating a romantic environment on Valentine's Day.

Another simple rite is lighting a candle, possibly one dressed with an oil and some herbs, and reciting a blessing as the light burns. To 'bless' something can be simply saying that you bless the item or substance you're using.

To bless a candle, you could cleanse it first, and then say over it: *I bless this candle by my own power.* You can also recite Psalms 23 over the dressed candle. It really can be this simple.

Going back to the power of your word, your breath also has power. This is why many practitioners do not blow candles out, particularly for magick used to bring things to you.

With magick to rid yourself of things or to cleanse, it's fine to blow out a candle as this can represent putting out the condition in your life.

You can pull into yourself fire energy. Some spiritual practices believe that every human has fire within them, represented by our ability to will ourselves to make things happen.

A safety tip. If you're doing a spell that requires burning anything and keeping the ashes, most practitioners use a cauldron, but if you don't have one, you can use tin foil. Just set the foil down on top of whatever plate or dish you're using and keep the fire burning on top. This gives you an easy way to collect ashes.

For Spell Casting

Before you can cast an authentic spell, there are a few concepts that we need to cover. First, spells are everywhere. Many practitioners consider the bible itself to be a spellbook.

Mantras are spells, as are the songs we listen to or music videos we watch. In this broader context there isn't really a process for casting a spell; they happen all of the time and often without our knowledge.

It's when you want to cast a spell with intention and with the help of Spirit that the work we've discussed gets involved. In previous chapters, we've mentioned bits and pieces of the process. Here's where we put it all together.

Living a Magickal Life: Before You Begin

You have to have the right energy. In Part One I described a worker who started clearing out their space even before they casted a spell. I'm going to continue with this example to describe how you want to create an energetic environment that will make your space conducive to doing work.

Getting rid of clutter is one way you can do this in your home (since this is where most work happens).

You want to make both your physical and your spiritual environments as clear as possible before casting a spell. This is why many workers do activities (rites and rituals) on a daily basis that keep them aligned, their space clear, and their connection with spirit strong.

I can't really prescribe what this will look like for you, your daily practice will be dictated by your relationship with spirit.

Your practice could involve elements of hoodoo and other magickal practices. This could look like exercising and meditating daily, speaking to your ancestors and speaking to the roots, and keeping a careful watch of your plants. You may sage your apartment or spray around a homemade cleansing water every week. Once in a while you might incorporate regular visits to a cemetery near your home where you leave coins at the gate. This is just an example.

The point is living a magickal life means that when it comes time to work, you're not completely starting from scratch. You will have started and built a strong relationship with Spirit and with your ancestors already, *before* you start your spell.

Pro Tip: Turn on the music! Your favorite music is an *excellent* way to build the right energy in your space before casting a spell. Anything that helps you to feel like your spirit is lifted and keeps your vibration high.

This is all about your preference. Music with lyrics might be distracting, or they could help you. Put together a playlist before starting your next spell.

What are you Saying?

Another thing you may want to prepare prior to starting your spell is knowing exactly what you're going to say, especially if you don't feel confident making prayers and statements of edification to spirit.

It's completely normal to feel nervous, but you also have to remember that *you* are a spiritual being as well.

The energies you are calling in are Spirit. They already know they are being called in to help you. Spirit is always with you. Breathe, get yourself to a calm and centered state, and remember your intention.

You won't completely ruin everything if you forget to do something or stumble on your words. Remember: Spirit understands *your intent*, first and foremost.

The Phases of a Spell

Most work happens in a sequence of phases. Generally, you open a spiritual channel, welcome the spirits that will help you, and communicate with them while working with your tools.

Keep in mind: each practice has a different way to complete each phase. Another practitioner might start with a smudge to cleanse their space and then use a wand to cast a circle. This circle is used to protect themselves as they open the energy to the spirit dimension.

After this, they will call the spirits from the four directions. This is one example of a common way spells are cast amongst witches in the Wicca tradition.

Phase #1: Incense, light, and water. Your first step in casting a spell is lighting a candle and having an offering, such as a glass of water, with you in your working space. This is so that when you call the spirits you're working with, they can see their way to you and are welcomed with your offering.

Before your spell, you may also want to consider using incense (in addition to the candle) to invite spirit into your space. More on this later.

In some types of spells, you want to use a candle of a specific color. Protection spells, for example, often call for black candles. Some of the spells below indicate what color of candle you will want to use.

Phase #2: Offering. Give something to the spirits you're inviting to help you with the work. As discussed in previous sections, this could be a song you sing, cigar smoke, incense smoke, etc.

Phase #3: The four directions. All magick honors north, south, east, and west in some way. These directions are also associated with the elements; earth, fire, wind, and water, respectively.

It is expected that before your work begins, you 'present' the herbs you are working with to the four directions. This will look like taking the ingredients in your hands and holding them up towards each direction with focus and intention.

For this phase, you might want to have a special dish you use specifically for herbs and roots. Otherwise, you can put some of the ingredients in your hand.

Phase #4: Your intention and prayers. This is where you pray over the herbs and say what it is you want for the work. In hoodoo, the bible is almost exclusively used for this.

At first you might want to start with the Psalms, but there are many chapters and books of the bible that can be used as prayers. You also want to speak from your heart, ensuring that you acknowledge the spirits involved and your ancestors.

Here's what this might sound like for a prosperity working. *Thank you, ancestors! Thank you for being here as I set out to do this work. I am ready to embrace prosperity in my life in all forms. I know that you are here with me, that I do this standing on the foundation you have laid before me. And with the power and strength you've given me, I ask that the spirit contained in these roots come to my aid. This work is to give life to financial blessings, success, money, new clients who pay on time, and are happy to do so. To the spirits of these roots: let it be so.*

Key Considerations. There is a time and a season for everything, magick included. Casting a spell requires a bit of planning.

- *Time of the month*. Spells for drawing something to you should be done during the waxing moon phase, usually a couple days after the new moon and a couple days before the full moon. A couple days after the full moon you can do banishing magic; any magick with the intent of ridding your life of some condition.

- *Day of the week*. Whether or not this is as important as time of the month is up for debate, but each day of the week is ruled by an energy and a spirit.

- *Time of day*. You don't have to get down to the hour and minute, but there are certain 'magickal' times of day.

- *Your notes*. Keep a note of all of the above considerations, plus the ingredients you use (you can copy from this book, but likely you'll have substitutions) and anything you felt before, during, and after the spell. This can be in the same notebook you use to keep track of your roots and herbs supply.

For each of the spells in this section, you will gather the herbs and ingredients listed and plan out when to do the working based on the key considerations. Give yourself enough time to gather everything and consecrate what you're using.

Spells for Keeping the Peace

There are many situations where you may need extra help with maintaining peace, either within yourself or your home. Just thinking of our current climate will probably provide you with a long list.

Before gathering your ingredients and writing your petition, it is important to know why the spell is necessary. With technology taking over more and more aspects of our lives, it seems stress and anxiety have risen exponentially.

I'm not going to get into the how's and why's too much, but in short, most of the apps and services we use on our phones are designed to make us feel like if we're not staring at the screen, we're missing out on something.

Many people are dealing with illnesses of all kinds. We know that stress and anxiety can either make you sick or worsen your health. In this case, keeping the peace can then have a direct effect on your health and your wealth.

While you might not feel the stress and anxiety of living in these modern times, or your health may be in check, the people you live with could be susceptible to any of these pressures. This will affect you and the energy in your space.

Often in homes where there are regular disturbances, in the form of abuse or addiction, there are *many* problems. The larger issue will trigger a domino effect, one that you can protect yourself against with the right perspective, and a little magick.

After your work is complete, you can do your best to know that peace is yours, regardless of what's going on around you. If you do your work and then continue to worry about whatever your situation, you are not practicing faith.

Continuing to feel anxiety or entertain thoughts of worry will not only reverse your work, but it will also lead you to cast another spell, then another, then another.

Once you cast your spell for peace, know that it *worked*.

Following your spell, you may find it helpful to use rituals with the intention of maintaining peace in your space. This is where you can use prayers, incense, essential oils like tea tree, or crystals. Below you'll find some waters, dirt, and minerals that are helpful to bring peace wherever you go.

For Home: A Candle Spell

This simple candle spell is designed to keep peace in your home. You will need:

1. A white or blue candle.

2. A candle holder or plate that will hold the candle as it burns.

3. House Blessing oil (you can use olive oil as a substitute, just be sure to consecrate it first).

4. Choose what you can from the following (use what you have on hand): basil, cilantro, coffee, coriander, or rosemary.

5. Rose or lavender petals.

6. A plate for the herbs and petals.

7. A plain piece of paper to write a peace petition on.

Instructions

Arrange the herbs and petals on the plate, with the candle and oil (still in the bottle). Pray over everything and consecrate using Psalms.

Write your petition down on the paper. While writing, imagine that the protection you are requesting is already done. Include all the names of the people in your household, if applicable, or your name.

If the paper is large and needs to be folded or ripped, do this action *towards* yourself. This is to signify drawing the protection energy towards you. (Conversely, if you are using a petition for a banishing spell, you would rip or fold away from you.)

Dress the candle with the oil, while instructing it what you want to do. Feel the energy flow through your hands and into the wax as you chant. Once the candle is dressed with oil, place it in its holder.

Dress the candle with the herbs and petals, again chanting and providing direction. Light the candle seeing your spell come to life.

Leave the candle burning for as long as possible. If you have to leave the candle unattended, snuff it out. Never blow it out (blowing out a candle is better for banishing magick).

For Your Space: A Knot Spell

The first at-home spell is fine if you live in a home where others know what you do and you can work without judgment or disturbances.

In other words, your whole home may be a safe space for you to practice magick. *Many* of the talented and powerful practitioners I know started their practice as teenagers, in homes where their parents or guardians were not supportive of their practice, if not downright hostile.

If you have at least a private space where you can practice, you can build the energy of peace within; a type of field that is protective and where you are in control.

Keep in mind that all of the materials used are there to represent spirit. In your private space, you can connect with any spirit without needing a physical root or seed.

This will require you to build some of your powers, like visualization. Some practitioners I've spoken to who used magick in tough situations consider their time in difficulty a gift for this reason. It forced them to become adept at their magick without relying on anything but their ancestors and guides.

Taking care of yourself and building your personal magickal power becomes even more important in this case. The more peace you can feel *before* doing the spell, the more effective it will be.

Of course, one of the best tools you can use in this situation would be a bible, if you have one. If you don't have one, you can find any book and chapter you need free online.

For this spell I'm going to assume you don't want anything that involves fire, smoke, or produces an odor. Do not think that these conditions mean you're limited in any way. With just a few roots and herbs, you can still do workings like mojo bags and spell jars. You can also use string for knot magic, which is the spell I'm going to describe below.

This spell is about 'tying' yourself and your space to the spirit of peace.

You will need:

1. String in a 'peace' color (see candle options above) or any type of string that is strong enough to withstand being tied into knots (i.e. not sewing thread). Twine is an excellent, neutral option.

2. Your petition and statements.

Instructions

Cut your string long enough so you can tie nine knots, and then double this over so you have one end that is a loop.

This spell is really about item #2. You want to have your intention so clear in your mind, that when speaking freely your words match up with what you want. This spell is about solidifying what you want as your hands tie each knot.

Tie three knots, close together making your statements. Then three more, and then the last three doing the same.

Your petition does not have to be the same for each knot. For example, for the first knot in this spell you may say something as simple as: *Peace now for me and my space*. The second knot: *Serenity now for me and my space*. The third: *Inner stillness for me and my space*.

If you need to be even quieter, you can say these in your mind, pray or meditate on what you want.

After your first nine knots are tied, continue to make ties until your string becomes a ball of ties. This is an optional step, but if your knots are broken or untied for any reason, that is in effect undoing the spell.

This means that if your string breaks, you will have to start again. This is why you'll double up the string before starting the spell; to better protect from breaking the string.

For Work: A Jar Spell

With more of us working from home than ever before, you may think a spell for peace in the home is enough to create peace in your work environment. For many people, the workplace and the home remain separate, and even if you do work from home, we know how important boundaries are.

In either case, a spell to encourage peace in the workplace may be necessary because of your manager or co-workers.

This spell is designed to be contained inside of a small, glass jar. You can use the same herbs and ingredients as I listed in the spell for your home. Aside from that, will need:

1. A glass jar small enough to keep at work or in the office.

2. A candle, keeping color correspondences in mind.

3. Seashells.

4. Sugar, brown or white will work fine.

5. Juniper berries.

6. Lavender essential oil.

If you have someone at the workplace who is particularly difficult to deal with, add a conjure oil to the recipe. You could include a Clarity, Stop Gossip, or Tranquility oil as part of your jar, but keep in mind how long you intend to keep the work for.

Jars can be used to improve a condition over a long or short period of time. With the wrong oil or ingredient, you could end up doing magick that could create unwanted results over time. Usually, this warning would be for any type of banishing magick. Keep the intention here clear: for peace in the workplace.

Instructions

Go through the four phases of your spell with your materials and ingredients. Once you're ready to put your jar together, charge each item before putting it inside by using your words and breath. Breathe your intention into each item and be specific about why you're adding it to your jar.

For example, for the seashell you might say: *Bring peace and tranquility to this spell, and to this work now and in perpetuity.*

Once you've finished adding all of your items, speak your intention into the jar one last time before closing it. Depending on the size of the jar, you can burn the candle on top of it or on a plate nearby.

If you're using one of the 4-inch candles that are common in magickal practice, you can stick it to the top of your jar by melting some of the wax on the bottom and holding it in place until the wax hardens.

Light the candle and let it burn out on top of the jar. You can also burn some of the wax around the lid of the jar to 'seal' it, but this is up to you.

Once you've made the jar, you have to 'work' the magick to keep the energy going. There are many ways to do this, but the simplest is to shake the jar while repeating your petition. It doesn't have to be the same one you used while creating the work; it can be whatever speaks to the intent.

Peace Rituals: Using Waters

Following your candle spell, an excellent way to maintain the peace in your home is by using waters. These can be sprinkled around your home, room to room in a clockwise manner. Start in the room furthest from the door and start by standing towards the west.

As you sprinkle, use your voice to ask the waters for what you want. You can say something like: *I invite peace and serenity in this space now*. Or just repeat words to conjure what you want, such as: *peace, serenity, love, harmony*.

With any rite, you want to feel gratitude and the peace that you want in your environment within yourself. Express gratitude to your ancestors and the spirit of the waters for responding to your requests.

Peace Water is perhaps the most obvious for this purpose. This, as well as all of the waters listed here, can be placed in spray bottles for a convenient peace spritz whenever you need it.

This type of water is great for calming the energy in your home down after chaos or following the visit from anyone suffering from an illness.

If you'd prefer a water that has more varied properties, you really cannot go wrong with **Florida Water**. It is so popular across many magickal traditions that you can now find it at some retailers as soap or hand sanitizer.

Gardenias Cologne. Can be used in a way similar to Peace Water, described above.

Lavender Cologne. Excellent if you're in a marriage or love relationship with someone you live with.

Cold Water. The type that comes out of a tap. Using a bowl of cold water, you can sprinkle *coolness* and *calmness* around your home or your workspace. This option works best if you are sensitive to smells, or live or work around others who are also sensitive.

Peace Rituals: Using Dirt and Minerals

I mentioned using **dirt from a church** in a mojo bag for love, but this can also be used to bring peace to your home or place of work (if these two spaces aren't one and the same).

Chalk or **Cascarilla** (pronounced kaws-kuh-ree-uh). An inexpensive powder made of eggshells that can be added to workings or sprinkled around a space.

Peace Powder. Sometimes this is the same as Cascarilla, but you can also find botanicals that make unique blends. For use in the home or at work.

Spells for Attraction, Love, and Relationships

Attraction, love, relationships, sex, and marriage are among the top reasons people either figure out how to do a spell on their own or hire a conjurer. If you've gone down either of these paths and what you wanted to happen didn't, it can be an incredibly frustrating experience.

The difficulty here is that often this magick is about controlling someone else's behavior. This is where it can become dangerous to have our minds set so fixedly on someone else, that we lose sight of the one truth of being human: that we all have free will.

However, love hoodoo is best used in situations where the emotions and love are there, but just need some assistance. Trying to cast a spell on someone who has never even looked your way only sets your work up for a very likely failure.

The same goes for spells cast on someone or for a situation where another person has not expressed any interest, or they've said they are not interested at all. Of course, it is possible to continue casting spells until your intended changes their mind, but these types of stories rarely end well.

It's for this reason that you want to cast a love spell with your first eye open. Are you using the spell to draw a specific person to you? And if so, is there a difference between the love you are fantasizing about and what it would be like in real life?

But in the case that you already have someone in your life that you are deeply in love with, hoodoo is excellent for strengthening that relationship and making it even stronger.

For Heating up Your Love Life: An Apple Spell

Apples are very common in love spells in hoodoo and some European magickal traditions. This spell is to heat up a relationship and add some passion to your love.

It is meant to draw these things to your relationship, and so I would recommend doing it during a waxing moon phase (after the new moon, before the full moon).

You will need:

1. An apple, fresh. Choose one that can stand evenly. You'll be putting the candle into the apple and you don't want to risk it tipping over.

2. A four-inch candle.

3. Coriander seeds.

4. Ginger root.

5. Marjoram.

6. Rose petals.

7. Sugar.

8. Love Me or a Marriage conjure oil.

9. A magnet.

10. Magnetic sand.

11. A photo of you and your partner.

12. A plate.

13. A bowl filled with holy or consecrated water.

You can use substitutions for many of the ingredients. Lavender petals can work instead of rose petals, but you want to know what each type of flower will bring to your work (meaning, what kind of results you can expect using one flower in substitution for another). Try to get fresh flowers.

Instructions

Keep the photo of you and your partner nearby, preferably somewhere you can see it while you're doing the following steps.

Stick the candle in at the top and press down just enough so it sticks out of the apple. Start your spell by speaking to the apple. Turn it clockwise while speaking your intention and desires into its skin and essence. Imagine your words going right into the seeds of the apple.

Place the apple in the middle of the plate. Anoint it with your hoodoo oil, again being sure to say what the work is for and what it is that you want. Next, place the magnet beside the apple on a side nearest to you. Sprinkle the magnetic sand on top. Now it's ready to be dressed.

Dress the apple by laying the coriander seeds, ginger root, marjoram, and sprinkle your sugar around it in a clockwise motion (to indicate drawing this hot energy to you and your relationship). Place the rose petals around next. Do this with intention. Take each item in your hand and connect with the spirit. After putting it around the apple, sprinkle some on top of the water in the bowl (including the rose petals).

Try to arrange everything on the plate with enthusiasm and creativity; take your time and make it appear pleasing to yourself.

Really feel the roots and plants that you're using. Touch and smell, imagine the heat, good feelings, and beauty being the same as in your relationship.

Every emotion you have while doing the work will show up in your magic, so make it count.

Light the candle, again with your intentions and prayers. As the flame burns, express gratitude! Thank the spirits for helping you with your work and being with you to see your spell come to life.

You will use the water to bathe with over the next few days. If you are working with a deity, choose a number of days that correspond with the spirit. Three is a number often chosen because it represents a holy trinity; father, sun, and the holy spirit, or Father God, Mother Goddess, and you.

History Traditions of Hoodoo Love Magic

If you've ever watched daytime talk television, you know exactly the kinds of situations folks used to go to hoodoo for. Love triangles, cheaters, unrequited love, getting dumped, wandering eyes, jealousy, loneliness, lust, sex, getting pregnant, getting others to stop interfering in a relationship, removing a third party, triggering a breakup (either for someone else or for yourself), the list is probably endless.

When it comes to magick, society used to be much more forgiving when it comes to questions of love. Advertisements for love potions were common in magazines and pamphlets in the 1920s and 30s.

A very special spirit many hoodoo practitioners have used for nearly 100 years to draw success in many areas in life, but particularly love, is called a 'lodestone'.

For love, you can get two stones; female/male, or male/male, female/female (depending on the retailer).

Although you can find these in crystal or metaphysical shops, these are not treated in the same way as your regular crystals or stones, like lapis lazuli or clear quartz. At least not in the hoodoo tradition.

Regardless of whether you get a pair for your relationship, or one to draw love to you, lodestones are more like pets than they are a crystal. They require care in a way unique from other stones to 'activate' them and their work for your situation.

As a beginner, your best bet may be to consult an expert about how to care for your lodestone since they will know how to program your stone for your situation.

As many stories as there are about how hoodoo was used for love in years gone by, there are cautionary tales. For example, a man who had a love powder that he wanted to give to a woman he loved but she didn't love him.

After she refused to eat the working (which was put in a slice of watermelon), he gave the food to some hogs. If he wasn't sure that the powder would work, he got confirmation because the hogs fell in love and ended up following him around![2]

Then there are ways, using nature and communicating with spirit, to get answers to burning questions (or just simmering questions). Some of these tactics are more dangerous than others. One method describes using knot magick; taking a string with a knot in it and having the couple pull each side. If the knot remains after being pulled, the two in love are in effect, 'tied together'.

Cautions and warnings in hoodoo love spells are just as old as the spells themselves. While we may not see advertisements for spells in our popular magazines and television shows, this work is real, that much we know.

However, no retailer can guarantee results in every situation. And without the right care and attention, unexpected results happen all the time.

Not all magick is used to cause changes in a situation. Sometimes, lighter spells and rituals are performed to find out where someone's heart lies. This doesn't mean that we approach spirit with a nonchalant attitude. Balance must be considered, as well as the potential for unintended consequences.

---

[2]Hyatt, H. M. (1970). Hoodoo, Conjuration, Witchcraft, Rootwork. Five Volumes (1st ed.). Self-published, 1970s.

Making and Maintaining a Love Mojo

A mojo bag is perfect for those who are hoping to draw love into their lives. You are supposed to already feel like you have love in your life. Feeling desperate or 'thirsty' indicates not being connected to your higher self.

You cannot feel desperate *and* be the magnetic, attractive person you are supposed to be. The two ideas do not go together.

With a mojo bag to draw love, you can connect to your inner magnetism. You can sit back and watch your love options be drawn to you, and then choose amongst the people who want to give you their heart. All you have to do is keep your eyes (and heart) open.

However, if right now you *feel* desperate to find someone, you will have to do your best to undo this way of thinking *first*. Before you decide to do a love working of any kind. Consider doing a self-love spell or building a relationship with your ancestors with the intention of getting help.

Not all mojo bags need to be maintained, but regularly feeding a mojo bag keeps the work working. This is important in love, especially as you may date many people and might need the hand for some time before you find someone you want to settle down with.

Or your love mojo bag may be about a way of life for you and not necessarily about finding someone to settle down with. It all depends on your intent.

If you're creating a mojo bag for a relationship, you want to have elements inside that connect to both you and your partner. This could be toenail clippings or hair from both of you.

This bag is a living, breathing spirit itself.

Once your mojo bag is created, you can feed it by anointing it with conjure oils or essential oils. This is placing a few drops of the oil on your hand and then on the bag, the specific spots being completely up to you. You can also leave your mojo bag on your altar and present offerings, in the same way you would with other spirits.

How often you do this is up to you. One easy way to plan how often you do this and when is to schedule around moon cycles.

Feel free to start with one of the mojo bag recipes in the section above, keeping in mind that your intent and your feelings are key.

Once it's made and you've had the bag for at least a week, maintaining the bag is a process of anointing it regularly, and adding mojo. This is literally opening the bag and adding ingredients, like you are literally feeding it. Ritualize this. Light incense and build your energy using music or your body. Keep your vibration high and your intention front of mind.

The specific oils you want to use for anointing will have to be high-quality conjuring oils. For this you may not want to go with a love oil, rather a Blessing or Abramelin Oil. This is about feeding your bag, which helps you with your mojo. Your intent isn't about what you want, this is about putting energy into the bag. This is about praising and uplifting the spirits aiding your mojo.

Aromatherapy for Hoodoo Love

Incense, colognes, oils, and perfumes. In case you were beginning to think scents are important in hoodoo, you would be correct. Scents are valuable in many magickal traditions.

Aromatherapy provides a simple and quick method to welcome spirits into your space. It's also a way to either change or lift vibrations ahead of a ritual or casting a spell.

One common way to do this is through the use of incense. Other forms of aromatherapy are through using essential oils in a diffuser, burning resins such as frankincense or copal (which is especially good for love work), cones and sticks.

Burning sage and palo santo are generally used for cleansing, but these are also forms of aromatherapy that open up your space to the invitation of spirit.

Your words work in the same way that smoke does, it floats up into the air and goes somewhere that becomes invisible to the human eye.

Spirits are attracted to spaces with good, clear energy (or at least the spirits that you want to invite to help you). Using aromatherapy will clear the way for your appeals and prayers.

Many people who practice hoodoo consider using an incense essential ahead of any spell.

Because of its ability to completely change the vibration of a space, aromatherapy is excellent when it comes to love. Burn some incense after an argument and ask that spirits lift you up or ease the tension. You could also use an essential oil like rosemary or lavender.

A simpler method to easing the mood in your home is by boiling one or two cinnamon sticks in water.

One practice that many in hoodoo and witchcraft are familiar with is creating custom incense. Be sure that by knowing the magickal correspondences of various herbs, roots, oils, and plants, you can become your own aromatherapist with a background in magick.

This means you can create incenses to fill your home with the mood of love, to dispel anger, or for reconciliation. Note that some magickal suppliers sell these incenses pre-made.

For some, creating an incense *is* the spell. Common tools for creating an incense or a mortar and pestle to mix ingredients, and a cauldron to light the incense.

While burning, you can use the smoke and the energy of the spirits to do work. You can think about what it is that you want, breathing in and out deeply. You can say your intention and send it in the air along with the smoke.

Don't think that the activities you do need to be highly complicated or ritualistic. Let the smoke do the work for you and allow your vibration to be carried upwards. You can write a letter to the person you're thinking of, if, for example, your relationship is fractured, or you have a lot of intense feelings.

You can also praise and rejoice! If you have been doing other spells to bring love into your life, light some incense, invite the spirits helping you with your work in, and dance and sing. Conjure the feeling that what you want has already happened and what you want will come to you even faster.

Spells for Money, Luck, Abundance, and Prosperity

The second most popular reason many people pursue hoodoo, is for work with the intention of improving an employment or career situation.

Hoodoo is great for any type of employment, whether you're working for yourself or someone else.

There are spells for nearly every aspect of your business that you can imagine, getting along better with coworkers or a boss, attracting clients, drawing more money to you, side gigs, finding work or finding new work, or changing any condition with your employment.

Some conjure oils for work include: Boss Fix, I Can, You Can't, Road Opener, and Steady Work. These oils might not be available at all retailers, but keep in mind you can create your own.

Most of us would not be surprised to know that money, success, and prosperity have their own spirit. You can make you and your environment attractive to these spirits, or you can repel them. The unfortunate thing is often we don't *know* when we've made ourselves unattractive to the spirit of money.

What the richest members of our society know is that wealth is an attitude, a vibration. It is something that everyone is free to choose, like any other. What follows, then, is that an attitude of poverty is also a vibration and is also a choice.

This isn't to say that those of us who are rich always have a prosperous mindset, or the other way around.

The problem is when a person wants more money or success, but they don't have the right attitude for it. This is literally a roadblock that will stop your chances before you even set out to start.

The good news is that you can use hoodoo to help yourself out of a contradictory attitude, so that the results from the work you do for more money or a better career will have a clear channel.

That being said, you might wonder about magick to stop other people from getting in your way. My response is, there isn't so much a concern about others in your way than there is energy.

Hoodoo cannot change fate; no magick can.

If there's a job you want that you aren't qualified for, no amount of incense or mojo will give you more experience or education. Preparing yourself puts you in a good position to see results in your work, but success requires balance.

The point about fate also points to the question of your life path, specifically the work you want to put out into the world and how you want to make money. Sometimes the obstacles in your way are there because the path you're walking is not quite right for you.

I see this often, working with clients who have conformed their nature to work in corporate environments, when in reality they crave a life of creativity and freedom that is inconsistent with working in an office.

They go from job to job, punishing themselves for not being more grateful that they've been able to find work, but miserable, nonetheless. Which only makes them feel even worse.

This is one of the issues that highlights the value of a close relationship with your ancestors, and the value of knowing who you are. Once you have these in place, any work you do for success will be very, very powerful.

A Jar Spell to Make Money Sweet on You

Earlier we went over a jar spell for peace in the workplace. Here, we'll cover another version of this spell: to help make money sweet on you. This one you don't have to keep in the workplace, it can stay in your home or on a money altar. For this spell, we'll go a little more in-depth than with the others. For the most part, I've tried to list items that are common in most homes.

Items from Your Pantry

- Sugar

- Honey

- Cinnamon

- Coffee* (especially if you drink regularly or daily)

- Rosemary

- Bay Leaves

- Thyme

- Star Anise*

- Peppermint

- Bee Pollen

Crystals

- Clear Quartz

- Citrine

- Bismuth (optional, see below)

- Pyrite

Curios

- Coins (stick to a certain number, denomination doesn't matter, but if you have coins from another country, feel free to use those).

- Dirt from the land around a bank or financial district in your neighborhood.

- A bill of some denomination (ditto re: foreign currency).

- Thread (green, though orange or purple could work).

Materials

- Candle of your choice.

- Marker (blue or green, but black will do fine).

- Incense of some kind to clear and raise energy.

- A plate for the work.

For the materials I would encourage you to get something from the natural environment in your neighborhood. In my area, helicopter seeds cover the sidewalks in the spring and into summer. You may have access to a garden or wooded area where many different types of plants grow, and nature generally thrives.

The soil from this area, or those helicopter seeds, would make an excellent addition to a money jar. Why? Because this spell is about making money sweet on you. I imagine that you want *lots* of money and adding these elements to your jar translates to an abundance of money coming to you.

As you know by now, it's not just about throwing these into your jar, sealing it shut and then going about your day. You have to speak your intention into everything you're adding to your work. This means telling everything you put inside why you chose it and what you want it to do for you.

For the helicopter seeds, you might say something like: *Money falls in abundance all around me and into my lap. Money surrounds me everywhere I go.* Or *Bring an abundance of money into my life.*

For the soil: *Make my business and my work fertile for all types of money and abundance to grow. Abundance is now well-rooted in my life.*

Let's talk about some of the items on the actual list above. Citrine is considered the 'merchant stone'. It is added to this jar for helping you to make wealth a solid part of your life, and to ensure that the wealth that comes to you is produced through positive means. It's also a great stone for dispelling negative energy.

Bismuth is a stone of transformation, and as such it may not be suitable for your money jar. However, I recommend it if you're looking for any kind of change to your financial situation. It's a stone associated with both the crown and root chakras, and as such can help you ground yourself if you tend to be 'in your head' or feel like you don't belong.

You have to program (speak into) everything before adding it to your jar, but this is especially true for clear quartz. This stone amplifies all energy, so you could add it to your spell as an overall booster.

Instructions

Optional. If you already have tarot cards or a crystal collection, use them to help you build the energy. Use larger crystals like malachite, or tree and moss agate. Likewise, use the tarot cards that speak 'money' to you: Wheel of fortune, ten of cups, ace of pentacles, nine of cups, etc. (Note I've used the Rider Waite names for these cards, but they might have different names in your deck.)

Light the incense and begin your spell using the phases described above.

Run all of the items from your pantry, the crystals, and materials through the smoke. Ask that it all be cleansed of negativity and blessed for your working.

Once everything is cleansed and your prayers have been said, it's time to begin. Start with the dollar bill. Put it on the plate and use the marker to write your name and date of birth. Draw a clockwise circle around it.

Anoint the bill with the honey, and then rub it in. (Taste it first, if you work with Oshun!) While rubbing the bill with the honey, you can say something like: *Money loves me like bees love honey!* You want to speak into each ingredient added to your jar in a similar way.

Once the honey is rubbed in and the bill is charged, put *you* on the bill. Add your hair, some toe or fingernails, and speak to the bill. These should stick to the honey and stick to the bill. This is what you want. Feel free to add more honey if you want.

Fold the bill towards yourself at least three times. Once the bill is folded into a small square, use the string to tie it closed. Speak to it one last time, and then add it to the jar.

Now you can start to add the ingredients from your pantry, the crystals, the soil and dirt, or whatever you got from your hood, and the coins. Do not forget to speak what you want as you work.

Feel the energy build.

Work it.

Embody the energy of what you want coming to life.

Once you've added the last item, mix the jar around and let everything sit for a while. You've created a working jar that will sweeten and bring money to you. Speak to the whole jar three more times before closing it.

Set the jar down and place your candle on top. Let the candle burn all the way through, and the spell is complete!

The last step: celebrate! Thank the spirits for their help and for coming to your aid. You can do this while you're cleaning up the space and putting all of your materials away.

As your hoodoo pantry builds, you'll no doubt collect mojo that will add some power to your jar. You can, of course, use what you have--and that is what you are supposed to do as a practitioner, but you may want to wait after gathering a few things.

Common herbs that are widely used in hoodoo, but that you may not have on hand include catnip, alfalfa, and high john the conqueror.

Spells for Success

Success can come to you in different ways for many different aspects of your life. You might want to see more success over yourself, as in, you want self-mastery to accomplish personal goals or remove a habit that no longer serves you.

You may have a specific situation in which you want to be successful, such as a presentation at work or a performance. You may want a success spell for a driver's test or a bar exam.

In each case, you can draw energies towards you, such as focus, or a boost in confidence. On the other hand, you may want to banish some personal trait that is at odds with your goal.

In addition to spells for success (either for specific issues or general), there are many rituals you can use to keep the energy flowing towards you and your home. Holy water is excellent for this. Not only will it clean your space and banish negative entities, but it can also be used to bless. To get holy water, you can go to a botanical or any shop that sells magickal items.

Many herbs can also be used to attract success, such as aloe, basil, bay leaf, and chamomile. These can be mixed and matched with other ingredients to make an incense for success.

One of the best things you can do for personal success is to carry and maintain a mojo bag.

Success by Banishment: A Simple Fire Spell

This is a spell that can be done using fire. For this reason, you want to use something that won't release toxic fumes in the air and that you can actually destroy.

Though you do not have to use fire, you can still destroy things with other methods, such as chewing.

While unpleasant, this alternative method involves biting and chewing an object that is charged with the energy you want to banish. For this spell, just remove references to burning and bite and chew instead.

You will need:

1. A banishing incense.

2. An object that you are okay with destroying.

3. A cauldron, fire-resistant dish, or a plate.

To really put the power into this working, try to find an incense that corresponds to what you want to banish. Usually, I would say use what you have, and that applies here as well, but if there isn't anything you have in your home that could be used as an incense, a little shopping might be necessary.

Here are some common examples:

- **Alfalfa** for banishing all forms of poverty from your life.

- **Asafoetida** for banishing negativity (does not smell nice).

- **Black Pepper** for banishing lower energies.

- **Cloves** for banishing hostility and gossip.

- **Curry** for banishing evil.

- **Gravel Root** for banishing discord or tense energies.

- **Peppermint** for banishing illnesses and lower energies.

- **Rosemary** for banishing negative vibrations.

- **Rue**, a popular herb in hoodoo. Burn to banish negative habits and energy.

- **St. John's Wort** for banishing demonic energy.

- **Thyme** for general banishing, specifically negative energies.

Hopefully, you already have one or two items on this list, and if that's the case, you can do this spell today. Provided the moon is in the right phase. As banishing work, this is to be done during a waning moon.

Instructions

Light your incense.

While the smoke rises, take the object and program it for the thing that you want to banish. If you're looking to banish jealousy or envy, asafoetida might be a good option if you can stand the odor, though cloves or rue do not smell as bad and will work as well.

If you can't find an item, get creative with some paper. Write down every detail you can about what you want to banish. Alternatively, you can draw something, or find an image online, print it out, and then add to it anything that helps with conjuring the energy of what you want to banish.

Put into the object all of the energy of the thing you want to banish. Keep speaking it through and talking until you are able to pinpoint the exact energy. This step requires some real focus.

Once you have the object programmed, add you. This can be some of your hair, spit, or toenails, but keep in mind that you will be burning the object.

Carefully light the object on fire and set it in the dish or cauldron. Burn it until all that is left are ashes. For this, make sure your space is well ventilated and you have some open windows. This is for safety and to clear your space of fumes, but it's also to clear your space of the energy you've burned.

You've finished the spell, and the thing you want gone from your life is banished. Success will now come to you swiftly, so the last step is: celebrate.

Success by Invoking: A Simple Candle Spell

Crown of success oil is a widely available conjure oil that can work very well in candle spells for success in any endeavor.

This is a basic candle spell that can be tailored and updated for any type of work you need to do. You will need to change the color of the candle, and the conjure oils you use, but knowing how to do a candle spell like this one will be important for your magickal practice.

You will need:

1. A candle that is wide enough to stand on its own and that you feel comfortable writing in. White candles can

be programmed for any use. Otherwise, a color that corresponds to your intent. For example, pink for a health-related spell.

2. Scissors or something sharp to carve with.

3. Crown of success conjure oil.

4. Your intent.

Instructions

Cleanse all of your materials. Carefully carve your name and date of birth into the candle using a sharp end of the scissors (or whatever you have to carve with).

On the opposite side of the candle, or underneath your name, carve in what it is that you want. If your petition is a little long for a candle, try editing it down to a couple words, such as 'dedicated subscribers'.

Anoint your candle with the crown of success oil, making sure to go from the bottom and upwards. Cover the wick, your name, and the petition with your fingers, which should have the oil on them.

Add your essence by speaking your intention into the candle before lighting it. Once it's lit, recite the Psalms and express gratitude. You can also speak to the flame and put into it everything you want.

This is something you want to think about *before* casting your spell: the type of problems that will follow when you achieve. Do you want these problems? Speak your anxieties or worries about achieving success to the fire. Ask Spirit and your ancestors for help with all that will come as your star rises.

Continue burning the candle until it goes out on its own. If you achieve your goal before the candle is finished, you can stop doing the daily ritual. I like to let the candle burn out on its own one last time and use the light as a reminder to keep a gratitude attitude.

If the candle goes out before you achieve what you're looking to achieve, consider the spell complete. Whenever you think about the spell or catch yourself worrying about results, remind yourself that you did the spell and the work is done.

I can understand the temptation to do another spell but do your best to resist doing another working. This will undermine the candle spell you've already done and undermine your magick overall.

You can, however, *continue* the work by anointing yourself with the crown of success oil, or burning the oil with an herb in a homemade incense.

When you speak about whatever you cast for, speak as if what you want has already happened, especially if you are speaking to yourself about what you want.

Never think of the spell as having "not worked". (It's fair to say this goes for any spell you do.) If what you wanted did not happen, think of how you can do things better next time. Or better yet, think of how the spell worked in any unexpected ways.

Success by Invoking: A More Complicated Candle Spell

A version of this spell appeared in the first volume of Hoodoo, Conjuration, Witchcraft and Rootwork, by Harry Middleton Hyatt. These volumes feature interviews of the earlier practitioners of hoodoo, and while it can be difficult to understand at times, it contains many spells that were shared among people via word of mouth.

As such, it is a highly valuable resource for anyone who cares to take a look.

This spell is for general success for something time-bound, like a test or if you want someone to pay you back quickly. Before I get into the spell, it requires lighting a perfume on fire, and then lighting a candle with that flame. I cannot control you or what you do, but I have to caution you on this because playing with fire is dangerous.

Last warning: be careful.

You will need:

1. Van van (a perfume).

2. A fire-resistant plate or a cauldron.

3. A lighter.

4. Three green candles.

Instructions

Do this spell on a Monday at 6 in the evening, during the waxing moon.

Put some van van in the fire-resistant plate.

Light the van van so there's a flame inside the plate. Light your first candle, speaking your intention, and let the candle burn until it is complete.

You will be repeating the same process using the second candle on Wednesday (at 9 in the evening). Use the third candle on Friday (at 12 in the afternoon).

Van van oil is another favorite among hoodoo practitioners, so if you end up getting some for this spell, you could use it in other ways for success that do not involve lighting it on fire.

One method is using the oil in floor washes. Adding it to the water you're using to mop with is a simple and effective way to pull in the energy of success into your space. This was reportedly a popular way of using van van among practitioners in New Orleans.

It also works when added to bathwater or for hoodoo baths.

You can also add the oil as a dressing for your candles and leave that on your ancestor or money altar.

Spells for Justice

Generally, when we think of spells for justice, we're thinking of court cases. However, justice applies in many, many areas of life. This is because justice is really about balance.

This is another area where hoodoo was and is very popular among rootworkers, especially in the United States.

These types of spells are also very useful in situations where you have been wronged by someone else, but you're not able to go through legal channels to balance the scales. This might be because going to a court or the police may incriminate yourself, or you want to ensure justice is meted out appropriately.

Many of us are very familiar with the legal system in the states. We also know that going through legal channels can often cause more imbalance, and more problems than it solves.

Luckily, we have hoodoo.

Another dose of realism is important here, as it is in love spells. Before you do any of these spells, you want to get a feeling that your spell has a chance of actually working.

For Court Cases: A Simple Fire Spell

This spell is a version of one from the folks at Yeyeo Botanica.[3] It is best used in smaller court cases, where you may have to appear as a member of a jury, or the issue is relatively minor. This is *not* for major cases where you are named as a major part of the case.

Read through the ingredients and description of how to do the spell below, and then ask your ancestors if this spell has a chance of working for your situation. Get all the facts and information you need and use your discernment.

You will need:

- A white 7-day candle (it's better if you can get one specifically for the purpose of your working, in this case, going to court).

- A conjuring oil, again, anything that speaks to your work, but snake oil is a good option, if you can find it from a reputable retailer.

- A copy* of the paperwork for the case.

- A black marker.

- Tobacco.

- A cauldron or plate with tin foil so you can collect ashes.

You may wonder why I'm recommending snake oil for this spell and not a court case or law stay away oil. Court case would work for this spell as well, but as a beginner, I am considering that after you cast this spell, you may have no need for a whole bottle of court case oil. On the other hand, a bottle of snake oil can be used for this and in other workings, like protection for example.

For tobacco, empty out the contents of a cigarette (use one from someone else if you don't smoke yourself). If having cigarettes is triggering for you, purchase a cigar from a local bodega.

---

[3] Yeyeo Botanica. (2020, February 19). Court Case Spell - Dismiss | Yeyeo Botanica [Video]. YouTube. https://www.youtube.com/watch?v=6_BMpZnxmK8

While there is a lot you can do with tobacco in hoodoo, when it comes to buying ingredients for this spell, I would recommend *not* going overboard.

Buying a whole pack of cigarettes just for this spell is not the message you want to send to spirit. It suggests you will have a lot in your life that you will need to do similar work on.

Approach this with a beginner's mind and just get what you need.

*You definitely want to use a copy of the court case papers because you will be burning it. Keeping the original will provide you with strong evidence when your magick works!

Instructions

Take the oil and use your fingers to draw a large 'X' through the content of the paper. Go from one corner of the page to the next.

Turn the paper upside down and take out your marker. Write down words that reverse whatever this case is about for you. Use your name and date of birth and continue writing words that oppose what is already on the page.

Avoid writing down anything that you desire. This is banishing magick. Everything you're using (the oil and fire, eventually) is about dissolving this situation. If you put down what you *do* want, you send confusing messages to spirit and risk including those good things within the banishing.

Think about what you want when you celebrate victory; *after* the spell is closed.

You will be coming back to this spell over the course of a specific number of days; generally three or seven. For this reason, you may want to set an alarm on your phone to remind yourself to come back to the spell. The day you start this spell is considered day one.

Dress your candle with the oil (place a few drops in at the top) and the tobacco. Light the candle, picturing the court case removing itself from your life.

Rip off a section of the court document copy. Rip the paper away from you.

You will rip a piece of the paper for each day of the working, so consider how many days you will do the work. Take your piece while leaving enough for each day you plan to work.

Set the paper on fire using the lit candle. Let it burn until the fire goes completely out and all that's left are the ashes.

Once all the paper has been burned, collect the ashes. In the traditional version of this spell, you would go to the courthouse and sprinkle all of the ashes there. If your case will be taking place over an online video conferencing platform, it is still possible to do this step. Remember, this work is about spirit. The correspondences still exist even as our world remains in flux.

If there *is* a courthouse address on your paperwork, use this. If there isn't an address, do a little research online to find a courthouse closest to you, even better if you can find a courthouse nearby where similar cases are handled.

For Personal Use: A Return to Sender Candle Spell

Being scammed is one of those situations that can be put into balance with hoodoo. It is very difficult to get your money back when you've been manipulated or tricked into giving it to someone else.

It will also work for situations where someone has done something to you that you know about but aren't able to remedy legally. For example, a manager at work who manipulates the truth to jeopardize your employment.

Before you take the measure to do a spell, you have to know that *justice is already yours*. You could decide not to move forward with the spell, and this would not change. The spell is an affirmation of this; of what you know already.

Remember that hoodoo is about bringing balance to circumstances. Evening the scales. You may be tempted to do *worse* to them than what they did to you, but keep in mind that the realm of justice is not something that you have to worry about.

You're not the one who exacts justice on the person or people who have done you wrong, that is spirit's job. As with all spells, this is about appealing to these spirits for work on your behalf.

You will need:

1. A black candle.

2. Van Van Oil.

3. Four Thieves Vinegar.

4. Black salt.

5. A knife or sharp object for carving into the candle.

6. A plate that the dressed candle will burn on.

7. Clover (optional, for incense).

Four Thieves Vinegar is especially good for personal protection, especially from negative people who may want to cause you harm. As such, it can be great for shielding you from people who will use you to dump all of their worries (also known as psychic vampires).

The reason I include Indigo Water as a substitute for this spell is because it has a wider variety of uses than vinegar *and* it can be used to keep negative energies from other people away from you. It is great for cleansing your home or space, and welcomes peaceful energy.

Van Van oil is an all-round key ingredient to have as a hoodoo practitioner, but if you don't have any or can't get access, Olive Oil can work just as well.

The black candle in combination with the black salt here is very much about protective energy, but remember that in magic, white is considered universal when it comes to color magic. If you don't have either candle or salt listed above, you can use a white candle and white salt and program it for your needs. Or, you can use a white candle with black pepper.

Instructions

Your glass of water can sit beside a glass of Four Thieves Vinegar or Indigo Water. Remember that over the duration of the next steps, you want to repeat your intention and what it is you want over and over again.

This spell is about keeping any and all negative energies clear, especially any sent to you by other people. Use specific names if you need to.

A sample incantation: *Every curse, evil eye, jinx, or hex, pack it up and send it back.*

You've called in spirit to help you. As you work you can tell the spirit what's happened and how things have fallen out of balance. Do not worry about speaking "holy", swear, roll your eyes, get emotional. Bring up everything that you want removed from your experience.

Carve an arrow in the candle, pointing up towards the wick. If you're using a tealight candle, a small arrow towards the wick works, or you can use a small piece of paper (such as a cue card) to draw the arrow and point it towards the candle.

Dress your candle with the Van Van oil, drawing the oil upwards, towards the wick.

Place the candle on the plate. Remember, if you need to make sure the candle will stay upright, you can melt the wax on the bottom and stick it to the plate. As the wax cools it will secure the candle.

Now you're going to draw a circle around the candle in a counterclockwise motion. Start at 12 and go around until you've completed the circle. Use enough salt so your circle is clear. I like to neaten the granules so none of the salt is too far off the boundary, and creates a solid barrier around.

Let the candle burn to completion and know that it is done.

Spells for Protection

If you're not used to having a relationship with spirit, one thing you may have heard is that once you've started to open up, you are open to *all* types of relationships. While this is true, it doesn't mean that you are vulnerable.

You decide if you are vulnerable or not. This is the power of your word.

There's a lot you can do to build and maintain a protective shield without an oil or candle. One tactic is surrounding yourself in a shield using your mind.

Much like creating a mental altar, you can create and maintain your aura with the power of visualization and prayer. The effects usually aren't quite immediate, but within a few minutes to an hour after your visualization, you will begin to *feel* protected.

Do not underestimate the power of cleansing when it comes to protection. This is because, as we've discussed previously, energies get attached to us without our knowledge or awareness. These energies can then weaken our fields, which leaves us vulnerable to more harmful spirits.

Cleansing here doesn't always have to be using an incense or Florida Water spritz. Meditation can be a form of cleansing. Same with exercise, showering, and chanting, yelling, or screaming. Simple, daily cleansing (and protection) can be done using the four elements: fire, water, air, and earth.

Sometimes removing those negative entities can be just a matter of screaming it out or putting your frustration on paper (both being examples of how you can cleanse using air).

Many hoodoo practitioners carry something on their person with the intent of providing protection. Usually, it's something small or inconspicuous (if not invisible) that most people who aren't familiar with magick wouldn't associate with anything spiritual.

This could be anything from a prayer, wearing an evil eye amulet necklace, to a mojo bag or nation sack (a type of mojo bag usually carried by women).

For each of these spells, cleansing is very important *prior* to the work. This is because the spells you will be casting are about containing what is already within your home or yourself. So cleanse, cleanse, cleanse, and then get busy.

For Your Home: A Spell Bottle

This is a great spell for overall protection. Though you could create it ahead of specific circumstances that require protection for the home and the people inside. This could be a new neighbor who is proving to be a challenge, or visitors coming in for a short period of time.

In this case, you would do your protection spell before the visitors arrive, and a cleanse after they leave (regardless of how long they're staying for). However, this bottle will continue to work even after your cleanse.

A spell bottle for your home is great if you have a lot of random visitors or energy passing by. If you live on a ground floor of a busy street, or you work from home and see patients regularly (whether in person or via online).

Depending on who is visiting and what their energy is like, you might feel the need to double up on protection. In this case you can use a spell bottle and then modify the candle spell above. Remember, in many cases, the simpler a spell, often the more effective it can be.

You will need:

1. A bottle that you can use *just* for this spell. It will not be reused or opened after the spell is cast.

2. Home Blessing oil.

3. Black ribbon.

4. Black candle.

5. Camphor.

6. Angelica.

7. Yarrow Flower.

8. Dragon's Blood.

9. Redbrick dust.

10. Holy water.

11. Frankincense resin (or essential oil).

Get a special bottle specifically for this working. This is one of those 'cast it and forget it' spells. That doesn't mean the spirits will forget about you or the work, but it does mean that you'll rarely (if ever) lay hands on or see the bottle again. So, you don't want to 'miss it'.

One thing you'll often see in hoodoo work is the use of skull and bone curios. This is to recognize the spirits that have come before us and have passed on and can be particularly effective in protective magick.

In this way, it's fortunate that the skull shows up in our daily life so much. It is not rare to find a bottle in the shape of a skull at a local liquor store, or a crystal molded into the shape at a metaphysical store.

While skulls work for many people, this imagery might not be what you want for a protection bottle. I encourage you to get creative with how you work this spell. Think of the bottle itself as being for the spirits you are calling in for your work. You can tie different objects and symbols to it using string or use the ribbon to wrap around the bottle and seal it with candle wax.

If you have trouble thinking of something you can add as a part of the bottle that will speak to spirit, go to your ancestors or the people in your family.

I'm willing to bet there's some image or association you have from childhood or that is relevant to your heritage that you can incorporate into this spell.

Instructions

Use the Holy Water on your hands and sprinkle it around your space. Light the black candle. You will leave it lit until it burns out on its own.

This spell is very simple to do, physically. You are placing each of your ingredients inside the bottle while doing your prayers and incantations.

Start with the heavier ingredients and layer them with the lighter mojo.

Once the spell is complete, find a dark, empty corner of your space and place the bottle there (ideally the bottle is small enough to fit). Whereas in other spells you would do the work every day, with this you *want* to forget that you cast the spell and the bottle exists.

Hiding it is important for this very reason. It's also important that other people--especially children! -do not touch the bottle or open it.

For Yourself: A Loving Protection Oil

As I've said before, a mojo bag is more than enough to provide you with protection on a daily basis.

The spell below is an oil for special circumstances, when you know you're going to be in the vicinity of someone who has trouble when it comes to the concept of *boundaries*. Physical or emotional.

Create this oil at least two weeks before you will be in contact with the person or situation of concern. Then, when you know things are about to go down, use the oil to anoint yourself. (You can use this oil on yourself at any time.)

You can use these oils to simply moisturize your hands. You can anoint candles with it ahead of meditation or prayer. You can pray over the oil and just chill with the spirit of protection.

It does have some romance, with the addition of rose petals. While they are beautiful and inviting, remember: every rose has its thorn.

When it comes to protection magick for the self, I always add at least a pinch of love in.

You will need:

1. A black candle.

2. A glass bottle.

3. Cinnamon sticks (you will be using one, make sure it can fit in the glass bottle).

4. Pink salt.

5. Castor oil.

6. Dried rose petals.

Instructions

Another simple spell, for this one we're going to layer the ingredients inside the bottle, starting with the cinnamon stick. You can follow the order above for the rest of the items.

You may also want to use Holy Water for this spell by putting some on your hands and sprinkling it around your space. This is optional.

The one "item" I did not include on this list is *you*. Before putting the cap on your bottle, add something of yourself to the spell. This can be some of your hair, nails, blood, or spit.

I do not consider this to be an ingredient, but if you do, it will make a fifth mojo for this spell. To some, five means change and upheaval, so you may want to consider adding an additional ingredient.

A resin-like Myrrh is both healing and protective, and associated with Mother Mary or the goddess Isis. An essential oil like rosemary can lend both cleansing and protective properties to your oil. It is spiky and has the ability to encourage clarity.

You don't need to add either of these to your bottle; this is where I encourage you to get creative.

As much as you might want to, do not use the oil right away. Let it sit for at least two weeks before using it. Let your work rest in a dark space away from sunlight (a medicine cabinet is perfect).

Part III

Eradication and Getting Professional Help

The Internet has made it possible for people to find out about powerful ways to get revenge and make things happen. Unfortunately, the speed of how we live today has also created this idea that results have to be visible, and they have to be quick.

Things can get out of hand for new hoodoo practitioners who are working without guidance or covering the basics.

News of folks who get wrapped up in working with spirits they have no experience with has made the rounds online, especially lately. These sensational stories trigger curiosity, enthusiasm, hope, and a little fear.

This is not how hoodoo works, most of the time. Often the real-life result is much smaller than those much-talked-about big stories. More than that, the person doing a spell or working experiences consequences they never expected.

One of the dangerous consequences of dabbling in magick without proper training is, in short, making a mess.

You can invite an entity into your life that won't leave, or you can become so obsessed with the work you do, you create a situation that looks and feels like a mental illness (in yourself, not an intended target).

In this case, it might be time to do a thorough eradication, or seek professional assistance.

Unhexing, Banishing, and Eradication Work

At some point as you practice hoodoo, it may be necessary to perform unhexing, banishing, or eradication work. It isn't always the work of someone else that you may have to banish or eradicate.

If you cast a hex on someone else, you will need to unhex yourself. These types of consequences have a short name: karma.

We tend to think karma is synonymous with punishment, but most of the time it is much deeper than that. Thinking fearful thoughts will cause you to feel afraid. This is karma.

Everything you do has a karmic return. Most of the time we don't recognize what the impact is because it happens in the realm of spirit, or deep within our mind.

In other words, feeling fearful often does not show up as karma because most people teach themselves to *accept that consequence.*

Most people don't know that karma follows just from thinking fearful thoughts. Instead, they think feeling fear is normal. And so, when that feeling shows up, they do not associate it with karma. Thus, continuing a karmic cycle.

Karma is *not* killing spiders and then having a spider lay eggs inside of a shoe. Any time you cast a spell, you are leaving yourself open to its impact, even if you do not notice or believe in what it should look like.

This is one of the reasons new practitioners are cautioned before doing any type of left-hand magick; the type of work where you want to do something to an enemy, for example.

What you do for a spell will have an impact on you. If you're buying a certain powder with the intent of doing work on an enemy, you will have them on your mind for much longer than it takes to do the spell. This could lead to creating an obsession, which doesn't hurt the "enemy" at all, it only hurts the person who is obsessed.

Feeling hate in your heart for someone else reduces your capacity to feel love for yourself.

In the same way, doing a hex on someone else means doing a hex on yourself. If you choose to go this route, after you've hexed another person you will have to banish that work immediately to remove it from your energy.

Before hexing another person, you need to decide if the blowback, however small it might be, is worth it.

As you can imagine this kind of work can get tricky. It is done in the shadows, and when it's dark it's not easy to tell what's coming back to you. Most of the time, your own cleansing and protection is sufficient, but there are situations where more work is needed.

I know we talked before about not having anyone else in your life who is open to concepts of magick or hoodoo, and in this case, that might be a good thing. The more people you have in your circle, the more opportunity there is for attracting negative energy.

This is one of the reasons many people shrink their social circles to the size of a dot, but one of the things I have learned on this path is that it's not the other people who are the issue, it's our idea of those people.

So even if you do have a lot of people around you, maybe others who also seem to be powerful, the only thing you have to be concerned about is your *perception* of those people.

I also have to add a caution here about thinking someone else is "more powerful" than you are. It doesn't always need to be someone who is an expert in hoodoo that may be the culprit of some work. We're *all* powerful, each of us given this power in equal measure. The difference lies in how we *use* that power.

Those of us who have more ownership over their power (which is all that is required to use it) are simply doing our work. And most of the time, we are not interested in hurting anyone else. It just does not appeal to us to put so much of our power on anything but making money and living our best lives.

People unknowingly hex each other--and themselves--all the time. Any time you send negative thoughts to someone else, or someone else thinks negatively about you, that is a hex. Add to these repeated thoughts, and that adds more and more energy.

This isn't anything to be afraid of, like I said it happens all the time. You'll go to the grocery store and notice other people in some kind of argument, or some stranger will say something to you, or an incident of road rage happens. The work we've talked about previously, the spells above and mojo bags, are excellent for protection against these kinds of minor disturbances.

These are also often the kinds of attacks on your aura that can turn into something bigger by the amount of energy *you* put into it.

Many people think that every minor offense, or even the suggestion of disrespect, is enough to get them riled up. I know what it's like to be like this, and if you don't, you probably know someone like this.

By now you probably won't be surprised to know that this energy, itself, is in effect a type of hex. We might not know or call it that. We think hexes are about tripping up over life, suffering from bad luck, or living a life of tragedy.

What is a Hex?

A hex is basically anything that is affecting you in a way that stops you from feeling peace.

And there is a very simple way to tell if there is an energy "on" you that needs to be removed: you do not feel peace or you have a very hard time feeling peaceful.

This could show up in your work, where you're having a hard time with coworkers or a manager. Or it might be emotionally, where you've lost motivation for your life. It could be in a relationship, where a once loving and warm space is cold.

Now if there are situations in your life that have been unsettled for a long time, your job is to take a close look to see if the reason behind these issues is something you've caused.

Did you decide at some point that you would never be able to make money doing what you actually love to do? Or did you decide to give up on love?

Most often, the answer here is inside of yourself. An issue in one area of your life is not what a hex makes, the same with minor issues, such as a flat tire or an upstairs neighbor making noise excessively.

Life will do what life does.

How to Know

If you have sudden and strange issues across multiple areas of your life, then you may need to start thinking about the possibility that someone has done work on you. The keywords here are 'sudden and strange'.

While it is true that the work might have been done years ago, if you've been hexed, the issues in your life will feel unusual in some way. It may also be that your regular spiritual self-care doesn't work to alleviate them.

Something always seems to be off; items break or are lost, communication with others always seems like it's happening through a foggy window or broken telephone. It might feel like you are never heard clearly, or that others do not *want* to hear what you have to say.

One place where you will really need to use your awareness is with yourself and with your thinking. Can you focus on completing tasks and go about your day or do you always seem distracted? Do you get confused when trying to figure out simple problems? Do you feel unable to focus? Have your job or employment prospects been affected negatively?

I cannot bring this question up without also talking a bit about mental health; the hot topic of the day. You will know if and when it's time to see a professional, or hopefully you have a network of support around you that can help.

Either way, it can be very difficult to stay neutral and centered if your mind isn't well. There's no way around this; your magick just will not work if your mind is unsettled. Living a life of health *is* living a life of magic.

But you have to do your best to keep yourself in balance. This means doing all of the physical-health stuff that can go neglected without regular maintenance. And it might require seeing a doctor or a therapist.

Don't make the mistake of thinking these activities aren't "magickal"; everything we have here on earth is for our help; not just the plants and roots. This includes the technology and resources, other people who have studied the mind, or who are willing to share their lessons learned. Even our problems all exist *for* us. It all depends on the way you think about it.

Look back at journal entries to see if there's a noted change or difference in what you write or the tone you use. Think over the past few months or years and make a list of any incidents that stand out to you, anything that seems negative and to have happened 'out of nowhere'.

Of course, this would be easier if you've kept detailed diary entries for more than a couple years. If you weren't convinced of keeping a hoodoo diary before, you may be now. Note anything that's happened to you that seemed out of place.

As a beginner, it's highly unlikely that you're going to require any clearing work beyond what you can do yourself. If you *have* gathered the evidence, consulted with your guides and found that you do need some major clearing work, the 3-day eradication ritual below is prescribed.

3-Day Eradication Ritual

This ritual is a complete reset for your spiritual life and practice. The cleansing and protection techniques described above are more for daily or regular use.

As a ritual that is designed to be repeated over at least three days. You need only do this once, but you may feel the need for this kind of ritual every few years, depending on your circumstances.

While the work might be serious, throughout this ritual, I want you to bring lightness, laughter, and joy to this process. On their own, joy and laughter have the power to dispel a lot of negative energy. For this ritual, we are going to use that power. And a little mojo.

That mojo will be in using hot water and herbs to make a spiritual bath.

Often, we hoodoo practitioners assume newbies have access to pots, pans, a bathtub, or be able to go outside to complete a ritual. I will warn you now: this will require you to do some things you've maybe never done before, and could invite looks, questions, if not downright interruption if you live with others.

If you don't think this is something you can do without inviting unwanted questions or comments, consider getting in touch with a professional who can help you do the work more discreetly. I'll discuss more about finding assistance in the next section.

Prior to doing this ritual, you will want to take a "regular" shower. During this shower, speak to the water and imagine your worries and troubles washing down the drain.

This ritual also requires air drying, which is not something most people are accustomed to doing. It is necessary, but some practitioners will forgo this step. If you want the full impact of this ritual, do not dry yourself using a towel. You *do* want to set things up in your space so you can sit or stand comfortably.

You will also want to wash and dry all of the clothes or linens you will be using after the ritual. This includes bedsheets and pillowcases, for when it's time to go to sleep. Wearing all white after the ritual is an ideal way to really absorb what it is that you're doing. This is completely optional and completely up to you.

After each bath, wash your tub with saltwater (recipe below). This is a little more than some salt mixed in with some water; you will need to purchase this from a hoodoo shop, get some from the sea (if this is accessible to you), or you can make some. I've included the ingredients for this below. The saltwater is very easy to make; mix all of the ingredients until all of the salt is absorbed into the water.

You will need:

1. Two white candles. You will be using these in the bathroom, so try to get either wider candles that can stand on their own, or holders that you can use in your space comfortably and safely. You'll also be in the bath with these candles burning, so you don't want to put them anywhere where they could fall while you're trying to focus.

2. A basin.

3. A smaller cup that you can use in the bath.

4. Lemon.

5. Sage.

6. Basil.

7. Rosemary.

8. Rue.

9. Florida Water.

10. Hyssop.

11. Angelica.

12. Mint.

13. Patchouli (essential oil is fine).

14. Dill.

15. Eucalyptus.

16. Himalayan Salt.

17. Saltwater.

For saltwater:

1. A pitcher of water (3 to 4 liters).

2. Two rocks.

3. 7 grams Epsom salts.

4. 81 grams table salt.

Instructions

Most of us do not have a bathtub or would prefer not to put all these herbs inside of a full bathtub, so I am going to recommend you fill a large basin with water and put all of the herbs inside.

You will be scooping out water and letting it run down your body thirteen times, so if you need to purchase a basin, get one that is as large as possible to hold the water and the mixture. And try to get something that's pleasing to you or that you *want* to use.

Start with the herbs you have (i.e. Leave out the Florida Water, salt, lemon, and any essential oils you're using).

For Dried Herbs: Mix in a pot on a stove with some water and bring to a gentle simmer while praying and speaking over the pot. Let the herbs cook until fragrant and remove from the heat. Let it cool before continuing.

For Fresh Herbs: Remove the leaves from the stems and mix in the basin with water. Rub the herbs in your hands as the water turns green. Speak and pray as you work the herbs.

Once the herbs have been incorporated into the water, add in the rest of your ingredients.

After they've been mixed, it's time to take your spiritual bath. Take the mixture to your shower and set it down. Light the two candles, on either side of you, and pray over yourself. Recite Psalms 51. Bless yourself, the process, and the spiritual bath you're using.

Get in the tub and stand in the middle. Start to say your prayer and continue to do so for the duration of the ritual. Take your cup and scoop out some of the bath. Pour it over your head, letting the water and herbs wash down from your head to your feet.

Repeat this 13 times, making the same statement each time.

This can be something like: *Remove all obstructions, eradicate all hexing, banish all negativity.*

Picture all obstructions, hexes, and negativity being removed from you as the water drips down into the tub. Get out and chill as your skin air dries.

You don't have to continue repeating your prayers after the bath is finished. You can just sit in silence or meditate.

Once you're ready to move on with your day, end the ritual by closing. You can simply clap once and say: *so be it.*

The leftover water can be used in a few ways; you can include them as a floor wash or as a personal cleansing spray. If you used fresh herbs, take these and leave them as an offering outside. Do not reuse the herbs for your next bath, start fresh each time.

If you feel like you need more cleansing, you can do this bath for more than three days. Seven is often enough for most situations, but some folks will repeat the ritual for 13 days.

After Your Bath

Clean your tub using the saltwater. The energies you've washed away are now sitting in the tub, and you want these to be completely out of your space before the next ritual.

You may notice that following the first day you are already feeling lighter, more focused, and more at peace. This is your confirmation that the spell is working! This leads to the next step: Feeling joy.

Once the ritual is complete, you are now free to live your life in the way you truly want, uninhibited by any work you've done on someone else, or anything someone else may have done to you.

Start to celebrate. There is nothing in your way, especially after your last ritual bath. See the roads in front of you clear and imagine your life unimpeded. *You are unstoppable*. Live an unstoppable life.

Over the course of the ritual, you will use your journal extensively. Record the ingredients you use and the time of month and day when you take your baths. Note the phase of the moon. Following each bath, write down anything that occurred to you while you were pouring the bath over your head.

Magick Mastery

Do not be too anxious to be rid of whatever was troubling you before the ritual. It's now when you have to do your best to not think of whatever the issues were that you were having before. Take on the idea that everything in life happens *for* you and make it as literal as possible.

Really, what you want is to learn to practice neutrality as much as you can. As I've mentioned before, you never want to think of any spell you cast or ritual you do as having "not worked". *Everything* you do works, it's just a matter of knowing *how*.

After your ritual, you'll be in a better place to remain neutral towards your life and circumstances: you are centered. This doesn't mean you're emotionally dead inside, it's quite the opposite.

It means you are better able to notice your emotions and things happening in your life without getting caught up in what's happening. From this position, you can take notes on your experience from a position of clarity.

The more you practice this, the easier it will get. The more you can ask for help from your guides and ancestors, the better you will be able to look at your life and know what's going on.

After the eradication spell, you may discover the ways in which you've given your power away by having an incorrect perception of someone else, or of yourself.

From a place of neutrality, you will also be better able to seek out help, if you need it. This next section on getting professional help is for those circumstances where you require work done that is out of your level of experience, or you need work done with tools that would be inconvenient for you to have.

Know that in most circumstances, you can do work on your own. But as a beginner, you may consider hiring an expert if your work involves outside entities, like a court or legal body.

Spiritual Activities Requiring Professional Help

Unfortunately, it is all too common to be scammed when looking for assistance from hoodoo practitioners. This is one of the reasons it is so important to develop a relationship with yourself and to trust your own instinct.

Before reaching out to any professional, get a clear answer from your guides and your ancestors *first*. If you're not sure of your answer, then the answer is simple: do not hire a professional.

How to Avoid Getting Scammed

If you're online and engaging with spiritually focused content in either the form of videos or on Instagram, you'll soon notice other accounts trying to get in touch with you. They may just follow your account or go so far as to try to send a message saying they can help with whatever you need.

These are scams. Always. Every single time.

You might think it serendipitous that someone contacts you saying they can help with your exact problem, but if you've left a comment on another page with details of your issue (or asking for assistance), whoever messages you saying they can help most likely read that comment and used it to market their services to you.

To be a little fair, this scammer probably did some homework but that doesn't change the facts. Most of the time, if you engage, a scammer will be more concerned about getting paid than they are helping you with your problem.

This is rampant in the spiritual community; however ironic and unfortunate it is.

Real experienced hoodoo practitioners *never* reach out to anyone to offer their services, especially online. (This goes for anyone who offers a service or product that is spiritual in any way, not just hoodoo.) The first and most obvious reason is that they are just too busy with their work and the people who are actually paying them to go out and find new clients.

While this creates a shortage, it also means that people who are desperate for help or answers will keep looking for someone or anyone to hire. This desperation makes it possible for scammers to exist.

The simple antidote: do not be desperate.

This is easier said than done, but there is no way of getting around it. Do not make the mistake of thinking you "need" help. All that does is help you muddle up the energy to resolve whatever your issue is.

Why Hire a Professional

Expertise. The most obvious reason you would hire a professional is to obtain the services of someone who is an expert and knows what they're doing. With this comes the convenience of not having to purchase curios you would only use once.

There are some spells and rituals that you must do for yourself. If you're dealing with a delicate situation where you do not want to risk making an error, consider getting professional help.

Karma. As I mentioned before, any work you do will come back to you in some way. For this reason, you may want to get in touch with an expert who knows exactly how to handle energy when it returns. This doesn't mean you won't be affected by the work at all, but an expert can and will help you to know what to expect after it is complete.

Advanced Eradication. Let's say you did the 3-Day Eradication Ritual described above and you discover through your notes and communication with your ancestors that more work is required to remove a hex.

This is one of the most common reasons many seek the services of a worker. They will be able to help you figure out exactly what is going on and the steps required to treat it.

Education. This book is not the final step in your hoodoo practice. As your reading continues, you'll come across many people who can act as guides and teachers. You can't just hire anyone to mentor you, but some practitioners are available for hire to teach you some specific techniques.

Mentorship is a much more involved relationship that usually evolves with the participation of at least two people.

Clarity. It is *very* easy to get confused as you begin your practice, especially when it comes to hearing the voice of your guides and ancestors, and listening to your intuition. This takes practice, and that practice never really ends. It's for this reason that you may, as you begin to open up to communication, decide to hire a professional to confirm what you're receiving.

There's another caution here, though.

At some point in your journey, consulting experts for clarity becomes redundant. You realize that you spent good money to hear things you already knew. Don't think of the money you spent as "a waste", rather it can provide you with a lesson in learning to trust what you already know.

It's at this point that you understand that seeing someone else for clarity undermines your connection to Divine Truth.

Before Your Appointment

Gather your notes and the information you have so that you can give a thorough overview of what the situation is. The first question the worker will ask you is why you came to see them. You want to have this answer clear and to the point. You also want to know, to an as specific a degree as possible, what work you want them to do for you.

This is not a therapy appointment. The more time you spend explaining and getting emotional, the less time they have to give you their read on what's happening. Approaching your appointment with clarity and focus will bring you resolution much faster.

In addition, if you have an hour and spend most of that time complaining or rehashing everything, you're going to be very disappointed at the end of your session when you're left with lingering questions.

Do not go into the appointment with too much excitement or nervous energy, get as calm and centered as possible.

I would also recommend doing a simple spell to remove negative energy from your aura and get more information on your situation. This work is super simple, all you need is a white candle, glass of water and a white egg (brown can be used, but white is better for this purpose).

Instructions

Light the candle and begin your spell.

Fill the glass with water. You're going to break the egg in the water, so you want the glass large enough so it will hold the egg.

Take the egg and hold it in between your hands to consecrate it. Express some gratitude, as this egg will absorb any negative energy in your aura.

Rest the egg at the top of your head and begin to pray. As you pray, gently roll the egg down your head.

Always go in a downward motion. This is to indicate removing energy. If you were to go up, that would indicate drawing energy towards you.

You can repeat this a few times before going to the next part of your body; begin at your crown and roll down the back of your head and neck, then the sides. Be sure to *lift* the egg off of your skin. Do not roll or draw the egg back up your body.

Then move to your back and arms, then to your chest.

Continue rolling the egg down your body, feeling the negative energy leaving you and being absorbed by the egg. Go over your chest, your hands, your abdomen and hips, legs, knees, making sure to get the front and back of your body as much as possible.

Go all the way down to the tops and the soles of your feet (you will want to move the egg over your palms as well, from your wrist to your fingertips).

Crack the egg and spill the contents inside the glass of water. You can dispose of the shell in compost or just leave it outside.

The egg inside of the water will give you an energetic read on yourself and your situation. You want to look for any cloudiness, bubbles, and blood. Take special note of any shapes or images inside. Seeing faces, symbols, numbers is common. They are things you want to be aware of, even if you don't know what they mean.

If you have at least a month before your appointment, you could do more than one egg cleansing, though I wouldn't recommend doing them too close together. Give it at least three days to a week between each cleansing. Take pictures and notes to help you see the changes over time.

Record whatever you notice with the egg in your journal and keep this information, for yourself and for your appointment. You can even take pictures of it and send it to the professional, so they see your results, provided they say this is okay.

Read the information from the egg with some neutrality. You might not be able to interpret what's going on, so start with just what you can see and what reveals itself to you.

It seems every practitioner has a different way of interpreting what's going on with an egg in water.

Bubbles and cloudy lines inside the water indicate negativity. Some say that bubbles, specifically, indicate negativity that was absorbed by the egg. Others say that cloudiness near the egg yolk shows that the cleansing worked.

Blood on the egg is not a good sign. If you see this on the egg or any spots, get checked out by a physician as soon as you can.

Working with Practitioners

The most important thing with heading into your appointment is to *have an open mind*. You are paying someone else to help you with a situation, denying what they say is like buying food and then throwing it out instead of eating it.

At the same time, even if you have an idea of what work you want done, the practitioner may recommend something completely different. This is why it's important to know what spell you want done, and why.

If there's something of specific concern and they recommend doing a spell different than what you expect, you can ask about what you wanted covered in the spell you chose. They may have a much better recommendation on how to get what you want.

For example, let's say you want to do return-to-sender work on a co-worker. But after hearing your explanation of what's going on, the practitioner recommends doing a spell to ease things between yourself and your manager.

You might ask about the work you want returned, but the practitioner intuits that this situation can actually be remedied with a stronger relationship with your manager. So, in addition to the spell, they give you some homework to cut ties to the situation and clear your way at work.

Take in what they tell you, no matter what it is. After the appointment you can consult with your ancestors and guides if there was anything you were unsure about or want clarity on.

You might be tempted to go back to the practitioner to ask more questions, but here again, I would encourage you to try as much as possible to intuit whatever additional information you need.

Ask, first, before sending an email with a photo, or any message over and above the correspondence you've already had. Be conscious that anything a worker has to do for your situation requires their time, which they should be paid for.

You might have purchased an hour consultation but exchanging money for time is really a crude way of putting a dollar value on what is actually being done.

The work usually takes much longer than that, considering what they receive from their guides about your situation, the follow-up, and any correspondence. Then there are materials they use if they do work on your behalf, the time it takes to do the actual work, and send you a summary.

Many practitioners charge less than what it actually costs to do work. They're not tallying up the time they've spent on your case down to the minute because that would be impossible. Spirit does not work with a timer (at least not one we would understand).

The other key consideration is to approach the work with some enthusiasm. Some people will get frustrated if they're asked to do something by the practitioner. They feel that they hired someone else for a working, and so the 'work' (in every sense of the word) should be done by them.

This is not the way to approach hiring a rootworker.

Your life is ultimately your responsibility, not that of the person you hire. Yes, you've paid them to do the spell, but to carry it forward and to *make it work* (again, in every sense of the word), you need to do your part or be willing to do your part at least.

Look at this as a learning opportunity as well. They may not have the time or resources to teach you everything they know, but they can help you to get to the next phase of your practice if you're willing to take in what they're offering you.

The End

Putting It All Together

We've gone over a lot in these pages: the history of hoodoo, working with spirits in nature, water, place, rootwork, herbs, waters, oils, rituals, when to do work, creating mojo bags, hoodoo lamps.

It's fine to pick up a couple concepts from this book and move on if you find hoodoo is not a practice you want to explore any further.

If, on the other hand, you've read the book from the beginning, you may have notes in many different places and be unsure of where to start. You may have already started your next book on the subject of hoodoo, or a different system entirely.

In this section of the book, we'll go over what your next steps will look like.

Start Communicating

When it comes to magick, your starting point is always the same: with spirit. In this context, that means going back to the beginning of this book and getting the basics solid before moving on to anything else.

I know that you want to get into casting spells now, and that is great, but remember: spellcasting happens all the time. Magick happens all the time.

If you have a specific issue that you want to work on, do not think that you absolutely need to do a spell in order to fix it. Even if you've already done a spell, there's always time to start fresh and revisit your understanding of the situation and what the solution may be.

Use the next spell you're planning to do as an opportunity to get acquainted with the basics of the practice.

You can begin by asking your ancestors and guides for their direction on the spell you want to cast and the situation you are working on. Start speaking to them and ask for their help in guiding you in even the smallest details: the colors used, where to purchase herbs and curios, what type of music to listen to, even the clothes you wear.

This might seem like small details that you have "handled", but if you're not already in communication with your guides, this exercise is about opening up to receiving. This is about knowing there isn't an issue too big or too small for spirit.

Knowing you are led spiritually on the smallest details of your life, you are building faith in the power of spirit, instead of faith in your problems. To reinforce this idea, start your practice by building an altar.

If you need some assistance with understanding the guidance you're receiving, consider trying one or two of the many tools of divination available.

Some hoodoo traditions use bones from animals, such as chickens, but do not feel that you must use this method. Tarot cards, crystals, or beads may be more effective for you and that is fine. Go with what you're comfortable with, or already know.

Get Organized

Another item you want to check off your list as soon as possible: get that notebook. Start recording your spells and work.

Give nature priority in your life. Go through your cabinets and what you have right now in the way of plants, curios, herbs, and roots.

Create a space in your home for the items you have that can be used in a spell or ritual, such as candles, incense holders, crystals, empty glass bottles, and containers. Special plates, dishes, and holders for spells are also important to keep easily available. Labels and Google are your best friends here.

Start looking up magickal correspondences of what you have. If there's something you're not sure of when it comes to magick, look it up! You'll be surprised at the variety and diversity of spells you can find online. While they might not all be hoodoo magick, they probably will help spark your imagination.

If and when you purchase something new for your magick, be sure to bless it before using it in any working, and then add it to your records. You may also want to note when you purchased it, if there's an expiration date, when it was blessed, and the moon cycle it was blessed in.

Hold whatever you've purchased in your hands and open up to the spirit of the item. Note down any feelings or messages you receive intuitively.

You also want to practice this communication with all of the herbs, roots, and items you already have that can serve a spiritual purpose. Your connection with the things in your life are there to serve you.

Remember this when you're going through difficulties or are experiencing confusion. The help you need is very often (if not always) within reach. The communication between yourself and the spirits helping you never stops.

Get Cleaning

Before you begin to practice magic, you may also want to start ritualizing your cleansing practices.

This might involve doing your spiritual cleansing of yourself and your home once every three months, or once a month during the new moon. I highly recommend getting your cleansing and protection rituals solid first, before moving on to doing any other types of work.

For a spiritual cleanse of the home, you want to use new tools; a new mop, broom, rags, and bucket.

Your first spells will (or should be, at least) cleansing and protection, such as a spiritual bath. Do not be too anxious about doing all of the steps and doing them "right". Your first time taking a spiritual bath will feel a little odd, regardless of if you're doing it with the guidance of an advanced practitioner.

This first bath won't be your only one. As you take more, you'll become accustomed to the practice, and will find your rhythm.

Remember there are a number of daily rituals and rites you can use for cleansing and protection. This could include imagining a light of protection surrounding you, using an oil every day, saying prayers, using a Florida Water spray, or doing an egg cleansing once a month. If you haven't already, I highly recommend that you be sure to check my other book called "Prayers and Protection Magick to Destroy Witchcraft; Banish Curses, Negative Energy & Psychic Attacks; Break Spells, Evil Soul Ties & Covenants; Protect & Release Favors" -- as this book will give you many prayer options to recite and to add to your practice. You can find it at https://www.amazon.com/dp/B096W6J97R

For this reason, many of the items you purchase for your practice will probably be with the intent of cleansing and protecting yourself and your space.

As effective as all of these tactics are, it's important to not overdo things. If your rituals are making it hard for you to go about daily life, they probably need to be revised.

Remember the rule of going down and going up. If you're removing something or cleansing, you always want to move in a downward motion. For your body, that means down from your head to your feet.

To invoke protection, you would move in the opposite direction (so from your feet to your head).

Get Focused

Cleaning and organizing go a long way towards clearing your mind. Same with taking care of your body. Our body is the channel through which we receive communication from our guides, from spirit, and from our ancestors.

But we have to be good with ourselves to make this channel clear. This means taking care of the channel.

I cannot prescribe what this will look like for you; it's different for everyone. Some people feel good if they go for a walk every day and to sit in direct sunlight. Others need a meat-heavy diet and a jog every morning. And for some, biweekly sessions with a therapist, six glasses of water and dancing every day is enough.

The point is to find what helps you to feel healthy and work every day at keeping your spine straight. This is what will put the power behind your work.

As you move forward with studying hoodoo, I would recommend an approach with going towards what is most interesting to you. If you want to study the cultural and religious origins of modern hoodoo, focus your attention there until you're satiated.

There are endless paths you can go with your study. And things can get confusing if you buy or borrow every book available on the topic so please be very discerning when choosing to follow any teachings by listening to your own intuition.

Keep Going

Many advanced rootworkers have been studying for many, many years. Their practice started when they were young children; before they even knew what the word 'root worker' meant.

They were lucky to grow up in 'root homes', where mothers, grandparents, uncles, and fathers respected the work. Nearly everyone they knew either had their own spells and techniques or had a reverence for people who did work.

For this reason, their lives are attuned to the practice. It is natural for them to live day-to-day in the omnipresence of spirit, and for this they are incredibly fortunate.

Your upbringing may have looked different than this. Instead of going to graveyards and taking spiritual baths, you may have spent Sundays in church, worshipping a God that you were taught would punish you for having sex before marriage.

Or you may have been raised to be afraid of life, dismissive of nature, and afraid to stand out among your peers.

It is for this reason that when advanced rootworkers try to teach people who have not been raised in the tradition, there seems to be a disconnect on what's considered "the basics" by new and seasoned workers.

Common questions I've heard new practitioners ask are: *How do I dispose of food on my altar? Where do I leave alcohol for my ancestors?* And *What the heck can I use [enter ingredient here] for?*

Advanced practitioners often forget or don't know novice practitioners don't live in homes where they have access to Van Van oil, cascarilla, or Frankincense resin.

I tried to keep this in mind when providing instructions and details for spells. In most cases, if you're buying something for a spell described in this book, that curio or mojo is powerful to use in more than one way. I also tried to use spells and information that would be easily incorporated into your day-to-day.

Whatever regular life looks like for you now or has looked like for you in the past, there is always room for magick. How much depends completely on you.

By now you should have a basis of knowledge with which to start a hoodoo practice as a beginner.

This book might not be enough to turn your home into a 'root home', but it's about starting on the path and knowing that nothing is closed to you regardless of your upbringing. Now you have the basics of what you need to move practice forward.

It's likely that as you study and explore, your magick will incorporate hoodoo and other systems, such as Wicca. You can also check out my other book called "The New Witch's Guide to Modern Witchcraft; Basic Wicca Starter Kit of History, Traditions, Solitary

Practice vs Coven Practice, Modern Day Magick Spells and Rituals with Crystals, Candles, and Herbs" if you choose to learn about Wicca.

Regardless of what other books you read, you will be connected with yourself and your ancestors first. This is the approach I've taken in writing all of my books.

My hope is that as your ability to listen and tune into your guidance deepens, you start to receive information about rituals, practices and direction that come from your guidance.

This is the beauty of this practice, and about being outside one defined system, you will learn to find your way and explore the world of magick available to you.

It starts with your connection to spirit. That is all the mojo you need to make hoodoo happen. And so it will be!

Last Message and small request from the Magickal Witches team:

We wish you nothing but magickal success and health on your journey of being a powerful witch! If you've enjoyed this book or found that it has been exactly what you've needed, please consider leaving the book a review here where you can find the book in Glinda Porter's author profile. You will also find all her other literature that you'd love to check out. We're sure of it!

All feedback is extremely important to us because it helps us deliver exactly what you want and it also helps other readers make a decision when deciding on the best books to purchase. We would greatly appreciate it if you could take 60 seconds to leave the book a quick review. You can also reach out via email to leave any feedback.

Email: magick@magickalwitches.com

Website: www.magickalwitches.com

Author Profile: https://www.amazon.com/author/glindaporter

Lastly, don't forget to claim the "Survival and Wellness Kit for Magickal Witches" where you will receive:

- 10 Elixirs For Detoxification and Aura Cleansing
- 12 Spell Jar Recipes For Protection
- Guide For Talisman Preparation For Use Outside Home
- 20 Daily Detox Tips To Keep Your Vessel Clear
- Master Ingredient Shopping List

Resources

A. (2012). Ancestor Paths: Honoring our Ancestors and Guardian Spirits Through Prayers, Rituals, and Offerings (2nd Edition). Oba Ilari Aladokun.

Clausnitzer, D. (2017). Adorned by Power: The Individualized Experience of the Mojo Bag. Religions, 8(10), 213. https://doi.org/10.3390/rel8100213

The Master Book of Candle Burning: How to Burn Candles for Every Purpose by Original Publications Spiritual Books & Supplies (1998) Paperback. (2021). Henry Gamache.

Hopkinson, N. (2003). Mojo: Conjure Stories. Aspect.

Riva, A. (2021). Powers of the Psalms - 365 Ways To Use Psalms (Occult Books). International Imports.

Teish, L. (1988). Jambalaya: The Natural Woman's Book of Personal Charms and Practical Rituals (Reprint ed.). HarperOne.

BOOK 3

Prayers and Protection Magick to Destroy Witchcraft

Banish Curses, Negative Energy & Psychic Attacks; Break Spells, Evil Soul Ties & Covenants; Protect & Release Favors

Introduction

Welcome to an entirely new realm of protection. In your modern world, there is a lot to worry about from the global-scale - climate change, political uncertainty - to the personal - a toxic ex, cyberbullying. Spell crafting can help you find comfort in a stressful world. This book will give you the tools to take charge and defend yourself mentally, physically, and spiritually.

The negative use of witchcraft, spell work, and psychic/energy work (collectively referred to as Black Magick) is a very real threat and has real-world consequences. These dark forces can be battled and defeated through the use of positive spell and energy work (referred to as White Magick). Within the chapters of this protection-focused spellbook you will discover how to banish bad energy; ward yourself against unpleasant/negative people; as well as defend your belongings; your spirit; and your space.

With over **50 spells and prayers for protection**, defense, and reversal magick; and a glossary of protective symbols, stones and other objects to keep on hand, this book will provide you with the weapons you need to cleanse your room and cast out old negative energies; put a protective and peace-preserving bubble around yourself as you ride the bus; deflect grumpiness and negative energy from people you work with - and so much more!

But negativity and curses are not overcome just with theory. It takes tangible positive action to address and undo tangible negative action. Through simple, understandable prayers and spells; through detailed explanations of the benefits of using magick to counteract magick; through lessons in how to correctly identify signs of witchcraft/psychic attack, you will be shielded and armed against Black Magick; you will hold the keys to destroying unholy agreements, and you will be versed in achieving and maintaining victory!

Magick has been hidden by its practitioners for hundreds of years, but now you can safely start your magickal journey with **information you won't find anywhere else**.

This book aims to be the shining light in the darkness - illuminating the path toward positivity, confidence, balance, and safety.

You may be thinking, "This sounds like some kind of Lord of the Rings, good versus evil, bull crap. Why would anyone hex or curse me?" We tend to believe that if we are good at heart and do not cause others harm, then everyone around us is doing the same. Unfortunately, that is not always the case. There are those, even in the seemingly supportive witch community, that perceive positivity and light as weakness and are all too ready to take advantage. There are also those who simply make mistakes and cast negativity accidentally. And finally, there are "dabblers" - people who may be temporarily angry or hurt and decide that reading a webpage on spell casting is enough research and end up putting something out into the universe which has far-reaching and terrible consequences for us. No matter the reasoning, the negativity placed on the unsuspecting recipient can range from annoying, to troubling, to devastating. We **need** to have an understanding of the ways to identify and destroy the negative effects that Black Magick can cause in our lives, whether it was intentionally or unintentionally placed.

Let me tell you about my first experience with negative, dark forces as a cautionary tale. In 1995, I was a wide-eyed, fledgling Wiccan. Wicca is a neo-pagan religion based on the worship of nature and universal forces. Not all Wiccans are witches, and not all witches are Wiccan. However, my intent was to practice spell work within the Wicca religion. Being new to the belief system and living in a rural setting, I did not have experienced Wiccans around me to provide guidance. Google did not even exist and the internet as a whole was still in its infancy. What I did have was access to a bookstore. So, I began to read everything I could to learn the ins and outs of the religion, as well as spell casting.

My third ritual ever was found in one of the many spellbooks I had acquired. It was presented as a spell to manifest an increase in light and happiness in the practitioner's life. I remember that there were many such spells, and I picked this particular spell simply because I already had the necessary ingredients. The spell included the casting of a protective circle, the common call upon the Goddess, and a few sentences which were described as calling upon a named Angel to deliver the "power of [its] light upon me". I followed the spell instructions and felt that it had been a successful casting session. Unfortunately, I was correct.

I had never heard of the Angel that the spell called upon. But, as I said, I was new, and I had no reason to think that any of the information in my prized books would be incorrect or dangerous. But that changed.

Within days of the ritual, I began to notice an increase in self-deprecating thoughts, along with a decrease in my natural confidence and sense of humor.

Within a month of the ritual, I had lost my job; withdrawn from friends; and fallen into a deep depression. Darkness had become a constant companion and hope was harder and harder to hold onto.

Within six months of the ritual, I found myself on the brink of total destruction. Nothing that I tried seemed to bring any joy. I was drinking at a very unhealthy level in an attempt to find relief from the constant weight of sadness. It was at this point that I was reading through a book on demonology I had just purchased. A passage in this book included, almost as an aside, a word that caught my eye. It was the name of the "Angel" which I had called upon in my ritual! For obvious reasons, I will not print the name here. Upon researching the being, I discovered that it was not the name of an Angel at all, but that of a Demon. My naivety and lack of research had led me to blindly call upon a Demon and request that it manifest its "light" in my life. That was the moment I realized just how powerful magick truly is. I have no idea whether the name of that Demon ended up in that book purposefully to cause pain, or if it had been a mistake by the author. But either way, the effect was the same. It nearly led me to become just another suicide statistic.

But the universe placed that demonology book in my path and, upon learning the truth and the cause of the train wreck my life had become, I immediately began to research how to reverse the ritual I had performed. The spell reversal I found was as simple as the original ritual had been. After gathering the ingredients, I performed the reversal and was immediately free of the oppression I had been under for so many months. My outlook on life brightened and my corner of the universe began to right itself.

And, yes of course, I have included that reversal spell within these pages! Not only did the experience highlight for me the power of magick, but also the need to be cautious in spell selection and casting; as well as the importance of understanding exactly what one is doing when performing a ritual.

This is not Harry Potter. Witches do not wave a stick, say some Latin words, and levitate people. Witches are manipulating powerful, universal forces to have real effects on their own (or other people's) lives. Those effects may benefit themselves or you, or they may be specifically designed to cause harm in your life. Once that threshold is passed and a witch is intentionally causing harm to another, the gloves need to come off. You can literally be fighting for your life.

You should know exactly how to protect yourself, your loved ones, and your property from astral attack. You should know exactly how to break a curse, a hex, evil soul ties, and unholy covenants. You should know how to be your own shield and your own sword. There may very well be no time to waste.

It is my solemn vow to you that after reading these pages you will:

- Understand the practical basics and must-knows of protection and reversal;

- Have the skills and confidence to level prayers/incantations which will lead you into protection, growth, and more awareness of and deeper understanding of self;

- Know how to identify signs of negative energy work; and

- Be able to destroy and reverse what needs to be destroyed and reversed.

Evil and negativity are not concerned with whether you believe in it or not. Darkness will affect you equally whether you are just starting out in the Wicca religion, are an experienced practitioner of Wicca, do not ascribe to any particular religion, or are a devout follower of a completely unrelated belief system. The tips, explanations, energy work, and spells included in this book are not aimed to make you a Wiccan, or a witch, or a pagan, or a believer of anything. This book is designed for YOUR protection and to provide you with armor against evil, darkness, and negativity aimed at you from any source. And you can rest assured that every aspect of the spells and prayers included herein has been properly researched. No demon names here!

Introduction

Quick Recommendation from the Magickal Witches team: We would like to make the magickal journey you are about to embark on as smooth as possible. As with any journey, preparations need to be made, and there are tools fit for each witch, new or experienced. In our case, we'd like to recommend the "Survival and Wellness Kit for Magickal Witches", which is completely free. Not using these tools is like making a trip to a rainforest and not taking any sort of tool to protect yourself from mosquitoes. You can do it, but the experience won't be quite as seamless as it could have been. It's discomfort that's not necessary and can even be risky. This analogy fits perfectly; if you don't have the right tools to go through with this process, it can be uncomfortable, and there is even a risk of not having a practice full of magick.

Please access the following link here or scan the code below: https://magickalwitches.gr8.com/

It may not be completely clear why these components are essential quite yet, but in further chapters, you will notice that this information will be very helpful. When you actually begin the practical side of the magickal work, you will come to understand. These tools are meant to alleviate some stress and obstacles that may show up along the way. For the time being, let's dive into understanding some theories that are meant to enhance the magickal journey you're here for.

Chapter 1

Knowing & Signs

So everything bad, unwanted, and unfortunate that happens in our lives has a supernatural cause? Of course not. I can make all the poor decisions I want and then undo the effects through the use of the spells and prayers? Definitely not. To tell the difference between natural occurrences and supernatural effects we need to understand the signs of being cursed, hexed, or being under the influence of negative energy work.

Luck, both good and bad, plays a part in our lives, as does the perfectly natural circumstances of cause and effect. It can be difficult sometimes to identify the true cause(s) of events in our lives. For this reason, it is extremely important that we do not jump to conclusions regarding what happens in our lives. We gain nothing when we try to cause a positive change in ourselves by attacking from the wrong angle. We need to determine the true cause of our troubles and take the appropriate action to counteract or destroy those causes.

Upon completion of this Chapter, you will have learned:

- To define and differentiate between a "curse" and a "spell";

- To demonstrate a working knowledge of;

  - Negative Soul Ties

  - Covenants

  - Agreements

- The dangers of practicing witchcraft;

- Psychic attacks;

- The types of witchcraft and curses;

- The signs of being under a witchcraft attack;

- The theory behind counteracting the power of witchcraft;

- The theory behind counteracting unholy agreements.

Here you will begin your journey into the world of fighting darkness with light, protecting that which is important to you, and no longer being a victim to dangerous, evil magick.

What is a "curse" and a "spell"?

A "curse" is defined as:

> "An appeal or prayer for evil or misfortune to befall someone or something."
>
> - The Free Dictionary

Honestly, that seems a bit too clinical to explain something so evil, fully encompassing, and broad. A curse can be placed on an object, an area, or a specific person. Its effect can be anything from loss of good fortune to death of multiple generations of family members.

As with most witchcraft, the intent of the witch casting the curse is crucial. One cannot "accidentally" cast a curse. Thankfully! The power of a curse does not come from the burning of a specific herb or the calling on a specific deity. The power of a curse is a reflection of the evil and harmful intent of the caster. To be successful in casting a curse upon an object, an area, or an individual, the caster must focus their rage, their dark desire, their destructive intent, every ounce of harm and hurt within them toward the goal of the curse. It is this wave of evil desire that the caster is sending out into the universe. Please understand that I am not being overly dramatic in my description. For most, the casting of a powerful curse is a very difficult undertaking because of the amount of focused intent required. It is not a matter of being momentarily hurt when you see your ex with a new lover. This requires serious, deep hatred. And luckily that kind of emotional output leaves a mark that links the curse with the caster - like when we touch any surface, we leave a fingerprint (a tiny bit of ourselves) behind on that surface, so it is the same with a caster and the curse they produce. It is this very link that will later help us to reverse the curse on the caster. But we have more to learn before we get to that point.

A "spell", on the other hand, is defined as:

> "The means employed to effect some kind of change, to accomplish some magical action, to bewitch someone or something, to influence a particular course of events or to inject magic into healing remedies or objects."
>
> - witchcraftandwitches.com

Spells are probably the best-known characteristic of witchcraft. They can be positive or negative, meaning that a "curse" is actually a type of "spell". A spell would usually involve the use of a protective circle, the calling of a deity or some type of supernatural being, the use of specific herbs or crystals, and an incantation or prayer.

Negative Soul Ties

Soul ties are created between two individuals through a powerful shared experience, namely sex and/or marriage. That's right. We are going to talk about the *horizontal mambo*.

Our modern society has taught us that sex is nothing more than a base, carnal, physical act. But that is not actually accurate. Sex is much more than that. It is a tridimensional experience - physical, mental, and spiritual. When we give ourselves to another sexually (casual, one-night stand or otherwise), we are actually forming a bond - a soul tie - with that person. We are exchanging a bit of our body, our mind, and our soul. Think about that for a moment. That means that, even in a casual sexual encounter where we think we are just craving human touch, we are deciding to give a part of ourselves to another human and, in turn, receive a part of them to carry with us.

I immediately flash to the Nancy Reagan era slogan, "Each time you sleep with someone, you also sleep with everyone they have ever slept with." Sure, that was meant to be a warning against indiscriminate promiscuity to avoid sexually transmitted diseases. But in a way, that slogan is correct on a number of different levels. In the same way that silly putty can pick up an image from newsprint, so too does each soul pick up or transfer an imprint of itself upon the soul of a mate.

This is not some diatribe against sex! Far from it. However, it is an explanation and warning that our carnal actions do have universal consequences. Many people use sex as a temporary fix; a Band-Aid to cover an emotional wound. When the next morning comes and the "relationship" ends, a residue is left - like the glue that is left behind when you remove the Band-Aid. That residue can cause very negative effects in the lives of one or both of the participants. The effects can range from an unfilled longing to the scariest of all events in a one-night stand - the dreaded "catching of feelings". Humans are very distinct and complicated animals. Our limbic system is responsible for both the physical sexual response and the release of the chemical compounds that make us feel love. In that way, we are predisposed to link love and sex to a certain degree. My father implanted me with a quote that I have remembered and have seen proven true again and again throughout my life. That pearl of wisdom was, "Men give love for sex. Women give sex for love." Mind you, that was back in a time period when "man" and "woman" were the only two options, so an update may be necessary for today.

But what happens when you end up with a soul tie that keeps you from fully loving anyone else in the future? Or what if you end up with a soul tie who is not able to let go and move on with their life without you? Or what if you are married, and yet create a soul tie with someone other than your spouse? These would be examples of **negative soul ties.** They affect your life in negative ways.

Covenants

Covenants are spiritual contracts. They can be either positive or negative contracts, but for our purposes we will be focusing on the negative contracts. Who would want to destroy a positive contract anyway!

Covenants are among the most difficult types of negativity to identify because the individual responsible for the covenant may well be dead and gone. A covenant with an evil entity can have effects lasting numerous generations past the maker of the deal. And the deal maker may not have even known that he/she was making a deal with evil. If you are familiar with the phrase, "a pact with the devil", an evil covenant is what is being referenced.

An evil covenant can be entered into by an individual on their own behalf or on the behalf of their child(ren). And the person making the covenant need not even have a full understanding of the terms of the contract, including the fact that the terms will result in destruction of future generations! Hey, nobody has ever claimed that the spiritual realm is fair, especially when dealing with evil forces.

As I explained in the introduction, as a new Wiccan, I myself accidentally entered into an evil covenant with a demon and was lucky enough to break the contract before the demon was able to succeed in taking my soul. It was a lack of attention to detail that very nearly cost me an eternity in Hell.

Like any contract, consideration must be received by both sides. So, the maker of the contract will receive whatever it is that they request, but the payment to the evil entity will ALWAYS far outweigh any worth the maker may receive.

The only purpose of a covenant, and thus the only consideration acceptable, to evil is absolute and total devastation of as many lives as possible. Humans never, and I mean never, are able to come out ahead in a covenant with evil.

However, because it is possible for a covenant to be causing negative effects in our lives many generations removed from the maker of the pact, it is important to know how to battle and destroy the link between us and evil. Ways to disconnect from the destruction will be discussed in Chapter 2.

Agreements

Negative agreements can be grounds for a demonic attack against our lives. These types of agreements between two individuals may seem innocent, and even true, at the time but later are dismissed. Something as simple as "Will you marry me?" answered with "Yes, I will marry you." is an agreement. Perfectly sweet and innocent at the time. But what happens if the agreement ends up being broken and one side decides to not complete the agreement? Spirits do not forget.

One side or the other of the agreement may decide to dismiss the agreement. Both may forget about the agreement and just go on with their lives. But the spirits who witnessed the agreement and the joining through agreement of the two souls may not just let it go. The souls can use the breaking of the agreement to afflict one or both sides of the agreement until the agreement is properly resolved.

Although these agreements are made between two humans, they are witnessed by and held accountable to the spiritual realm. Your word truly is your bond. To break that agreement opens you to the possibility of demonic interference and attack in your life. Prayers for properly dissolving these agreements will be discussed in Chapter 2.

Psychic Attack

A psychic attack is an intentional attack by a witch to cause a change in an individual's luck, thought patterns, or emotions. It isn't necessarily a spell cast to cause harm (a curse) but could also include a love spell for instance. A love spell designed to manipulate one's emotions into loving another individual is a form of psychic attack. Another example of a psychic attack may be a spell designed to turn an individual's luck bad. Although a psychic attack is not specifically cast to cause "harm", it is a perfectly understandable possibility. For instance, a person may be deemed "lucky" if an air conditioner falls out of a 7th story window and narrowly misses them. However, if that individual's luck has been affected by a psychic attack, that same air conditioner may very well not miss.

The Dangers Of Witchcraft

Witchcraft is truly not for everyone, and it is certainly not for the faint of heart. It can be terrifically dangerous for both the witch and for their client or target. We must realize that we are dealing with forces that are far too large to "control". The caster is merely "directing" the forces. As soon as a witch becomes overconfident in their abilities and understanding, the universe and magic itself have a tendency to remind us just how human we are. In my opinion, albeit humble, there is no more spiritually dangerous activity than "dabbling" in magick. Witchcraft and magick demand our full commitment and respect.

A story from London, England, tells of a mother and daughter who became convinced that the 75-year-old woman who lived in the apartment next to their own was a witch. They also fully believed that a rash of recent bad luck and illness they had experienced had been directed at them by this woman. And so, they began to hold nightly, 9-hour, sessions of chanting toward the wall which separated the two apartments. The chants were loud enough to keep the elderly woman awake throughout the night and she was forced to sleep only during the day. The mother and daughter began to include more deadly and evil language, until they were heard chanting "Death by fire to the witch" for three straight nights. On the fourth day, the mother and daughter were discovered by a family friend. Both appeared to have burned to death in their beds, although there was no fire damage anywhere else in the apartment, nor even to the mattresses which the two women were found on. The story was relayed to British authorities by the old woman who was in no way found to be involved at all in witchcraft. The mother and daughter had misattributed their woes to a curse and had, in turn, actually become the very witches they were incanting to burn. Is this some antiquated, medieval story passed through generations as a fable? No. This incident took place in 2015.

The above incident also goes to show that witch harassment is still alive and well in modern society. Witches may not be hanging in towns and villages, but the uneducated and knee-jerk reactions to the unknown still pose a big threat to witches today. These are the dangers that keep witchcraft secret and still only being practiced in the shadows.

There is also the danger of being swindled and scammed out of huge amounts of money. Fake faith healers, fake witchcraft supply stores, and fake clairvoyants are all big businesses. These unscrupulous scammers prey on the weak, the frightened, and the sad. Fake faith healers will take people for all they are worth with promises of miracle, supernatural cures. These scammers can be found across nearly every religion and in every corner of the globe, but are extremely prevalent in the holistic and charismatic Christian communities. With all of the evidence and information available to us with the click of a button, it surprises me that these sham "healers" still continue to be successful, but desperation can make otherwise rational people do some very irrational things.

Fake clairvoyants are of the same ilk as illegitimate faith healers, except clairvoyants are usually sought out by even more desperate individuals. Those who seek out easy-to-find, sham clairvoyants tend to have lost someone in their life and will believe almost anything that gives them some sense of peace. Through broad questions and reading of body language, a good scam artist can appear to have come into contact with some very accurate information. Not only that but they are well-practiced in keeping you coming back for more. With each session being worth up to $150-$200, even a fake can support a very comfortable lifestyle. Not to mention, some "clairvoyants" can even manipulate their clients into believing that a curse has been placed upon them that only the "clairvoyant" has the power to break…for a healthy fee of course.

And those are dangers if the witch is NOT legitimate. There are also dangers inherent in the practice of Black Magick. Any spell or ritual performed to cause harm to another person can, and often does, have repercussions on the casting witch as well. This is due to the Rule of Three. The religious tenet of the Rule of Three states that whatever energy a witch puts out into the universe, be it positive or negative, will be returned to that witch threefold. Witches casting black magick spells/curses, use a protective circle in the attempt to shield themselves from the effects of the Rule of Three. However, there are no guarantees when it comes to the Rule of Three. When we focus our intent on negativity, it leaves a stain behind; an indelible mark on the witch's soul that forever changes them and invites the Rule of Three.

Brief History of Witchcraft and Wicca

Although witchcraft and witches have been a presence since before the Middle Ages (references date back to the 13th century), the religion of Wicca is a relative newcomer to the world scene.

The "father" of modern Wicca is Gerald Gardner, although he never actually called his belief system "Wicca" because he preferred the more ancient term "Witchcraft". In 1920, Gardner was initiated into the New Forest Coven in Britain. It was Gardner's belief and claim that the New Forest Coven was a surviving group of original witch-cult members.

In 1946, Gardner feared that witchcraft was a dying and disappearing practice. So, he began his own coven, calling it the Bricket Wood Coven, with another former member of the New Forest Coven, Edith Woodford-Grimes. Gardner and Woodford-Grimes became the High Priest and High Priestess of the Bricket Wood Coven. Gardner implanted in his new tradition a lasting foundation of Wicca - the notion of an equal God and Goddess (this was terrifically unique and intriguing within the patriarchal, male-dominated society of 1940s Britain.) In this same year, Gardner initiated Alex Sanders into the Bricket Wood Coven. Sanders would later leave Bricket Wood Coven to form a new system of belief known as Alexandrian Wicca.

Woodford-Grimes only stayed with the Bricket Wood Coven for 6 years, citing concerns over the publicity that Gardner was attempting to bring to the religion. Prior to Gardnerian Witchcraft, all aspects of witchcraft were practiced in extreme privacy for the safety of the practitioners. Gardner, however, aimed to change the pact of secrecy of the religion and to gain popular understanding and acceptance. This proved to be a brilliant and well-timed strategy, but it did tend to make some traditionalists rather uneasy.

In 1953, Gardner initiated Doreen Valiente into the Bricket Wood Coven and she became the new High Priestess of the coven. With the assistance of Valiant, Gardner wrote the Bricket Wood Coven Book of Shadows. Many of the rituals in the Book of Shadows came from late Victorian-era occultism, but much of the spiritual content is derived from older pagan religions and includes both Hindu and Buddhist influences. Valiant was able to rewrite many of the spells and incantations into poetic verse. The partnership with Valiant was also short-lived, as she left the coven due to Gardner's continued publicity hunt and the new rules and restrictions which he began placing on the Bricket Wood Coven and the other covens following Gardnerian Witchcraft.

Gardnerian Witchcraft was brought to the United States in the 1960s by a British Airways employee named Raymond Buckland and his wife. The Bucklands were initiated into Witchcraft in Britain by Monique Wilson, a Gardner adherent. Upon their move to the United States, the Bucklands began the Long Island Coven. The Bucklands continued to lead the Long Island Coven until 1973, at which time the Bucklands stopped strictly following Gardnerian Witchcraft and formed a new tradition called Saex Wicca. Saex Wicca combined aspects of Gardnerian Witchcraft with Anglo-Saxon pagan iconography.

In 1971, American Zsuzsanna Budapest fused Wiccan practices with the burgeoning feminist ideals and politics to form Dianic Wicca. This tradition focused exclusively on the Goddess, Diana, and was completely made of female practitioners.

Although there are many different offshoots of Wicca and types of witchcraft, as we will soon see, Gardnerian Witchcraft was the first to step out of the shadows and show itself as a legitimate religious belief.

Types of Witchcraft

One could write an entire book filled with nothing but "types of witches". It seems that there are as many categories, sub-categories, and specializations as there are practitioners! But let's focus on 7 categories.

Folk Witch - A "traditional" or "Folk Witch" practices the magick of his or her ancestors, or of their general geographic region. The Folk Witch tends to take their magick as historical because it would have been practiced well prior to the formation of Wicca as a religion. The Folk Witch would most likely be a wealth of local information, having access to local availability of talismans, crystals, herbs, charms, and spells. Many Folk Witches have begun to blend the use of their "traditional" magick with more updated beliefs and modern tools.

Green Witch - The Green Witch focuses on their interaction with nature and the magic to be garnered daily from nature itself. A Green Witch is typically a rural witch and highly influenced by folk magic, with the center of their magical world being the home. The use of herbal remedies tends to be the specialty of most Green Witches and they often grow and harvest the herbs themselves, as opposed to purchasing herbs from vendors. Also, Green Witches are usually quite versed in aromatherapy using local herb blends.

Gardnerian Wiccans - Gardnerian Wiccans are one of only two forms of modern witchcraft that can trace its lineage back in an unbroken line to the very beginning of Wicca, i.e., Gerald Gardner. Although not all Wiccans are witches, Gardnerian Wicca is a British form of Wicca which is bound by oath to practice reasonable witchcraft. Gardnerian Wicca tends to be extremely practical with very little ceremony.

Alexandrian Wiccans - Alexandrian Wiccans are the second form of modern witchcraft able to trace its lineage back to those early days, i.e., Alex Sanders. Alex Sanders was one of Gerald Gardner's very first initiated into Wicca. Alexandrian Wicca is typically a blend of ceremonial and Gardnerian Wicca.

Eclectic Witch - Eclectic witchcraft is a catch-all term for witchcraft that doesn't specifically fit into any other category. The Eclectic Witch may be a blend of many different traditions, faiths, and folk practices. The Eclectic Witch can be thought of as the consummate do-it-yourselfer. They may take some traditional beliefs, some things read online, some things learned from a workshop they attended, and their own personal experiences; roll them all together, and come up with a practical method of witchcraft that works for them.

Ceremonial Witch - Ceremonial witchcraft, also called High witchcraft, uses very specific tools and incantations to call upon the deities and entities of the spirit world. Ceremonial witchcraft is a blend of ancient occult/pagan teachings. This type of witchcraft is held highly secret and many practitioners do not even identify with the word "witch" at all out of an abundance of caution.

Hereditary Witch - Hereditary witchcraft is a belief and practice system in which the knowledge is handed down from one generation to the next (mother to daughter; father to son). It is very unusual for any family outsider to be included in Hereditary witchcraft and it is just as unusual for the existence of such knowledge to even be discussed in the presence of an outsider, including sons-in-law or daughters-in-law. The relationship need not necessarily be a genetic one, as adopted children are seen as worthy candidates for Hereditary witchcraft. It is more a family tradition basis than a strictly biological tradition.

Angels for Prayer

Praying to angels for protection is quite literally as old as the first humans. More specifically, we are talking about archangels. An archangel is an angel of the highest rank. In Abrahamic religions, the archangels were created before any others and are seen as "leaders of angels" in their various tasks.

Angels are seen as the bringers of messages to humanity. Since the expulsion of Adam and Eve from the Garden of Eden, God does not come and speak with humans directly. Instead, angels are used as intermediaries. It was an archangel, and his angelic forces, who physically visited and ensured that Adam and Eve left the Garden; it was an archangel who visited Mary and informed her that she would be pregnant with Jesus.

However, archangels also have roles to fill directly assigned by God. Some are protectors, some are healers, etc. Not all angels are relevant to our topic of protection from evil and so we will focus on the relevant angels only. However, feel free to explore the others and add them into your prayers as you see fit. Just remember, from personal experience, you must research the names thoroughly and use pronunciation keys if necessary. Most demons were, after all, angels themselves before the fall of Beelzebub. And we certainly do not want to mistakenly call on a fallen angel to enter our lives.

The following are archangels named in the Bible and their assigned roles:

- Gabriel-

Gabriel was the first angel created. The name "Gabriel" means "God is my strength".

Gabriel's ministry is promise and mercy. It was Gabriel who God sent to deliver the news of the coming of Jesus.

- Michael-

Michael is listed as the Chief Prince of Heaven.

Michael's roles include: leading a host of angels in a victorious war over Beelzebub and protecting the angels during the end times. Also, Michael works to oppose Beelzebub in his rebellion against God and his attacks upon humanity.

Michael is a warrior and a champion. He can be called upon in times of battles against evil.

-Raphael-

Raphael is among the highest-ranking archangels. The name "Raphael" means "God heals".

Raphael stands before the throne of God. Some of his duties include presenting the prayers of the saints and entering into the presence of the glory of God. It is also his work to heal the earth defiled by the fallen angels.

-Uriel-

Uriel is an angel of wisdom. He is an archangel who watches over thunder and terror. In modern Christianity, Uriel is an angel of the divine presence, repentance, and archangel of salvation. Uriel means "God is my light."

Christians depict Uriel carrying a book or a papyrus scroll which represents wisdom.

-Azrael- Azrael holds the role of the angel of death. He does not *cause* death. Instead, he is responsible for helping the soul detach from the physical body after death and leading the soul to judgment.

-Phanuel- Phanuel is the throne bearer of God and the archangel of repentance. Phanuel is responsible for ministering truth and serves as the angel of judgment. Phanuel means "Face of God".

-Zadkiel- Zadkiel is the archangel of freedom, mercy, and benevolence. He also serves as the patron angel of all those that forgive. His influence on humans helps to inspire forgiveness to allow them to attain spiritual freedom. Zadkiel means "Grace of God".

-Camael- Camael is the archangel of strength, courage, and war. Camael is the leader of the forces that physically removed Adam and Eve from the Garden of Eden. Camel means "He who sees God".

-Jeremiel- Jeremiel has various roles, including assisting humans with clairvoyance and prophetic visions. He is also an angel of emotions and assists people to take a closer look at their lives. Also, he serves as the gatekeeper of heaven and watches over the holy deceased in their afterlife journey.

-Ramiel- Ramiel is the archangel of hope. He fills the roles of assisting with divine visions and guiding the faithful's souls into heaven. Ramiel, represents the mercy and eternal compassion of God. Ramiel means "God's thunder".

-Ariel- Ariel is the angel of nature. Her role is to oversee the healing and protection of animals and plants. Ariel also is charged with taking care of the earth's elements, including fire, wind, and water. Since she is a messenger, she punishes everyone that harms the creation of God. Ariel means "Lion of God".

-Barachiel- Barachiel is the patron angel of family and marriage. He is responsible for watching over converts to Christianity, referred to as God's adopted children, and helping them with their lives.

-Haniel- Haniel plays the role of divine communicator and acts as a direct passage between a human's lower energy and the higher energy states of the celestial realms.

-Jehudiel- Jehudiel is the angel of work. His role is to guide those in positions of responsibility by ensuring they work to glorify God.

-Jophiel- Jophiel is known as the angel of beauty and wisdom. She is the patron angel of artists and artistic illumination. She teaches the outer consciousness of Power of Light within oneself and sends fresh ideas to people.

Types of Curses

As with the types of witchcraft, there are MANY types of curses. However, given the fact that we are all living in a fast-paced technological world, there is less and less time available to perform curses that may take multiple days or weeks to complete. Therefore, instead of boring you with details on magick that is extremely rare, we will discuss 5 much more likely quick curse types. It is important to be aware and familiar with the types of curses when it comes to successfully spotting the signs of being cursed!

Spitting Curses - Yep. The least hygienic way to possibly curse someone. The most effective spitting curses are performed by actually spitting directly on the target. But, thankfully, that is pretty tricky to get away with in modernity… and definitely in the age of Covid-19! However, these curses can also be performed by spitting in front of or behind the person with the proper intent. Or even on something the target is likely to touch, like a door handle or keyboard. If you are a germaphobe, I apologize for putting these images in your head, but knowledge is power. Moving on!

The Evil Eye - It may sound like some kind of punchline to a Golden Girls episode, but it is all too real. The evil eye is a large output of evil intent directed while staring at the target of the curse. Because we have learned that intent released into the universe is really the backbone to all spells and curses, this should make sense. Gathering all of the evil, wicked intent and imagery the witch can muster and releasing it all at once toward a target he or she is in visual contact with is actually quite a powerful and dangerous weapon.

Verbal Curses - Pretty self-explanatory probably. These are short incantations that can be repeated over and over while releasing the evil intent of the curse into the universe. It is frightening just how simple it is to find ready-made verbal curses with just a quick Google search, not to mention that some of the most powerful and appropriately directed verbal curses actually spring from the creativity of the casting witch!

Written Curses - With written curses, the casting witch can write the evil intent on a slip of paper and conceal the paper on or near the target. Written curses are actually quite powerful, especially if combined with an accompanying verbal curse to add to the destruction.

Object Curses - Object curses are probably the most common type and, unfortunately, also the most long-lasting. An object curse is not directed at a specific person but is instead placed on an inanimate object. This allows the curse to affect anyone and everyone who comes into contact with the object. That's right folks. We are talking about the kind of curse that was attached to the lava rock in *The Brady Bunch - Hawaii* episode! And if you don't know what I am talking about, are you sure you are old enough to be reading this book?!

There are two big issues when it comes to object curses. First, they may have been unintentionally cursed. If the object was very near or extremely special to an individual who exuded or was a victim of rampant, sustained evil, the object may have picked up the evil by transference. Murder weapons used for bludgeoning or cutting a victim to death are notorious for becoming "cursed objects". Not because they were cursed by a witch, but because of the evil which was poured out through them.

The second issue is that the object may not be "cursed" at all but may instead be haunted. Many times, this is the case with "cursed" dolls. Instead of having a curse placed on them, dolls are actually ripe vessels for demons or evil souls to inhabit. Real examples of haunted dolls with "cursed" histories include "Annabelle" held by the Estate of Ed and Lorraine Warren; "Robert The Doll" exhibited by the East Martello Museum in Key West, Florida; and "Harold The

Doll" held by Zack Baggins in Las Vegas, NV. Removing a "curse" from a haunted object will have no effect whatsoever, except perhaps to anger the already demented spirit within.

Reading the Signs: How to know if you are under a witchcraft attack

First and foremost, witchcraft or psychic attack should not be among the first things you assume is wrong with you! If you are having physical symptoms, go to your doctor. If you are having psychological symptoms, go to your therapist. It is absolutely imperative that you rule out natural, logical causes before moving on to otherworldly, supernatural ones. Usually, there is a perfectly legitimate and understandable medical or psychological reason for what is happening.

The keyword in that sentence is "usually". Let's assume that you have ruled out any cause for your distress here on this plane. What next? Well, it is time to take a look at your life for signs of a psychic attack through witchcraft.

Signs that you are under attack can vary wildly based on the type of curse, the intended result, and the knowledge of the caster. For instance, a curse designed to cause you depression and increase your self-loathing will have different signs than a curse designed to cause physical damage to your heart. There are, however, some general signs which are common to all curses. These are the signs we will be taking a look at.

Planting the Seed - Curses, and magick in general, become more powerful when the target is aware of the intent. So, if the caster is determined to cause the desired effect in your life, they may very well tell you about the curse. Or, if they have an outwardly positive relationship with you, they may merely hint at the possibility of a curse just to plant the seed of thought in your mind. If someone tells you that they have cursed you, it is safest to believe it and act accordingly.

Unexplainable Physical Sickness - If you develop some kind of physical ailment that your doctor is unable to explain and control with modern medicine, someone may be attacking you. Headaches/migraines are a common physical symptom of psychic attack. But remember, we only get to this point by ruling out the more probable medical reasons. It is also common for a new and unexplainable hormonal imbalance to arise. This is because the pineal gland (otherwise known as the Third Eye) in the brain is responsible for hormone regulation. If our Third Eye is sensing an ongoing psychic attack, our hormonal balance can be greatly affected.

Lethargy and/or Inability to Sleep - Although it just sounds like a normal day of Covid quarantine, blobbing out on the couch and not being able to form much desire to do anything is actually a sign of psychic attack. That type of extreme lethargy can be coupled with the inability to actually get restorative sleep. If these symptoms are a result of a psychic attack, the purpose may be to destroy your quality of life, affect your physical and mental health, or even cause you to lose your job. However, these are also symptoms of depression, which highlights the importance of seeking medical guidance first.

Nightmares - As our conscious mind rests, our subconscious mind processes and plays out the inner dialogue of the psyche. When our guard is down and we are not able to consciously process or control our experience, curses can be very active. Now, not every occasional nightmare is a sign of a psychic attack. The nightmares we are talking about here are persistent and recurring. If you are having the same type of nightmare repeatedly, nightly, you may be experiencing a psychic attack.

Depression/Oppression without cause - Despite adequate nutrition, counseling, and medication, something just keeps weighing you down. This odd feeling of being unsettled can be an indication of the presence of negative energy or an evil attachment.

Paranoia - This type of mental effect usually manifests as a feeling of being watched, or a feeling that your thoughts and the thoughts of those around you are being invaded or monitored by someone else. These feelings can, and are actually designed to, convince you and those around you that you are going insane and cannot be fully trusted. It is a truly surreal situation to be in when you no longer are sure you can trust your own senses, your own inner dialogue. Again, paranoid delusions are a well-known psychological disorder so make sure to rule out any such pedantic explanation first.

Patterns and Symbols - These are the types of things we tend to think about as signs or omens. These can take an endless number of forms, but the most important part is that they will be most apparent to the target. Our Third Eye can filter mere coincidence from true patterns and symbology. For example, if you wake up on your own at 4:18 a.m. every morning for a week and look at the clock, your pineal gland will discern whether it just happened that way or if it is a sign. Follow your instincts when it comes to patterns and/or signs. Go with your gut.

Loss of Time and Memory - You may experience gaps in your memory where you cannot account for the amount of time that has passed. This occurs as your worldly outlook begins to steadily turn inward. Time becomes irrelevant because you are dealing with so many other, seemingly more pressing, issues. You may have no memory of meeting people, going to places, or the things you have done during these periods. It is as if you exist on a separate timeline from those around you and can lead to some very disturbing and awkward situations.

Animals acting oddly in your presence - Animals are far more emotionally intelligent than we commonly give them credit for. There is a reason that animals have been used as "familiars" by witches stretching back into antiquity. They have a very strong connection to the spirit world and are able to sense when something is not quite right. A change in an animal's behavior when they are around you may signal that you are under attack from the spirit world.

Destroying the Power of Witchcraft & Unholy Agreements

Now that we have discussed definitions, types, dangers, and signs of witchcraft interference in our lives, it is time to begin arming ourselves against attack. No one deserves the terrible consequences that can arise from a psychic attack.

The negativity - the evil born into the universe as a result of a curse - is an abomination and an affront to the purity and light of the universe.

Agreements made with dark and evil forces, demons, whatever you wish to call them is equally as destructive and unnatural as a curse. Holding true to an oath and following through with one's word should not be an exception, but the accepted rule in all things. As such, a broken agreement that invites darkness and evil into the equation must be properly undone.

The power to fight against and destroy these forces within our lives, along with the devastation and soul-crushing darkness they bring, resides in each of us. What vanquishes darkness? **Light.** What has the power to sever the chord holding us hostage to the whims of a curse-casting witch? **Prayer** and **Incantation.** Through the power of releasing light (good intentions) into the universe by way of prayer or incantation, we hold the ability to end psychic attacks against us. And through the power of releasing good intentions into the universe via prayer or incantation, we have the ability to successfully break agreements that have invited evil into our lives.

Chapter 2

Prayers & Protection Spells

Throughout this book, it has been my intention to completely avoid discussing religion. However, we are now in a section where it is going to be pretty much impossible to ignore it. Please understand that the power of the prayers and spells in this chapter do not come from the language used, but from the focused intent of the person reciting the prayer. If you find a prayer that resonates with you but contains the name of a deity to which you have no connection, there is no reason you cannot substitute a deity from your personal belief in its place. Or even simply use the term "universe".

With that being said, I will attempt to provide prayers and spells directly from as many religious backgrounds as possible. Read through each section and find those prayers or spells which speak to you and your experience.

As a specific note to my Christian brethren, I implore you not to skip over the "spells" in this chapter. While it is true that the faiths of Christianity and Wicca/Paganism/Occultism have been at odds for…well…more than 2,000 years now, demons and evil do not care if you believe in it or not. Quite frankly, a strong Christian faith actually puts you in more danger of a psychic attack from evil forces because Satan would most assuredly enjoy watching a saved soul squirm. In other words, just as Jesus worked in the supernatural realm, or should I say he came from the supernatural realm, you must be willing to fight for your health, safety, and well-being wherever it is being challenged.

The powers of evil and personal destruction that accompany a curse, a negative soul tie, an unholy covenant, or a broken agreement can be extremely strong and grow like a tumor, embedding themselves deep in our lives and psyche. It may, and most likely will, take more than one prayer or spell to free ourselves from this type of darkness.

This is not a one-and-done situation. I visualize curses and the other types of psychic attacks much like a mangrove tree. What appears on the surface to be a large swath of mangrove trees of many acres, or even an entire swamp, can actually be only one large mangrove tree. As the roots of a mangrove grow, they spread in all directions, not just down into the earth, and produce periodic shoots back above the surface. These become what appear to be separate and distinct trees but are actually part of the original root system.

So, it is the same with curses and darkness in our lives. What might appear to be unconnected traits or instances of negativity may, in fact, all be fed by the same curse. Just as you would not expect to kill a 4-acre wide mangrove system by chopping down one of the trees on the surface, we cannot expect to break a widespread curse that has pervaded many aspects of our lives by saying a prayer once and then moving on.

That is why we need to see the fight against darkness as an ongoing war and not just a single battle. We need to be willing to fight for ourselves, our destiny, and our bloodline. It may take repeating the same prayer once per day, or once per week, over an extended period of time to finally dig out the last effects of a curse in our lives. It may take performing the same ritual on successive new moons for a number of months to break a strong curse. It may even take a combination of the two! But please know that we are on the side of good, of light, of love, and of righteousness. We WILL prevail.

When you should utilize these prayers is completely up to you and your needs. The line of prayer is always open. That is the beautiful thing about prayer, it takes very little preparation and there is never a bad time to pray. It is important to focus and calm your spirit, open your heart and mind, and pray. Pray with all your heart. Pray often. And pray hard.

Utilizing these spells and rituals is slightly different. Spell work is normally performed at night, under the light of the moon. Unless otherwise noted within the spell, it is safe to assume that the spells and rituals are meant to be performed at the time of the waxing moon. Also, there is a specific way to maximize the power you are putting out into the universe - try to perform your ritual near running water (i.e., a creek, a river, an underground spring, etc.). The electromagnetic energy created by running water is a natural, measurable fact. It is electromagnetic energy that powers our intentions into the universe and into the spiritual plane. Therefore, if you are able to be near a source of electromagnetic energy, your intention will gain strength merely by being in the location. As you are preparing yourself for the ritual, focus your intention and calm your spirit, cast your protective circle, and make your intentions known.

How can we tell if our prayers and rituals are actually working? Well, have you ever tried to organize and clean out a garage? I always end up with boxes and piles of stuff sitting all over the driveway and yard at first. It pretty much becomes just a mass of controlled chaos because there is so much to unpack and go through to make sense of it all. It actually gets worse before it gets better. But then, the useful items get matched together, while the items which have gone bad or are no longer necessary are discarded. Order starts to form out of the chaos and, slowly but surely, everything starts to fall back into place nicely.

That is essentially how the breaking of psychic attacks and removal of evil from our lives will work as well. At first, things may seem to get worse. It may seem counterintuitive, but that means you are doing something right. Satan, evil, darkness - whatever you choose to call it - does not give up and release power easily or willingly. As you begin your work to rid yourself of negativity, darkness will double down. STAY STRONG. STAY THE COURSE. Positivity and light will begin to reign in your life. Order will begin to form out of the internal chaos and a feeling of peace and freedom from oppression will fall back into its rightful spot within you.

Cleansing and maintaining victory will be discussed in Chapter 3. Do not believe that once you have broken a curse or negative soul tie, you are free and clear. There will still be work to be done.

The Right to Reverse A Curse

In the following pages, you will find prayers and spells to break curses, and prayers and spells to reverse curses, negativity, and evil. To "reverse" a curse means to send the negativity back to the individual who placed the curse on you. You can think of reversal as sliding a mirror in between you and whoever placed the curse. The negativity reflects off of the mirror and shoots back in the other person's direction. Reversal is a wonderful option to rid yourself of negativity and to do so in accordance with universal laws. These universal laws include the concept of "like attracts like" and The Rule of Three.

In case you feel that you should never reverse black magick, let's discuss a bit about how the spiritual plane functions. On the spiritual plane, like attracts like. This means that it is not unusual to find negative energy zipping back and forth. When an individual performs a ritual or places a curse on you, your family, or your belongings, they are quite aware that the concept of "like attracts like" means that performing black magick opens one up to darkness. The focus and evil intent that it takes to saddle another individual with a curse announces to the universe that this person is open to negativity. Just as we can manifest good and light in our lives through focus and visualization, black magick uses the same concept to manifest evil and darkness in their life through their actions.

Further, any witch who is powerful and versed enough to successfully place a curse will also be aware of the Wiccan Rede (aka Rule of Three). A "Rede" is not something that a Wiccan or witch repeats as part of a spell or incantation, it is more of a guiding principle, or advice passed on from an adherent to a new follower. The Wiccan or witchcraft Rede states:

> "Bide the Wiccan Law ye must,
>
> In perfect love and perfect trust.
>
> Eight words the Wiccan Rede fulfill:
>
> If ye harm none, do what ye will.
>
> What ye send forth comes back to thee
>
> So ever mind the Law of Three.
>
> Follow this with mind and heart,
>
> Merry ye meet, and merry ye part."

The Wiccan Rede decrees that whatever type of energy one puts out into the universe will be returned to them threefold, be it positive or negative. The Rede stands as a warning against the use of black magick to avoid the threefold return of evil into their lives. However, humans tend to be greedy and spiteful creatures. And so, against all advice and against the Rede, humans will continue to flaunt the rules at every opportunity. Their insolence will lead to the return of their own punishment threefold.

For these reasons, there is no need to feel hesitant about reversing black magick onto its practitioner. It is completely natural and within the universal laws to do so. Because "like attracts like" the energy or evil will find its way back to the castor. The castor, the person who casts the curse, quite literally manifests or creates evil and darkness in order to mold it into the curse they want, it does not exist on its own or in a vacuum. Every curse needs a castor to come into being. This is why there is an undeniable and unearthly link between a curse and its castor. It is not wrong, evil, dangerous, or even shocking to return a creation to its creator. When we reverse a curse or evil intention placed on us, that is what we are doing - returning it to its creator (in threefold form).

Now, finally, let's grab our armor and sword and step into the fight.

Prayers To Destroy The Power of Witchcraft

#1

I thank you, God (or Goddess, Universe, Angels, Spirit, Ascended Masters, Protectors, etc.), for giving me authority and power to defeat the kingdom of darkness. I thank you for the authority that I have in you to overcome and defeat witchcraft, Jezebel, and their father the devil.

Through our Lord (or Goddess, Universe, Angels, Spirit, Ascended Masters, Protectors, etc.), you have given me authority to trample on snakes and scorpions and to overcome all the power of the enemy and nothing will harm me.

You have decreed that whatever I bind on earth will be bound in heaven, and whatever I release on the earth will be released in heaven, and that if two of us on the earth agree about anything we ask for, it will be done for us exactly as we agreed.

Amen and Blessed Be

==============================

#2

My Lord (or Goddess, Universe, Angels, Spirit, Ascended Masters, Protectors, etc.), I have authority and power over the spirits of witchcraft, Jezebel, wickedness and disfavor. I have power over the decisions and activities of the powers of darkness at all levels. As I stand in this divine agreement and pray this day, I will accept my victory over witchcraft and the works of darkness in my life and in my family.

I reject every form of authority of the devil and of authority of the witchcraft world over my life and family.

Let the walls and defenses of evil witchcraft against my life, my destiny and my family be torn down. Frustrate every witch; every wizard; every Jezebel against my life and my family.

I break the power of witchcraft's deception, seduction, sorcery, domination and intimidation over my life and my family. I command every evil seed in the form of strife, quarrels, disfavor, hatred, nightmares, illnesses, and confusions planted in my life or in my family be uprooted by fire this moment.

Amen and Blessed Be.

================================

#3

I hold myself as a being of light. I declare myself to be kept free of the captive and limiting power of darkness. I do hereby rebuke the use of all malicious and harmful magick for any purposes. Let not what I rebuke be used upon or against me; my family; my destiny; or my possessions.

The balance of nature shall be found elsewhere other than within the pure splendor and blessings of the light which shines from and upon me.

Allow my goodness to prevail against any evil settling upon me either in my past, present or future.

Amen and Blessed Be.

================================

#4

Lord (or Goddess, Universe, Angels, Spirit, Ascended Masters, Protectors, etc.) I ask that you forgive me in any way I have surrendered myself to men or women who come in your name but are using evil powers. I believe that I did not listen enough to you, which was why I submitted to their tricks. I believe you tried to warn me, but perhaps I placed my own needs far above your instruction.

Lord (or Goddess, Universe, Angels, Spirit, Ascended Masters, Protectors, etc.), I am now asking for restoration. Please restore my health; peace of mind; fruitfulness; property and breakthrough. Restore to me whatever has been tampered with in my life as a result of the witchcraft of false visioners and false preachers. I break every bond, tie and spiritual connection between me and demonic entities.

I declare a total restoration and healing of any part of my life that has been tampered with by my ignorant submission to the Great Deceiver.

Amen and Blessed Be.

Prayers to Destroy Curses and Spells

#1 - Prayer designed to destroy self-inflicted curses

This is the prayer which I used to break my own self-inflicted curse. Although it is rather rare to accidentally curse one's self, it is common enough for there to be a recommended prayer! Remember, the tip of the day is: Research any "names" you are unfamiliar with before throwing them around! Just in my personal experience, I repeated this exact prayer every day for 10 days before I felt the relief from this curse.

Heavenly Father (or Goddess, Universe, Angels, Spirit, Ascended Masters, Protectors, etc.), You have said that the power of death and life is in the tongue; and that we will be justified or condemned by our words. Lord (or Goddess, Universe, Angels, Spirit, Ascended Masters, Protectors, etc.), I know that Your words are ever true. Heaven and earth will pass away, but Your words will not.

Lord (or Goddess, Universe, Angels, Spirit, Ascended Masters, Protectors, etc.), I acknowledge that I have used my words in ways that were not decent and pleasing to You. I have used my words to hurt others, speak negative things about my life, partner, children, family, and nation. I now ask You to forgive all my wrong use of words from the past to present.

Sanctify my tongue and purify my heart. Empower me to be a carrier and speaker of life, health, encouragement, and peace from today onwards.

Whatever pain and hurt I have brought upon myself, my family, my career, my children, and my family as a result of my wrong use of words in the past, heal and restore me today.

I decree that no corrupt word will proceed out of my mouth again. I willingly command myself to put away all forms of bitterness, wrath, anger, malice and evil speaking from today. I command myself to be kind to others, tenderhearted, forgiving, and ever ready to be a blessing.

I break any curse I have imposed upon myself ignorantly, through my use of negative words, anger, fear and anxiety. I replace all self-inflicted pains and events in my life today with God's (or Goddess', Universe's, Angels', Spirit's, Ascended Masters', Protectors', etc.) favor, peace and deliverance.

I bless myself from now onwards; I bless my home; I bless my career; I bless my family; and I bless my children. When and where others are saying there is a casting down, I will be there to ensure there is a lifting up.

Amen and Blessed Be.

===============================

#2 - Prayer designed to destroy curses placed on parents

Today, Lord (or Goddess, Universe, Angels, Spirit, Ascended Masters, Protectors, etc.), I thank You for my parents and guardians. I thank You for giving them the grace to bring me into this world. I thank You for enabling them to care for and protect me and my siblings over the years.

I ask forgiveness for my actions which in any way dishonored or disrespected my parents or guardians in the past. I was ignorant. Please have mercy upon me now.

I pray today that You heal and restore my relationship with my parents and guardians. Give me the grace to forgive them if, in any way, I feel they have not treated me right in the past. As I take new steps to make amends with them, may Your power prevail in our hearts and may Your peace and love be established in our hearts once more.

From this day forward, I declare a break to every curse, negative word and evil pronouncement from my parents or guardians in the past. I receive deliverance from the consequences of these statements from today. And I decree healing and restoration from every hurt and pain affecting our lives as a result of these past statements.

Today, I exercise myself into forgiveness and willfully forgive my children, grandchildren, and anyone whom I cared for in the past that offended me. I drop all burdens against every one of them and release everyone from whatever curse is happening in their lives as a result of this harbored pain in my heart.

Amen and Blessed Be.

===============================

#3 - Prayer to break a multi-generational curse

Lord (or Goddess, Universe, Angels, Spirit, Ascended Masters, Protectors, etc.), I call upon you to give thanks for all of the blessings you have bestowed upon me. Your light, your love and your power has given me comfort and refuge throughout my life.

I rely on your promises Lord (or Goddess, Universe, Angels, Spirit, Ascended Masters, Protectors, etc.) now as I ask for relief. An ancestor has broken their relationship with you or gone against your demand or has been attacked by evil which follows me through the blood. I beseech you relieve me of this curse; this evil which has plagued those of my blood for untold generations.

You are my protector and my strength and I will follow you all the days of my life.

Amen and Blessed Be.

================================

#4 - Spell to break a multi-generational curse

What you will need:

- A small bag or locket-style necklace

- Sea or Mineral Salt

- Coriander (Cilantro)

- A small drop of your blood (to be harvested during ritual)

- A black candle

- A Selenite crystal

Instructions:

It is an extremely important portion of this spell work that you be as cleansed as possible prior to performing this ritual. You should bathe in saltwater, cleanse your energetic aura with incense, focus your intention, and calm your mind.

This spell should be performed on the night of a full moon.

First, cast your protective circle. Light the black candle. Use the flame to calm your spirit and set your intention - you will be undoing powerful dark magic that is transferred through generations. When you feel focused, place a small amount (a pinch) of the sea salt into the bag or locket. Harvest the small drop of blood and put the blood onto the salt. Next, add the coriander (cilantro). Take up the Selenite crystal. Slowly moving the crystal above the bag or locket, recite the following:

"A darkness has followed

in the blood of rich and poor.

I purify with salt and fire

to be accursed nevermore."

Next, add one drop of wax from the candle. Tie the bag closed or close the locket. Keep this bag or necklace on your person every day until the next full moon. At that time, you may decide whether to dispose of the bag/locket or to keep it.

It is most assuredly odd to include blood into a white magick spell. The reason blood is included in this spell is due to the type of curse (multi-generational). The power of the curse and the negativity is transferred and travels through the bloodline from generation to generation. Therefore, the only way to break the curse is to cleanse the blood of the curse. That is done through the purifying salt and the Selenite crystal. The cilantro is meant to contain the curse within the bag. There are times when the necessity of using bodily fluids in white magick does come up, but as you read other spell books or Books of Shadows, be aware that most uses of blood or bodily fluids are linked to the dark uses of black magick.

===============================

#5 - Prayer to break a curse and reverse the evil

I call upon the power of the earth; the power of the air; the power of the fire; and the power of the water. I call upon the power of the high God and Goddess (or Lord, Universe, Angels, Spirit, Ascended Masters, Protectors, etc.). I call upon the power of the sun and of the moon.

An evil has been levied against me from the realm of darkness; a magick of torment and pain. I hereby break the power of this witchcraft and rebuke the Caster of Darkness. No form of evil or torment shall be given foothold within my life, the life of my family, nor my current or future objective holdings.

In light and love

I implore of thee

Return this evil

With the Rule of Three.

Amen and Blessed Be.

==============================

#6 - Prayer to break a curse and reverse the evil

Dear Lord (or Goddess, Universe, Angels, Spirit, Ascended Masters, Protectors, etc.), you have told us, your faithful, that your protection is infinite and that your love is boundless. You have never given us any indication that you will ever let us down, that you will ever turn your back on us. I call upon you now at a time in need. Lord (or Goddess, Universe, Angels, Spirit, Ascended Masters, Protectors, etc.), I ask that you step between my soul and the curse which has been placed as my personal burden. Whether this curse has been placed on me, my family or my property, I ask that you remove this darkness now. Shine your light and love upon the darkness which has been placed upon me and send it running.

Lord (or Goddess, Universe, Angels, Spirit, Ascended Masters, Protectors, etc.), as in your teachings that one should not suffer a witch to live, I ask that you send the darkness placed on me back to the witch whom birthed this abomination. This person should be forced to feel the negativity and evil which has been unleashed upon your child. Protect me oh Lord (or Goddess, Universe, Angels, Spirit, Ascended Masters, Protectors, etc.) and free me from this curse.

Amen and Blessed Be.

==============================

#7 - Spell to break a curse and reverse the evil

You Will Need:

- A mirror

- A piece of paper

- A black pen

- A white candle

- A piece of white fabric

Instructions:

Sometimes just breaking a curse is not enough and doesn't give you closure on the attack. Instead, we aim to break the curse and send the negativity back to the cursing witch.

Cast a protective circle. Light the white candle. Lay the mirror on the altar, reflection side up. Next, on the piece of paper, write all of the symptoms you are experiencing from the curse. Then, lay the paper upside down on the mirror and cover it all with the fabric. Recite the following:

"Your magick delivered

A curse unto me.

I remove and return

Your curse back to thee."

Press on the mirror through the fabric until it breaks (or smash it with a tool).

Gather all of the pieces for disposal. Be careful not to either cut yourself on the shards, or see your reflection in any of the shards.

Close the protective circle.

==============================

#8 - Prayer to break a curse

Lord (or Goddess, Universe, Angels, Spirit, Ascended Masters, Protectors, etc.), it is written that they shall gather together, but their gathering is not of You. Whoever gathers against me shall scatter and fall.

I, therefore, command this day, let a furious east wind from heaven confuse, scatter and paralyze every evil gathering against my life and my family.

Amen and Blessed Be.

==============================

#9 - Prayer to break a curse

I come to you on my knees Lord (or Goddess, Universe, Angels, Spirit, Ascended Masters, Protectors, etc.). Having prostrated myself before you I ask that you fulfill your promise to your people, that no evil shall assail us if we are with you. Lord (or Goddess, Universe, Angels, Spirit, Ascended Masters, Protectors, etc.), I am under attack from the powers of darkness. Break this attack. With a snap of your mighty fingers, you have the power to undo all that has assailed me.

My life is your Lord (or Goddess, Universe, Angels, Spirit, Ascended Masters, Protectors, etc.). I am assured by your word that you will free me from these bonds of evil.

Amen and Blessed Be.

===============================

#10 - Prayer to break a curse of judgment

I decree this night, let every satanic altar and court existing against my life and family, raising accusations and counter-accusations against me and my destiny, be destroyed.

Every demonic lawyer and judge giving judgments against my life, family and destiny, in the spirit wherever you are, I command you all to die by fire.

I nullify every evil judgment and decision that has been made and is being carried out against my life and family. I command all those carrying out such judgments against my family and me to become frustrated.

Let the imagination of every satanic monitor fail and tumble into the abyss. Let every witchcraft mirror monitoring my star break and scatter.

Amen and Blessed Be

===============================

#11 - Prayer to break curse

Lord (or Goddess, Universe, Angels, Spirit, Ascended Masters, Protectors, etc.), I will live to eat the fruit of my labor. Any man or woman, witch or wizard, who has vowed that I will not see good in life, let fire from heaven visit them and destroy their curses.

Amen and Blessed Be

===============================

#12 - Prayer to break curse or negativity

Deliver us Father (or Goddess, Universe, Angels, Spirit, Ascended Masters, Protectors, etc.), from the everyday attacks on our conscious, health, relationships, and beyond. From what we can see coming and from what we would never expect, protect and deliver us from anything that threatens to throw us off your course for our lives. Give us strength to love people that are seemingly unlovable without compromising our character. Build a confidence in us that is unstoppable and immovable, but guard our hearts from pride. Deliver us from our distorted thoughts, sickness, debt, sadness, struggles, hunger, pain, fear, oppression, conflict and unbelief, for we proclaim your peace over our lives through prayer.

Amen and Blessed Be

===============================

#13 - Brute force spell to break curse

You will need:

- Air drying clay

- Water charged with the sun's energy (solar water)

- A slip of paper and pen

- Bay leaf

- Black candle

- Fire-safe container

- Toothpick

Instructions:

Perform spell at night during the new moon.

Cleanse yourself and your protective circle. Anoint yourself with solar water. Light the black candle. Write down on the slip of paper all of the effects that the curse has had on you (be thorough and specific). Fold the paper around the bay leaf. Set the bundle on fire and place it in the fire-safe container.

When the ashes are finished smoldering, set them aside. Take a portion of clay and anoint it with a drop of solar water. Mix the ashes into the clay thoroughly. Roll the clay into a ball and then flatten it into a disk shape. On one side of the disk, use the toothpick to inscribe: *"No more befouled, again unbound, again unbidden"*. On the other side of the disk, inscribe a symbol to represent the curse (it can either be a sigil or just a simple doodle that represents the curse to YOU). Close your protective circle, blow out the candle and allow the talisman to dry.

Once the talisman is dry, take it outside and allow it to sit and charge in the sun. Carry the talisman with you constantly to allow it to absorb the energy from the curse. On the next new moon, take the talisman and smash it, rendering the curse that the talisman has absorbed broken. Dispose of the shards outside of your home. Be sure that no residue of the talisman remains in your home or on your person.

===============================

Prayers to Destroy Unholy Covenants and Agreements

#1 - Prayer to Destroy Unholy Covenant

God (or Goddess, Universe, Angels, Spirit, Ascended Masters, Protectors, etc.), I come before you to confirm by faith that I stand on and agree with Your word; that I am crucified with Christ; nevertheless I live and that Christ is alive in me. Therefore, God (or Goddess, Universe, Angels, Spirit, Ascended Masters, Protectors, etc.), my testimony is this: Through the blood of Jesus, I am redeemed out of the hand of the devil, in spirit, in body, and in body. Thank you Jesus that your blood speaks for me before God night and day on the mercy seat. Thank you Lord for grace and mercy.

I come before you and I renounce, rebuke, revoke and cancel all unholy covenants and agreements I have ever made in my life and the lives of my ancestors, going all the way back to the first people. I repent, God (or Goddess, Universe, Angels, Spirit, Ascended Masters, Protectors, etc.), for these unholy covenants and agreements in my life and my ancestors lives and I ask for your grace, mercy and forgiveness. Wash away my sins and wash my ancestral bloodline clean.

I decree today that the only covenant I am in from this day forward is only holy covenant and agreement with God (or Goddess, Universe, Angels, Spirit, Ascended Masters, Protectors, etc.). I also decree this over my bloodline.

God (or Goddess, Universe, Angels, Spirit, Ascended Masters, Protectors, etc.) I ask that all records of unholy covenants and agreements be wiped from my record books and the record books of my ancestors in the courts of heaven and remembered no more.

God (or Goddess, Universe, Angels, Spirit, Ascended Masters, Protectors, etc.) I also ask that me and my bloodline be released and set free from all consequences of these sins. I ask that the new holy covenant that I have with you God (or Goddess, Universe, Angels, Spirit, Ascended Masters, Protectors, etc.) be written and decreed in my record books in heaven.

Amen and Blessed Be.

===============================

#2 - Prayer for Release from Unholy Covenants and Agreements

Lord (or Goddess, Universe, Angels, Spirit, Ascended Masters, Protectors, etc.), I ask You for grace and strength to obey Your word henceforth. Help me by the Spirit and keep me in constant reminder that I do not have to make promises and pledges to please men, but to obey You.

As I begin to work towards fulfilling my pledges from today, grant me wisdom and speedy breakthrough from this day forward.

Amen and Blessed Be.

===============================

#3 - Prayer for Release from Unholy Covenants and Agreements

God (or Goddess, Universe, Angels, Spirit, Ascended Masters, Protectors, etc.), through your forgiveness and your grace, I come humbly before you requesting that you grant me release from my unholy covenant. Lord (or Goddess, Universe, Angels, Spirit, Ascended Masters, Protectors, etc.), I made this covenant in error, against your wishes. Please forgive me for not trusting you to provide all that I may need. I ask that you free me from the bonds of the covenant so that I may devote myself, in body, soul and mind, to your praise.

Amen and Blessed Be

===============================

#4 - Spell for Release from Unholy Covenant

You will need:

- Mugwort

- Salt

- Red Candle

- Small Bowl

Cast your protective circle. Light the red candle.

Add a small amount of crushed Mugwort to the small bowl while reciting, *"With herb I signify the power of my word."*

Add a small amount of salt to the small bowl while reciting *"With salt I signify the purity of my word."*

Drip the liquid candle wax into the small bowl while reciting *"With wax I signify the binding of my word."*

Once the wax has hardened, it should contain bits of the salt and Mugwort.

Take the disk of wax into both hands. Holding it outside of the bowl, break or tear the disk while reciting *"Through freedom sought. Through freedom found. My word revoked. No longer bound. So mote it be."*

Keep the two parts of the wax from touching each other and bury them outside of your home separate from each other.

==============================

#5 - Prayer for Release from Unholy Agreement

I come before you Lord (or Goddess, Universe, Angels, Spirit, Ascended Masters, Protectors, etc.) and confess my foolishness. Your word says that those who do not fulfill their vows and pledges are fools and that You do not delight in them.

How foolish have I been all this while!

Lord (or Goddess, Universe, Angels, Spirit, Ascended Masters, Protectors, etc.) I sincerely apologize for saying things and making commitments that I could not keep afterwards. Please forgive me and set me free from the restrictions from this attitude.

Amen and Blessed Be. ==============================

#6 - Prayer for Release from Unholy Agreement

With my mouth, I confess that I am seated with God (or Goddess, Universe, Angels, Spirit, Ascended Masters, Protectors, etc.) in the heavenly places, far above all principalities and powers. I have been translated from the kingdom of darkness in the kingdom of light. I am a bringer of light and a salter of lives and destinies. I am moving from glory to glory even now and forever.

Amen and Blessed Be.

==============================

Prayers for Deliverance from Destructive Habits

#1 - Prayer for Deliverance from Destructive Habits

Every bad habit in my life causing a barrier between me and the power of God (or Goddess, Universe, Angels, Spirit, Ascended Masters, Protectors, etc.), let your fire destroy them this moment.

From today, Lord (or Goddess, Universe, Angels, Spirit, Ascended Masters, Protectors, etc.), plant in me an everlasting hatred for every work of the flesh as revealed in your word. I claim my freedom from every destructive habit.

I declare that I am forever free from all spirits of anger, lust, dishonesty, lying, spiritual laziness, pride, exaggeration, alcoholism, smoking, gossiping, and criticizing.

I command you all to leave my life now and return to the abyss.

Amen and Blessed Be.

==============================

#2 - Prayer for Deliverance from Destructive Habits

Lord (or Goddess, Universe, Angels, Spirit, Ascended Masters, Protectors, etc.), whatever evil effect is happening in my life, resulting from my character, past mistakes, or addictions to negative thoughts, words and actions, please set free.

Whatever curse and obstacle my wrong association and friendships have brought upon my life, Lord (or Goddess, Universe, Angels, Spirit, Ascended Masters, Protectors, etc.), let them be destroyed today.

From now onwards, surround me with the right people; surround me with people who will challenge me towards a Godly and excellent life.

I commit myself never to walk in the counsel of the unholy, nor stand in the way of sinners.

Cause me by your Spirit to find delight in seeking You and following holy counsel. Make me like a tree planted by the riverside that will bear fruit in all seasons.

Amen and Blessed Be.

==============================

#3 - Spell for Deliverance from Destructive Habits

You Will Need:

- A small box with a lid

- 1 clove of garlic

- 1 sprig of rosemary

- A handful of graveyard dirt

- A symbol of the destructive habit (needs to symbolize it to you)

- A roll of pennies

- Shovel

Instructions:

During a full moon, leave the box you have chosen outside to allow the moonlight to charge the box.

Over the following two weeks, whenever you think about the destructive habit, place one of the pennies into the box. At first, you may go through A LOT of pennies, but it will start to lessen as the days go on.

On the first night of the waning moon, add the rosemary and garlic to the box. Take the symbol of the destructive habit into your hands. Tell the symbol that you *"Will not allow this to have any effect in your life ever again."* Place the symbol into the box. Secure the lid onto the box with glue or nails.

Take the box and the small amount of graveyard dirt to a location off of your property, but near a moving body of water. Dig a small hole and place the box inside. Sprinkle the box with the graveyard dirt and then bury the box with the rest of the soil. When finished, walk away and do not look back.

================================

Prayers for Protection

#1 - Incantation for Protection of Body and Spirit

This quick incantation and visualization let you protect yourself when an unexpected threat appears.

Recite the following incantation (even if under your breath):

Power of the Goddess (or Goddess, Universe, Angels, Spirit,

Ascended Masters, Protectors, etc.).

Power of the God (or Goddess, Universe, Angels, Spirit,

Ascended Masters, Protectors, etc.).

Cool as a breeze.

Warm as a stove.

Flowing like a stream.

Solid as a stone.

So mote it be!

Repeat the incantation a total of seven times. During each incantation, visualize an electric blue ring of flame encircling you until you have a seven-ring spiral from head to toe.

================================

#2 - Spell for Spiritual and Mental Protection

You will need:

- A golden candle

- A pair of earplugs

- A flat stone, or a piece of wood, or a piece of metal (as amulet)

- Gold paint and a brush

Cast a protective circle. Light the candle and say, *"This is the power of silence."* Put in the earplugs. Concentrate on the power of spiritual and mental stillness as is found in the candle flame. When you feel calm and still, paint the bindrune on the amulet. Feel the power of the silent stillness flowing from the candle, through you, and into the amulet. Close the protective circle.

Wear or carry the amulet whenever you feel the need for spiritual and mental protection. The amulet can be recharged from time to time by using a new golden candle.

================================

#3 - Prayer for Spiritual and Mental Protection from Evil

Dear Lord (or Goddess, Universe, Angels, Spirit, Ascended Masters, Protectors, etc.), lead me not into temptation, but deliver me from the Evil One. Open my eyes to see the temptations and evil in this world for what they are. Give me a discerning heart, eyes that can see clearly, and ears that can hear you. Help me to resist the lure of temptations that lead me from you and keep my life firmly rooted in light. Protect my loved ones from temptation and evil, surround them with your hedge of protection Lord (or Goddess, Universe, Angels, Spirit, Ascended Masters, Protectors, etc.). Help us to suit up in your armor to withstand the forces of evil in this world. Lead us away from temptation and protect us from the evil in this world.

Amen and Blessed Be

================================

#4 - Prayer for Protection from Evil

Our loving Heavenly Father (or Goddess, Universe, Angels, Spirit, Ascended Masters, Protectors, etc.), I pray that you protect my family and me from all the evil, as well as from those who would seek to harm us. Guard us and protect us from all the evil which surrounds our lives. Give us your shield of safety and security and place guards at our home door. Lord (or Goddess, Universe, Angels, Spirit, Ascended Masters, Protectors, etc.), please keep our hearts fearless and fill us with your peace, which surpasses all of our understanding.

Thank you for being our refuge and strength. You are the omnipresent help in difficult times. In your faithfulness, we will not be afraid of all the world's dangers. Stay with us wherever we go and keep us in your loving hands.

Amen and Blessed Be

================================

#5 - Prayer for Protection from Evil Enemies

God (or Goddess, Universe, Angels, Spirit, Ascended Masters, Protectors, etc.), hear my voice and my prayer. I pray that you save me from my enemies and their evil ways. Help me to recognize their bad intentions. Do not let the false and hurting words of them touch me. Protect from devastating enemies' actions. Please do not let evil destroy and triumph over my life. God (or Goddess, Universe, Angels, Spirit, Ascended Masters, Protectors, etc.), I can rely only on you this bad hour and only you can save and protect me. I believe and trust you and you alone.

Amen and Blessed Be

================================

#6 - Prayer for Protection from Evil - The Lord's Prayer

Our Father who art in Heaven, hallowed be thy name. Thy kingdom come, thy will be done on Earth as it is in Heaven. Give us this day our daily bread and forgive us our trespasses, as we forgive those who trespass against us. Lead us not into temptation, but deliver us from evil. For thine is the kingdom, the power and the glory forever and ever.

Amen

================================

#7 - Spell for Protection from Evil Enemies

You will need:

- A piece of paper

- A black pen

- A piece of black string

- A small amount of water

- A freezer (if not performed in sub-freezing outside temps)

This spell is best performed during a new moon.

Instructions:

On the piece of paper, write the name of the person(s) affecting you. Tie a single knot in the middle of the string. While tying the knot, focus on the negative effects this individual has been causing in your life.

Fold the paper up with the piece of string tucked into the middle. Moisten the paper (you do not want to soak it and obliterate the name or names). Place the paper in the freezer (or in a protected spot outside if performing the spell in sub-freezing temperatures) and leave it there until the situation has passed and the individual is no longer affecting your life negatively. ================================

#8 - Protection of Home

The Witch's Bottle - Witch bottles have been used for at least 400 years to protect the home by creating a magickal double of yourself. The supplies needed are a bit odd, but this is ancient magick after all.

You will need:

- A bottle with a tight cork or cap

- Nails and pins (preferably bent)

- Broken glass pieces and/or broken mirror pieces

- Pieces of string, knotted multiple times

- Your own nail, hair clippings, and bodily fluids (i.e., urine)

- A red or black candle (just to seal the bottle cap)

Put all solid materials into the bottle while reciting *"Harm be bound away from me"*. Add the liquid. Close the bottle and seal with the wax.

Bury the bottle upside down outside the front door of the home, or under the floorboards, or hidden in a remote corner of the lowest point of your home.

The idea behind a Witch's Bottle is that the evil spirits are drawn to the bottle instead of you, and then get trapped by the nails, pins, and knotted string and confused by the broken glass/mirror (like a funhouse mirror maze).

==============================

#9 - Protection Spell for Friends and Family

You will need:

- Salt

- Rosemary

- Angelica

- White Dandelion Fluff

- Small Crystal of Either Blue Lace Agate, Carnelian, or Garnet

- Slip of Paper with The Name Of The Person To Protect

- White Sachet or Small White Bag

Instructions:

Place the salt, rosemary, angelica, dandelion fluff, crystal, and the slip of paper into the sachet/bag.

Focus on a visualization of the person. Speak the words, *"I send you protection from all that may harm you. I send you the wish of safety. I send you the energies to keep you out of harm's way."*

Tie your sachet/bag shut and gently kiss it focusing on your desires to send your friend or family member protection.

Place the sachet/bag in a slightly open window to help send the energies to the friend or family member.

Leave the sachet/bag untouched for a minimum of one hour. Following removal from the window, the sachet/bag can be emptied and cleaned for future use.

==============================

#10 - Protection Spell for Traveling

Car Mojo Bag - A car mojo bag is a simple but effective way to protect yourself, your passengers, and your vehicle while you are driving. It is also used in a number of other traveling protection spells. I have mine hanging from my rearview mirror, but the car mojo bag can be kept anywhere inside the vehicle. If you do keep it hidden away, be sure to periodically place it on your dashboard at night so it can recharge with moonlight.

You Will Need:

- A small cloth bag (red for machine reliability; orange for travel; or dark blue for luck and long-distance travel)

- A silver paint marker

- A small cup of saltwater

- Choose from the following ingredients, keeping an eye toward balancing elements and properties :

    - Fire: An iron nail (protection; dill (protection); cumin seeds (anti-theft)

    - Earth: Coffee (alertness); barley (protection); dried corn (protection); malachite (traveler's protection)

    - Water: Marjoram (protection); aloe (protection); willow wood (protection); moonstone (traveler's protection)

    - Air: Parsley (protection); anise (protection); mint (travel)

Instructions:

The car mojo bag should be created during the waxing moon.

Using the silver paint marker, draw a crescent moon on each side of the cloth bag.

Cast a circle of protection.

Place each ingredient in the bag. As you place each item, announce its purpose. (i.e., "You are for protection.")

Consecrate the bag by sprinkling it with saltwater while reciting:

> *Safety from harm. I am protected.*
>
> *Safety from theft. I am protected.*
>
> *Safety from attack. I am protected.*
>
> *Safety from error. I am protected.*

Safety from accidents. I am protected.

Safety from hate. I am protected.

Safety from losing my way. I am protected.

Going to each cardinal quarter direction, hold your mojo bag high and recite: *"Safety from dangers from the East/South/West/North. I am protected."*

Close the protective circle.

==============================

#11 - Spell to Protect Against A Dangerous Driver

Road rage is not good for anyone. We are all flying around each other in these mechanical death traps as fast as we can. But when one of the drivers on the road begins to make it blatantly clear that they are in no way interested in maintaining the social contract we all have to drive carefully, they become a threat to everyone else on the road. Something should be done to protect ourselves from harm.

You will need:

- Your car mojo bag

- To keep both eyes on the road!

Hold your car mojo bag in one hand.

Take a deep breath; focus your energy while keeping your eyes on the road.

Visualize the deity of justice of your choice. Personally, I visualize Athena, Goddess of Justice. Athena carries a helmet, spear, a shield, and sometimes an owl with her.

As you exhale, let go of the mojo bag, point at the dangerous driver, and demand justice by literally speaking, *"Justice!"*.

===============================

#12 - Prayer for Protection Throughout Long Distance Car Travel

Father (or Goddess, Universe, Angels, Spirit, Ascended Masters, Protectors, etc.), I pray that you will guide and protect me (us, my husband, etc.) as I travel a long distance today. Please send your protection to guard me through every turn and every stop. I know that you are able and that you will do all which is in your will.

I believe that you have heard my prayer Lord (or Goddess, Universe, Angels, Spirit, Ascended Masters, Protectors, etc.) and that you will grant me protection all the way until I arrive safely at my destination. Thank you for being a loving and protective God (or Goddess, Universe, Angels, Spirit, Ascended Masters, Protectors, etc.).

Amen and Blessed Be

===============================

#13 - Prayer for Protection During Airplane Travel

Dear Lord (or Goddess, Universe, Angels, Spirit, Ascended Masters, Protectors, etc.), I pray over the trip we are about to take on this airplane. I pray that no mechanical errors or emergencies will occur. I pray for our pilot, that he or she will be alert, have sharp eyes, and steady hands throughout this flight. I pray for our flight attendants that they will be friendly, alert and adequately prepared for the trip. I also pray for my fellow passengers, that everyone will be in good spirits and in good health. I pray that everyone will make it to their destination safely and under your protection.

Amen and Blessed Be

Chapter 3

Cleansing Rituals & Maintaining Victory

Performing cleansing rituals is a vital task in sweeping away the last remaining bits of negativity and darkness that may remain after breaking a curse or any type of psychic attack. Picture it this way, you had been shackled to darkness, chained to evil. When you break or explode from a chain, there are tiny bits or shards of metal that go flying off. They may be too tiny to see with your eyes, but if you walk around in bare feet you are guaranteed to end up with a sliver. Breaking a curse, negative soul tie, evil covenant, or agreement tends to leave behind tiny shards of that negativity and evil. If you allow it to remain in your space, your soul is guaranteed to end up with a sliver. When you get free - stay free.

There are many thought processes and beliefs surrounding cleansing rituals. Every religion from Catholic to Hindu to Rosicrucian has its "own". However, the truth is that, when viewed as a whole, they share more similarities than differences. As a result, there is really no harm to be done by trying one, two, or even all of the ritual examples which follow. All are designed to do the same thing: rid the space (and thus the people within the space) of negative energy and ward against the re-emergence of evil. So explore. Find what works best for you, your space, and your lifestyle.

Unlike the majority of tasks in the spiritual realm, a successful cleansing will result in **immediate** relief. Oftentimes, although not always, when there is a negative presence or evil remnants are left from the breaking of a curse or spell, a general feeling of heaviness or unease will pervade a space. The stronger the negativity, the stronger the feeling. When you are able to rid your space of the negativity, the feeling of unease, and the heavy atmosphere will disappear along with it. You will know that it worked because you will feel that it worked.

It is extremely important to continue cleansing until all the evil and negativity have been removed. An evil or negative entity can be further enraged and empowered by a half-hearted attempt at cleansing it. The cleansing rituals quite literally hurt and weaken the entity. If the cleansing is not carried through, the entity will resume its prior actions with much greater resolve and a newfound revenge-filled rage. Remember, we are making things better, not worse.

Cleansing Rituals

1. **Smudging**

Smudging is probably the most widely accepted and practiced cleansing ritual. Smudging is the burning and smoldering of herbs wherein the smoke is used as the cleansing agent. The most commonly used herb for smudging is a bundle of sage, specifically white sage. Sage is the kryptonite of dark entities (whether they be demons or restless spirits). However, a variety of different herbs have actually proven equally effective, including basil, lavender, and clove.

The "ritual" is actually extremely simple. It is one of the few rituals to preferably be performed during the daylight hours.

A smudging session should begin with a prayer or call for protection for anyone who will be in the home during the session. Next, the aura and body of each person present for the session should be cleansed. This is done by lighting the herb bundle and, once it is smoldering, tracing the outline of the person with the bundle; allowing the smoke to rid the aura and individual of any attachments they may be carrying.

Be sure to have at least one window or door open on each floor of the home. The negativity must be given a way to escape or it will be trapped and further enflamed.

Next, the smudging bundle should be carried into each corner of each room and public space in the home. Carry something to catch any of the smudge bundle ashes that may drop off (I use an abalone shell). Do not forget closets, basements, attics, side rooms, enclosed porches, etc. Once each and every space has been cleansed, you have finished the ritual.

There really are not any specific words that <u>must</u> be said during a smudging session. It is really up to those present to use visualization to help the smoke guide the negativity out of the home. However, some tend to give a short prayer or incantation within each room. If you choose to speak, commit to it being in each space and keep it simple. Perhaps something like, *"In the name of the Father, the Son, and The Holy Spirit, I implore all negativity and evil to leave this space. You have no right here."* or *"Through the power of the Spirit, no negativity or evil shall remain in this home."*

Smudging is not even a ritual that should be used only to cleanse from a brush with evil. I smudge myself and my aura once every two weeks and my home 3-4 times per year. It is a great way to maintain a clean aura and stay free of unguided attachments by evil entities and to keep my home clear of pockets of negativity. (Speaking of pockets of negativity - I have two teenagers, so when I finish smudging my home, I always run upstairs and "make sure they are both still there". That gets an eye roll EVERY time! Sometimes, a sense of humor is a witch's best friend.)

2. Salting

Salting is a widespread practice in eastern cultures, but it is quickly becoming accepted by the west as well. Salt has long been known as a purifier. Like quartz, salt's crystalline structure has the ability to hold and trap negative energies. It is a passive way of cleansing your environment of darkness.

There are a few different ways of deploying salt as a cleansing agent.

- A bowl of salt beside the front door (perhaps on a foyer table) can be used to attract and trap negativity or evil from individuals entering your home.

- Salt can be sprinkled in the corners of rooms in order to draw the negativity. Be sure not to touch the salt while it is deployed as a cleanser. After 4-5 days, vacuum or sweep up the salt and dispose of it.

- Salt can be used to encircle the outside of a home as a protective measure against the invasion of evil.

- Lastly, salt can be added to bathwater to create a cleansing soak for the individual working with the spirit realm.

It is important to note that I am not referring to common table salt. Table salt has been processed with iodine. Iodine affects the structure and clarity of the salt crystals. You will want to use whole or shaved pieces of unrefined sea salt or unrefined mineral salt. Don't worry, it is not as difficult to find as it sounds! A simple Google search will bring up many inexpensive suppliers.

3. Incense

The use of incense began, as far as we can tell, with the Egyptians who used it in healing rituals and the Babylonians who relied upon it when conferring with their divine oracles. The use of incense arrived in Japan in the sixth century - where it was used in purification rituals for the emperor and his court.

Today, incense can be found in a large number of scents and forms. Not to mention incense holders ranging from simple to amazingly intricate.

Incense is best used for personal and small area cleansing. Much like smudging, the smoke is the cleansing agent. However, unlike smudging, incense remains situated in one room.

Just light the tip, blow out the flame and place the incense in the holder.

4.   **Tuning Fork**

Sound and music have been used in healing rituals for thousands of years. Early civilizations used singing bowls for sound therapy and Greek physicians used instruments and vibration to treat sickness and combat insomnia. Using a tuning fork for cleansing is merely an extension of the same idea. Tuning forks vibrate at specific frequencies. The frequency of 417 Hz is known as a "Solfeggio frequency" and has been found to rid the body, mind, and physical space of negative energy. It is not an absolute "must", but a fork tuned to the frequency of 417 Hz would undoubtedly be the most useful.

Find a comfortable spot within each room of your home. Set your intention for a cleared, renewed space. Lightly tap the tuning fork against something solid. Close your eyes and let the sound vibrate around and through you; allow it to clean all of the negativity and evil out of the room and you. Move on to the next room and repeat the process.

==============================

What cleansing is NOT?

I felt that this point was important enough that it required its own section. Blessing a house and home exorcism is NOT what is meant by "cleansing". Let me be very clear because I do want to allow room for any ambiguity on this point: Do not, under any circumstances, attempt to perform your own "Home Blessing" or "Home Exorcism". A blessing or exorcism should only ever be performed by an experienced priest, clergy member, or shaman.

Let's discuss why. The most dangerous work you could possibly undertake is attempting to remove a demon from your space. And remember, you do not need to believe in demons because they certainly believe in you. If goodness exists, it must have a counterpart. If goodness exists, evil must exist as well. Therefore, we are going to simply assume that you believe in the concept and reality of demonic forces.

The cleansing tactics explained previously are useful and safe for removing the shards, the pieces, and remnants of evil left behind after a psychic attack is broken. They are not, however, designed to remove a full evil presence - a demon - or even a fully negative soul.

An attempt by an individual who is not appropriately protected, shielded, and fully prepared to bless or exorcise a home or space can easily result in very unwanted effects. These types of half-hearted attempts have led to a sharp increase in the intensity of the evil attack, the opening of a portal allowing other evil entities to gain access to the space, personal evil attachment, or even full possession of the living by a demonic entity.

It is not just ill-advised, it is not just probably something you should be careful of, and it is not a good way to show off for friends and flex your spiritual muscles. It is something you should completely rule out right now and steer clear of. The very last thing that I would want to occur is for one of you, my friends, my family, or anyone to ever be hurt as a result of not understanding the dangers of blessing a home or attempting to exorcise a home. Be smart. Stay safe.

===============================

Symbols, Stones, and Protective Objects

There are a handful of symbols, stones, and protective objects that you may want to be aware of and/or have on hand if you have been touched by evil. We are not going to get into a fully comprehensive guide to symbology and crystals because that could easily fill two or three other volumes, however we should at least touch on a few of the highlights.

Symbols

We live in a symbolic world. Because symbols hold the power to be immediately recognizable and to mean paragraphs worth of information, they were being used prior to the development of language to transfer information and ideas. We are going to briefly discuss three symbols that can definitely be of use in protecting ourselves from all forms of psychic attack: The Pentacle; The Triquetra; and The Eye of Horus.

The Pentacle

The Pentacle, a five-pointed upright star within a circle, symbolizes white magick; light, goodness, and intellect. It is often used or worn as a talisman.

The Triquetra

The Triquetra, or "Triple Moon", symbolizes the threefold nature of reality - the balance between mind, body, and spirit.

The Eye of Horus

The Eye of Horus (the left eye) is related to the moon. It symbolizes protective powers coming from the deflection of evil forces.

Stones and Crystals

Stones and crystals are nature's magickal gift to us all. Formed in many different ways over unimaginable spans of time and under unfathomable conditions, these amazingly powerful objects wait patiently to be used for their intended purposes. They can be beautiful, smooth and shining with what seems like light from within; they can be rough and bulky, they can be as dark black as any starless night, or glimmer with a rainbow full of colors. No matter what form they take, stones and crystals have earned the respect and recognition they have received throughout the centuries as true magickal miracles.

We will only be exploring a few of the thousands of stones and crystals which hold magickal significance because there are thousands of reference books out there dedicated solely to the subject. For our purposes, however, you should have a working knowledge of the following stones and crystals.

- **Black Tourmaline**

  - Black Tourmaline is a powerful healer and protector crystal. Specifically, it is useful in blocking psychic attacks and negative thought patterns. It is even used as protection against harmful electromagnetic radiation caused by modern electronics.

- **Black Obsidian**

  - Black Obsidian is formed when molten lava is cooled very quickly, such as when it comes into contact with water. It works wonderfully as a protective shield against negativity and evil. It soaks up bad energy like a sponge and holds it. Because of its retention ability, you will want to cleanse your obsidian regularly by simply holding it under running water and visualizing all of the negativity washing from the stone, down the drain, and out of your life.

- **Selenite**

  - Selenite has been a favorite among crystal lovers dating back to Ancient Greece. Some Greeks actually made windows from thin slabs of Selenite. It is found deep in the caves of Mexico, Morocco, and Madagascar, and the raw crystal formations in the caves can reach up to 35 feet long. The caves are absolutely beautiful, assuming you would find Superman's Fortress of Solitude to be beautiful! Selenite is very useful in cleansing and clearing a home or office because it dispels negative energy and creates calm in any space. Selenite lamps are also a great alternative to Himalayan salt lamps because it not only looks great when lit but is also self-cleansing and can cleanse other crystals in its environment.

- **Amethyst**

  - Amethyst has been used since the middle ages as a healing crystal. It is widely used for its ability to protect its bearer emotionally and spiritually by helping to break anxious or addictive thought patterns and ties to stressful energies. Also, a piece of amethyst on your nightstand or under your pillow can help protect you from nightmares.

- **Carnelian**

- Carnelian is an absolutely beautiful, polished stone with swirls of red, orange, and brown. It is a great way to stay energized but calm at the same time. It will keep you grounded even when the atmosphere around you is buzzing. Carnelian can make you feel comfortable without the effects of laziness or complacency.

- **Clear Quartz**

  - Clear quartz is an extremely dynamic and versatile crystal. It is useful in both deflecting negativity and attracting positivity. Also, clear quartz is easily able to pick up and funnel intention. Just as it does in its use in laser functionality, in television projection tubes and in early computer motherboards, clear quartz is a ready-made energy storage and amplification device.

- **Smoky Quartz**

  - This opaque gray crystal is a personal favorite. Smoky Quartz helps you in manifesting your desires out of the ethereal plane and into the material world. But the beautiful part is that, once you have made your ideas into reality, smoky quartz will also protect those intentions from any evil or negative energies that may attempt to get in the way.

- **Black Jade**

  - Black jade can help you stay clear of negative people and situations by helping you tune into the root source of the negativity. Sometimes it is just easier to avoid contact with negativity than it is to try to rid yourself of it. Black Jade is also known to assist you in tapping into your intuition.

- **Smithsonite**

  - Smithsonite is a soothing stone that can help calm your emotions and connect you to your center. Having a calm mind and a grounded center is absolutely vital to the success of many of the spells, rituals, and prayers we have discussed. Plus, who couldn't use some help relaxing after a stressful day or event!

- **Limestone**

  - Any witch who already practices, or spiritualist familiar with crystals, is undoubtedly confused by this addition. Limestone is not usually included in a list of stones or crystals used in any kind of spell work. However, limestone is very special. Limestone is found as bedrock in non-sandy environments and is often used to build the foundation of many of the homes in these non-sandy environments. And a special quality of this common stone is that it contains natural clear quartz and silica. Within the metaphysics community, limestone is seen as a storage vessel for energy. There is also the paranormal theory that limestone allows for storage and release (playback) of high-energy situations. For these reasons, I always include a piece of limestone with me during a cleansing session and keep one nearby during meditation.

Protective Objects

There are also protective objects that can be helpful in dissuading curses, evil energies, and psychic attacks. We have actually already spoken about three of them: The Witch's Bottle, The Car Mojo Bag, and The Pentacle. There are just a few more objects that I tend to keep on hand in case of a psychic attack. They are Black Salt, Amulets, Talismans, and Candles.

- **Sea Salt or Mineral Salt**

  - We have already discussed how useful sea salt or mineral salt can be in cleansing you or your space. However, salt is useful in any number of rituals. It is the ultimate purifier. Salt represents purity, goodness, and light. I personally use sea salt when casting my protective circles in order to protect myself from any negativity getting too close to me while working in the spirit realm. I also circle my home with a sea salt line once per month to keep all negativity and evil spirits out of my living space. It is believed that evil is unable to cross a salt line because of its purity, unless carried or attached to a human.

- **Black Salt**

  - Black Salt is a useful ritualistic tool used in a number of protection spells to keep unwanted energies at arm's length, though not as mystical and mysterious as it sounds. Black Salt is, essentially, just ashy sea or mineral salt. If I find myself low on black salt, I will typically make my own by burning some pinecones to ash. Then I collect the ash and add it to a bag of moistened salt, mix it around, and spread it out to dry in the sun. You can also add complementary herbs to the mixture if the black salt has a specific purpose.

- **Amulets and Talismans**

  - First of all, the terms "amulet" and "talisman" can and often are used interchangeably. Their definitions, however, do differ. An amulet is an object with natural magickal properties. As such, crystals and stones would be considered amulets. A talisman, on the other hand, is a created object which must be charged with magickal powers by its creator. Talismans are usually created for a specific reason, whereas an amulet would be used for general protection from evil and negativity.

- **Candles**

  - Individuals who work with the spirit realm have candle collections to rival any Yankee Candle Co. outlet! Candles are used in every practice from casting a protective circle to aromatherapy and everything in between. The color of the candle is very important in spell work as the color itself is used symbolically. The flickering flame can be used for divination or to facilitate a meditative state, as well as obviously for burning paper. Scented candles are rarely used in spell work, however they are extremely useful in aromatherapy applications and for placing a person in the proper state of mind for carrying out their work in the spirit world.

Understanding Blessings and Prosperity

So many times, I have seen people who have successfully broken curses or defended themselves in a psychic attack be afraid to follow through and manifest the blessings and prosperity in their life. They seem to feel like being given the help and blessing of the broken curse is really all they could have hoped for. But there is no such limitation placed on our blessings from the universe or any deity. We should never be hesitant to request our fruits. They are FOR us.

Should we be treating the universe or God or the Goddess, etc. as a lottery ticket? Absolutely not. Let's be honest here, if we could guarantee the next Mega-Millions jackpot by praying hard or by performing the right ritual, there would never be a week without a winner! That is just not how the spiritual plane works. Our blessings and our prosperity do not necessarily mean financial gains. The very concept of money is a human invention and has no value on the astral plane. The blessings and prosperity that await us are much more likely to be in the form of "shalom".

Shalom is a Hebrew term that means peace, completeness, soundness, and welfare. I think of *shalom* as being comparative to grace. Grace is that which affords joy, pleasure, delight, goodwill, and reward. It is the kindness and benevolence of God (or Goddess, Universe, Angels, Spirit, Ascended Masters, Protectors, etc.).

Manifesting our fruits, our blessings, our prosperity is all about living and walking in the favor afforded us by the universe. There is really nothing more powerful than being in a position of positivity and light wherein we are receiving the blessings meant for us. The curses, the negative soul ties, the covenants, and the agreements we have learned to escape have kept our blessings and prosperity from raining down on us. However, now that we have been freed from the evil weighing us down, the universe is once again in a position to smile upon us.

To manifest and receive the blessings and favors which have awaited us, we need to know how to request them. And for that, we need to discuss some prayers and spells to assist in the manifesting of our fruits. And then we will review some crystals and crystal combinations that can assist you in getting your intention for blessings out into the universe.

Prayers for Manifesting Your Fruits

#1 - Prayer for Manifesting the Fruit of The Spirit

Dear Lord (or Goddess, Universe, Angels, Spirit, Ascended Masters, Protectors, etc.), I desire to remain rooted in you, bearing fruits that lead others to the light of your love.

I desire to walk in love, forgiving others at all times and gifting God's (or Goddess, Universe, Angels, Spirit, Ascended Masters, Protectors, etc.) blessings in my life with others, just as you have done for me.

I desire to walk in joy every day of my life, thereby drawing from the well of salvation.

Please remind and help me at all times to love and be joyful as I live.

Amen and Blessed Be.

===============================

#2 - Prayer for Manifesting the Fruit of The Spirit

Dear Lord (or Goddess, Universe, Angels, Spirit, Ascended Masters, Protectors, etc.), I desire to bear the fruit of goodness so that I may lead others to the path you have shown me.

I desire to be faithful at all times with whatever God (or Goddess, Universe, Angels, Spirit, Ascended Masters, Protectors, etc.) blesses me with, so that I may stand before you in the end and receive the rewards of faithfulness.

I desire to be gentle with myself and others, in thoughts, words and actions, so that I may be an instrument of encouragement and uplifting to others and not discouragement.

I desire to walk in self-control in food, dressing and in everything so that I could win the race set before me and not be cast away after teaching others.

I call upon you to empower me every day to bear these fruits as I live, serve God (or Goddess, Universe, Angels, Spirit, Ascended Masters, Protectors, etc.), and relate with others.

Amen and Blessed Be.

==============================

#3 - Prayer for Manifesting the Fruit of The Spirit

God, (or Goddess, Universe, Angels, Spirit, Ascended Masters, Protectors, etc.), you are the way and the substance of all life; all that is good, and as your child all that you are is within me.

I now understand my divine birthright and I call it forth letting your everlasting abundance manifest in my life.

You are the source that ignites my dreams and meets my every need in perfect order. I am truly blessed.

Amen and Blessed Be.

==============================

#4 - Simple Spell for Manifesting Your Fruits

The first step of this spell should be performed during a new moon.

You will need:

- A slip of paper

- A small box or small bag

- A piece of Clear Quartz, or Citrine, or Amethyst

While holding your crystal, focus your intention on manifesting the fruits of your Spirit (the goodness, the light, the fortune, the luck, the positivity).

On the piece of paper, write what you want to manifest in your life as if you already have it. For instance, if you are attempting to manifest peace in your life, you would write "My life is peaceful. My mind is calm."

Fold the piece of paper and place it, along with the piece of your crystal, into the box or bag. Close the box or bag.

Every day, or every night if more convenient, open the box or bag, remove the paper and the crystal. While holding both, focus your intent again on what you are attempting to manifest. Read what you had written followed by the words, *"So mote it be."* Place the paper and crystal back into the box or bag. Do this every day or night a minimum of nine times. If you feel that you have not yet seen the manifestation you want, keep reading it daily and focusing on your intent.

Once you see the manifested fruit you desired, burn the paper and spread the ashes outside your home. There is no need to cleanse the crystal or the container. Feel free to use both again immediately if you wish.

================================

Stones and Crystals for General Abundance

- **Aventurine**

    - Aventurine is known as a crystal of abundance. It can be charged with your intent or combined with other crystals to lend abundance to them.

- **Bloodstone**

    - This aggressively named stone is actually more like a bank vault than a gusher. Bloodstone will help you in conserving your money. It is perfectly suited for carrying with you on shopping trips, keeping you under control on yard sale days, and for deflecting spells cast to separate you from your wealth.

- **Citrine**

  - Citrine is known as the Merchant's Stone because it is meant to assist with cash flow. Keep citrine in your wallet, your purse, or above your shop door to see your financial intentions manifest in your life.

- **Jade**

  - Jade has long been associated with success. It excels in its ability to focus your intent to manifest luck, prosperity, and good fortune.

- **Stibnite**

  - Stibnite crystals are not exactly a common commodity. However, if you see one of these metallic black crystals for sale, snag it! It is an amazing ability to keep our attention and intentions focused on our manifestation goals. It can also be combined with other crystals to keep us laser-focused. It may not win any beauty contests, but what a powerful crystal!

Combinations for Specific Abundance

- **Aventurine & Rose Quartz**

  - The combination of Aventurine and Rose Quartz can be used to attract the right people into your love life. These two crystals combine to bring us meaning and fulfillment through the right people or even just that one right person.

- **Pyrite & Amethyst**

  - The combination of Pyrite and Amethyst is used to bring an abundance of spiritual knowledge and enhanced mindfulness. Because amethyst is the ultimate stone for spiritual advancement, this duo is perfect to accelerate the effects of your meditations, spiritual learning, and path to peace.

- **Emerald & Rhodonite**

  - This Emerald and Rhodonite combination is perfect to manifest an increase in popularity and an uptick in your social life. And the best part, both of these crystals correspond to forming *healthy* relationships.

- **Bloodstone & Garnet**

  - This is your ultimate health and fitness combination. You will find that the combination of Bloodstone and Garnet can provide you with the motivation you need to get fit and healthy.

- **Citrine & Carnelian**

  - This beautiful combination is something that I refer to as the "Unstoppable Muse". With Citrine for abundance and Carnelian providing its powers of creativity, this duo will fuel your artistic side and provide that inspiration and abundance of ideas all artists need.

===============================

Maintaining Your Victory and Deliverance

Once you have broken a curse or spell, destroyed evil soul ties, covenants, and psychic attacks, cleansed yourself and your space of negative energy and evil, and have begun to manifest your fruits, you would think you are done and could just sit back and relax. But no. Just as evil never stops chasing us, we must never stop being vigilant to avoid it.

The next step is maintaining our newfound victory over evil and celebrating our deliverance from its clutches.

Have you ever wondered where the idea arose of demonic entities referring to themselves as being "legion"? Well, it comes from what happens after evil is removed or cleansed from our lives. The Christian Bible describes it this way in the book of Matthew:

> "When the unclean spirit has gone out of a person, it passes through waterless places seeking rest, but finds none.
>
> Then it says, 'I will return to my house from which I came.' And when it comes, it finds the house empty, swept, and put in order.
>
> Then it goes and brings with it seven other spirits more evil than itself, and they enter and dwell there, and the last state of that person is worse than the first. So also will it be with this evil generation."

Not exactly inspiring, I know. This passage pretty much boils down to, exorcising an evil demonic entity will lead to being haunted or possessed by that same entity plus seven others that are even worse. Exorcise one of those 8 and you end up with 15 and so on and so on. You can see how the numbers could quickly get out of hand, especially considering that they are each eviler than their predecessor.

However, this does not need to be the outcome. We are given instructions right in the passage.

First, **do not keep your spirit empty**. It is important to fill your mind, body, and spirit with positive thoughts and positive vibrations. Work out a system to read or recite positive affirmations every day. It can be just 10 minutes out of your day, but it is part of the process of keeping the evil from gaining an even stronger foothold than before.

Second, **exercise your faith by sharing your testimony.** You have been victorious! You have defeated evil on a plane that believed you had no chance! Do you need to hide? No! Become active in your faith, whatever faith that is. Be vocal, be joyous, be a beacon of positivity. You have earned the right to be proud of your freedom and the duty to tell others how you achieved it.

Thirdly, **keep a positive outlook on life and speak positivity into your life.** Now is certainly not the time to allow depression or negativity into any small crack or crevice. Positivity attracts positivity, just as negativity attracts negativity. So, the more positive you are about your future, the more positivity you will create in your future.

But, I believe the most important sentence in this passage is, "And when it comes, it finds the house empty, swept, and put in order." So, when the evil returns to the person, it finds a hospitable and waiting home for it and 7 of its evil brethren. We do not want it to find an acceptable home when evil comes sniffing around us again. We want evil to find us already occupied by God, by light, by spirit. We want to make evil very uncomfortable. That is why we need to maintain our victory and ward ourselves against future attacks.

Once we rid ourselves of an evil, we will ensure that it cannot simply return with backup and take up residence yet again. And we can accomplish this maintenance with prayer.

Prayers to Maintain Victory

#1 - Prayer to Maintain Victory

Heavenly Father (or Goddess, Universe, Angels, Spirit, Ascended Masters, Protectors, etc.), I praise you with all my heart. You are my shield. I take refuge in you all the days of my life and I am safe. Even though the enemy comes like a flood, you have set a standard over my life and I always remain victorious. I call to you Lord (or Goddess, Universe, Angels, Spirit, Ascended Masters, Protectors, etc.), for you are worthy of all praise and I am saved.

Amen and Blessed Be

==============================

#2 - Prayer to Maintain Victory

God (or Goddess, Universe, Angels, Spirit, Ascended Masters, Protectors, etc.), I confess that I have been too concerned with the physical world and have neglected the spiritual. But through victory and deliverance, you have shown me peace and strength. Open the eyes of my heart that I may become all the more aware of the spiritual battles taking place around me. Never allow me to forget that there is a real enemy seeking to destroy me so that I may remain alert and vigilant.

Use the Spirit to awaken me that I may become more attentive, watchful and sober-minded. Grant me wisdom to earlier discern the ways the enemy is attacking me so that I may become more intentional in choosing righteousness.

Amen and Blessed Be

==============================

#3 - Prayer to Maintain Deliverance

Lord (or Goddess, Universe, Angels, Spirit, Ascended Masters, Protectors, etc.), I praise you. This world is hard. It threatens to crush us in many ways. Physically, we cannot always outrun the ailments of our bodies. Sickness and injury take hold of us and we are always healed to the original state of our health. Mentally, we are bombarded and pulled at by unfiltered thoughts threatening to run away with our self-esteem on a daily basis. Spiritually, you promise us a battle in this life. You bring our hearts to focus on your truth at the start of each day, expecting a battle, but also promising deliverance.

Father (or Goddess, Universe, Angels, Spirit, Ascended Masters, Protectors, etc.), in overwhelming moments help us to always recall the truth. Remind us of the great gift you have given us through deliverance; deliverance from all we have battled and fought. Your protective hand of deliverance has guided me into deliverance and light. You are always faithful.

Amen and Blessed Be

==============================

#4 - Prayer to Maintain Deliverance

Heavenly Father (or Goddess, Universe, Angels, Spirit, Ascended Masters, Protectors, etc.), you call us to action, to stand firm in our faith. Help us turn from shame, make a way for kindness, and rise up for those who cannot speak for themselves, and find a way to make sure those who are burdened by distorted thoughts of who they are may experience the deliverance which you have given to me. For you assure us that when we seek you, we will find you if we seek you with all of our hearts.

Father (or Goddess, Universe, Angels, Spirit, Ascended Masters, Protectors, etc.), we are grateful that you hear us and care for us beyond our understanding. We prayerfully proclaim deliverance in our own lives, and in the lives of those suffering next door to us and around the world. We cry out to you in faith that you will continue your promise to deliver us from our physical pain and mental anguish.

Amen and Blessed Be

==============================

Conclusion

Do you feel armed and prepared to do battle in the spirit realm? Do you now feel that you have the tools to protect yourself, your family, and your belongings against psychic attacks through curses, spells, negative soul ties, evil covenants, and agreements? Do you understand the importance and the ways to cleanse yourself, your home, and your surroundings of negativity and evil? I sincerely hope that you do. You have been empowered to break the chains that bind your soul to these evils. You can go on living your life free of the negative entanglements caused by evil, whether you brought it on yourself or it was thrust upon you by other individuals. And you can rest in the assurance that you have the power to prevent the return of evil and destruction from returning. Walk in confidence.

That is what I hope you take with you from this book - the ability to walk in confidence. Although it is strange to say, I honestly hope you never need to use any of the prayers or spells contained here. I would never wish that anyone ever come into contact with negative or evil forces. However, since you have decided that you need to take this journey, your path has most likely already been crossed by evil. The good news is that now you see that you're not powerless to stop the effects. You do not need to simply accept it or try to mitigate the negativity in your life. You, my friends, can remove it.

We all know people who seem to be beaten down by life. Over time, they have come to expect things not to work out for them. They are no longer surprised when plans go awry or they are passed over when something positive happens around them. In my life, I refer to these unfortunate souls as "Eeyores". They just kind of plod through life, content taking the hits and negativity that daily life offers. Willing to feed off the scraps left behind by the energized, forward-looking individuals. It has happened to them so often that it becomes a mindset, a way of life. Well, I say, NO MORE!

In the spirit realm, vibrations cause reality. An example on this plane with which we are all familiar would be sound waves. Sound waves are essentially vibrations in the air caused by the disturbance of silence. These vibrations hit against our eardrums and are interpreted by our brain into meaning. In the world of spirit, vibrations in the stillness caused by our mindful intentions are able to manipulate reality, as if reality were a universe-sized eardrum. The universe then interprets our vibrations and discerns meaning - which changes the reality of our lives.

A little too deep? It boils down to this - How we feel and our focused intent (what is most prevalent in our mind) is the "vibe" we give off. If we give off a positive vibe, we receive positivity in our lives. If we give off a negative vibe, we receive negativity in our lives. Within the ethereal, like always attracts like.

Through the use of the prayers and spells you have learned, you can give off a confident, fearless, positive vibe. You have gained the strongest armor anyone can possibly have against attack - the knowledge of how to be victorious in any style of battle. Not only do you hold the power to repel evil, but you also hold the keys to keeping it away. Forever. Not only have you learned how to wield a sword against evil, but you have also *become* the sword against evil.

You are familiar with the prayers to invoke the power of God or Goddess, Universe, Angels, Spirit, Ascended Masters, Protectors, etc. into the war for your freedom from oppressive negativity and evil.

You are familiar with the spells to fight fire with fire on the spiritual plane.

You are familiar with the stones and crystals which can focus and amplify your intentions or trap negativity themselves.

You are familiar with the Archangels who you can implore for assistance in a time of crisis.

You are familiar with the symbols from antiquity that can be used to strengthen your defenses against negativity and evil.

You are familiar with the objects you may want to keep on hand to immediately rid yourself of new negative or evil attachments.

You are familiar with the prayers and tactics you should use to maintain your victory over curses, spells, evil soul ties, negative covenants, and agreements.

You are familiar with the tools and tactics necessary to cleanse your aura and your space of negativity or evil.

You have become your own shield and your own sword. Your life is your own to live on your own terms. The universe wants the best for you and your family. The time has come to reclaim your peace and your space. And now, you know exactly what to do.

Last Message and small request from the Magickal Witches team:

We wish you nothing but magickal success and health on your journey of being a powerful witch! If you've enjoyed this book or found that it has been exactly what you've needed, please consider leaving the book a review here where you can find the book in Glinda Porter's author profile. You will also find all her other literature that you'd love to check out. We're sure of it!

All feedback is extremely important to us because it helps us deliver exactly what you want and it also helps other readers make a decision when deciding on the best books to purchase. We would greatly appreciate it if you could take 60 seconds to leave the book a quick review. You can also reach out via email to leave any feedback.

Email: magick@magickalwitches.com

Website: www.magickalwitches.com

Author Profile: https://www.amazon.com/author/glindaporter

Lastly, don't forget to claim the "Survival and Wellness Kit for Magickal Witches" where you will receive:

- 10 Elixirs For Detoxification and Aura Cleansing
- 12 Spell Jar Recipes For Protection
- Guide For Talisman Preparation For Use Outside Home
- 20 Daily Detox Tips To Keep Your Vessel Clear
- Master Ingredient Shopping List

Resources

https://thefreedictionary.com

https://witchcraftandwitches.com

Abundance Crystals. Retrieved from https://satincrystals.com/pages/abundance-crystals

Big Issue North. April 26, 2021

Lipp, Deborah. *The Complete Book of Spells - Wiccan Spells For Healing, Protection, and Celebration*. Rockridge Press, 2020.

Moons, M. Spell to Break a Bad Habit (Banish). Retrieved from https://moodymoons.com/2019/10/31/spell-to-break-a-bad-habit

Mutuku, R. Names of Angels In The Bible and Their Duties. Retrieved from https://yen.com.gh

Okpara, Daniel C. *Prayers That Break Curses & Spells & Release Favors & Breakthroughs*. Better Life Media, 2016.

Okpara, Daniel C. *Prayers To Break Negative and Evil Soul Ties, Agreements and Covenants*. Better Life Media, 2016.

Okpara, Daniel C. *Prayers To Destroy Witchcraft Attacks & Release Your Blessings*. Better Life Media, 2016.

Phillips, G. Something Wiccan This Way Comes-Part 1 of 2. Retrieved from https://musingsfromtheuniverse.com/2021/04/09/something-wiccan-this-way-comes-part-1-of-2

Russell, Jeffrey Burton, and Brooks Alexander. *A History of Witchcraft, Sorcerers, Heretics & Pagans*. Thames & Hudson, 2007.

Skon, J. Sidestep Negative Energy With These 6 Crystals. Retrieved from https://mindbodygreen.com/2020/02/11/sidestep-negative-energy-with-these-6-crystals

Thank you!

I want to end this book by sending you so much gratitude by saying thank you for taking the time to learn from my teachings on the subject of Hoodoo. I hold this practice very near and dear to my heart and I am very grateful to have had the opportunity of putting it in book format for all of my fellow practitioners out there. I would love to hear your feedback about the book and how much you enjoyed it. You would be a legend if you could leave the book a review as I read every single review with an open mind and heart. Thank you!

~Glinda Porter

Milton Keynes UK
Ingram Content Group UK Ltd.
UKHW051550150124
436065UK00012B/229